Architecting Composite Applications and Services with TIBCO®

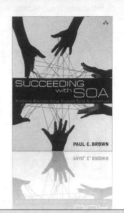

Architecting Composite Applications and Services with TIBCO®

Paul C. Brown

✦✦ Addison-Wesley

Upper Saddle River, NJ • Boston • Indianapolis • San Francisco
New York • Toronto • Montreal • London • Munich • Paris • Madrid
Capetown • Sydney • Tokyo • Singapore • Mexico City

The publisher offers excellent discounts on this book when ordered in quantity for bulk purchases or special sales, which may include electronic versions and/or custom covers and content particular to your business, training goals, marketing focus, and branding interests. For more information, please contact:

U.S. Corporate and Government Sales
(800) 382-3419
corpsales@pearsontechgroup.com

For sales outside the United States, please contact:

International Sales
international@pearson.com

Visit us on the Web: informit.com/aw

Library of Congress Cataloging-in-Publication Data

Brown, Paul C.
  Architecting composite applications and services with TIBCO / Paul C. Brown.
    p. cm.
  Includes index.
  ISBN 978-0-321-80205-7 (pbk. : alk. paper) — ISBN 0-321-80205-5 (pbk. : alk. paper) 1. Composite applications (Comuter science) 2. Application software—Development. 3. Computer network architectures. 4. TIBCO Software Inc. I. Title.
  QA76.76.A65B78 2012
  004.2'2—dc23   2012016968

ISBN-13: 978-0-321-80205-7
ISBN-10:   0-321-80205-5

Text printed in the United States on recycled paper at RR Donnelly in Crawfordsville, Indiana.
First printing, July 2012

To Michael Fallon and the TIBCO Education Team:
Thank you for your perseverance teaching me
the fine art of knowledge transfer.

Contents

Preface

About This Book

In composite applications and services, multiple components collaborate to provide the required functionality. These are distributed solutions for which there are many possible architectures. Some of these will serve the enterprise well, while others will lead to dead-end projects.

The Dual Roles of an Architecture

At the core lies an understanding of the dual role that architecture plays in a distributed design. One role is as an expression of an overall design: how the components collaborate to solve the problem. The other role is as a specification for the components and services that are part of that design. Understanding this dual role leads to an understanding of the information that must be present in an architecture document in order to effectively play this dual role.

This dual perspective on architecture is recursive: Dive in to a component or service and you'll find that it, too, has an architecture that must play both of these roles. It describes how its sub-components collaborate to provide the capabilities of the component. At the same time, it serves as a specification for each of its sub-components. And so on.

This perspective is so important to success that the better parts of three chapters (1, 5, and 6) are devoted to its exploration both by discussion and by example. All of the examples in the book are documented in the same manner.

Design Patterns

The architectures you define provide solutions for your enterprise. Many of these require solutions to well-known problems. To aid you in this work, this book covers a wide variety of design patterns for addressing common challenges. These include partitioning interfaces and business logic; incorporating rules into your design; asynchronous interactions involving multiple consumers and providers; providing services with both synchronous and asynchronous coordination patterns; distributing workload with and without sequencing constraints; managing replicated data; creating composite components, services, and applications; fault-tolerance, high-availability, and site disaster recovery; and federating services. These build upon the basic service and integration patterns covered in the book *TIBCO® Architecture Fundamentals*.[1]

Relevant TIBCO Products

Components and services need to be implemented, of course, and to do this appropriate technologies need to be selected. TIBCO provides a number of products that are intended to play specific roles in composite applications and services. This book provides an overview of these roles for TIBCO ActiveMatrix® Service Bus, TIBCO ActiveMatrix® Service Grid, TIBCO ActiveMatrix BusinessWorks™, TIBCO Hawk®, TIBCO® Managed File Transfer components, TIBCO® mainframe integration products, TIBCO BusinessConnect™, and TIBCO Collaborative Information Manager™.

Best Practices

A good architecture is a living thing that evolves gracefully over time as the demands facing the enterprise change. Facilitating this evolution requires careful consideration of service and data structure versioning, naming standards, modular data structure design, and the federation of services. This book devotes a chapter to each of these topics.

Performance and Tuning

Your solution must perform well enough to meet the needs of the enterprise. Assuring yourself that you have achieved the performance goals requires suitable benchmarking, and one chapter is devoted to the conduct of such experiments and the interpretation of results. Hand in hand with benchmarking goes tuning, and one chapter is

---

1. Paul C. Brown, *TIBCO® Architecture Fundamentals*, Boston: Addison-Wesley (2011).

devoted to the tuning of ActiveMatrix® Service Bus and ActiveMatrix BusinessWorks™.

Service Federation

Services will arise in many contexts both within and external to your enterprise. Some of these services will be intended for local use, while others will be intended for more widespread use. One chapter is devoted to service federation, which focuses on organizing services that arise in these different contexts.

Documenting Solution Architectures and Service Specifications

Finally, all of your architecture decisions must be captured in a form that can be communicated to all interested parties, from the business people who chartered the project to the technical teams that will implement, deploy, and operate the components that comprise the finished solution. One chapter is devoted to documenting solution architectures and another to documenting service specifications. Augmenting these chapters are online templates for each of these documents and a worked example of each. These may be found at informit.com/title/9780321802057.

In summary, this book is a guide to successfully architecting composite applications and services employing TIBCO technologies. It presents a comprehensive approach for architecting everything from the overall solution to the individual components and services. It builds upon and extends the basic design patterns and product information presented in the book *TIBCO® Architecture Fundamentals*.

TIBCO Architecture Book Series

Architecting Composite Applications and Services with TIBCO® is the second book in a series on architecting solutions with TIBCO products (Figure P-1). It builds upon the material covered in *TIBCO® Architecture Fundamentals*, which provides material common to all TIBCO-based designs. Each of the more advanced books, including this one, explores a different style of solution, all based on TIBCO technology. Each explores the additional TIBCO products that are relevant to that style of

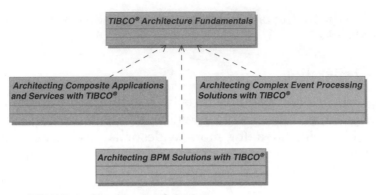

Figure P-1: *TIBCO Architecture Book Series*

solution. Each defines larger and more specialized architecture patterns relevant to the style, all built on top of the foundational set of design patterns presented in *TIBCO® Architecture Fundamentals*.

Intended Audience

Project architects are the intended primary audience for this book. These are the individuals responsible for defining an overall solution and specifying the components and services required to support that solution. Experienced architects will find much of interest, but no specific prior knowledge of architecture is assumed in the writing. This is to ensure that the material is also accessible to novice architects and advanced designers. For this latter audience, however, a reading of *TIBCO® Architecture Fundamentals* is highly recommended. It explores basic concepts in greater detail. This book provides a summary of that material in Chapter 2.

TIBCO specialists in a center of excellence will find material of interest, including background on the TIBCO product stack and design patterns showing best-practice uses of TIBCO products. The material on benchmark testing and tuning ActiveMatrix Service Bus and ActiveMatrix BusinessWorks lay the foundations for building high-performance applications based on these products.

Enterprise architects will find content of interest as well. The material on architecture documentation, component and service specification, versioning, namespace design, modular data structure design, and benchmarking can be used as a reference for defining or reviewing enterprise standards in these areas. The collection of design patterns, in conjunction with those presented in *TIBCO® Architecture Fundamentals*, provide the basis for a baseline set of standard design patterns for the enterprise.

Technical managers will also find material of interest, particularly the description of the content expected in architecture documents and specifications. The guidelines for conducting benchmark tests will also be of interest.

Detailed Learning Objectives

After reading this book, you will be able to

- Create and document architectures for solutions, component and service specifications, and component and service implementations.
- Describe the intended roles for ActiveMatrix Service Bus, ActiveMatrix® Service Grid, ActiveMatrix BusinessWorks, Hawk®, TIBCO Managed File Transfer components, TIBCO mainframe integration products, BusinessConnect, and TIBCO Collaborative Information Manager in composite applications and services.
- Define a manageable approach to versioning services and their artifacts.
- Establish practical standards for naming services and related artifacts.
- Design modular and manageable data structures.
- Conduct and interpret performance benchmark tests.
- Tune ActiveMatrix Service Bus and ActiveMatrix BusinessWorks™.
- Identify and select appropriate design patterns for
    - Separating interface and business logic
    - Incorporating rules into an architecture
    - Supporting asynchronous interactions involving multiple consumers and providers
    - Simultaneously supporting synchronous and asynchronous coordination patterns
    - Distributing workload with and without sequencing constraints

○   Managing replicated data

○   Creating composites of components and services

○   Fault-tolerance, high-availability, and site disaster recovery

○   Federating services

Organization of the Book

This book is divided into four parts (Figure P-2). Part I begins with a discussion of components, services, and architectures that provides the conceptual foundation for the book. It next reviews the material covered in *TIBCO® Architecture Fundamentals*, which is foundational material for this book. Next comes a discussion of some TIBCO products not covered in *TIBCO® Architecture Fundamentals* that play prominent roles in composite applications and services. Finally, the Nouveau Health Care case study is introduced. This rich case study will be used as the basis for many of the examples in the book.

Part II covers the basics of designing services. It starts with a discussion of observable dependencies and behaviors—the externally observable characteristics of a component or service. This understanding is next incorporated into a discussion of service-related documentation. The following three chapters address issues that greatly impact the flexibility of the architecture: versioning, naming standards, and data structures.

Part III describes a number of common design challenges and architectural patterns that can be used to address them. It starts with a number of general building-block patterns. Next are patterns for load distribution, with and without sequencing constraints. Patterns for managing replicated data are then followed by patterns for composing components and services.

Part IV addresses advanced topics. The conduct and interpretation of benchmark experiments are key for achieving performance goals, as is the tuning of key products. Fault-tolerance, high-availability, and site disaster recovery are discussed, followed by a discussion about federating multiple service domains. The book concludes with chapters covering the documentation of a solution and a service specification.

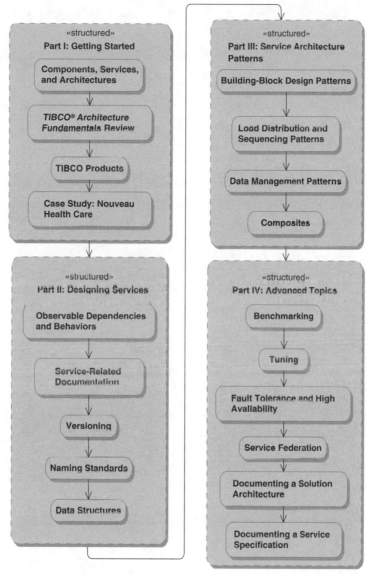

Figure P-2: *Organization of the Book*

Acknowledgments

Knowingly or unknowingly, many people have contributed to this book. Chief among these are my fellow global architects at TIBCO, particularly Kevin Bailey, Todd Bowman, Richard Flather, Ben Gundry, Nochum Klein, Marco Malva, Heejoon Park, and Michael Roeschter. Many of the other members of the architectural services team have contributed as well, including JenVay Chong, Dave Compton, Roger Kohler, Ed Presutti, and Michael Zhou. My thanks to these folks and the rest of the architectural services group—you're a great team to work with.

The educational services team at TIBCO has played a key role in conceptualizing this book, along with the accompanying course and architect certification program. More broadly, they have taught me the fine art of knowledge transfer and greatly influenced the manner in which this material is presented. Particular thanks to Alan Brown, Michael Fallon, Mike Goldsberry, Robert Irwin, Michelle Jackson, Lee Kleir, Madan Mashalkar, Tom Metzler, Howard Okrent, and Ademola Olateju.

The folks in TIBCO engineering have been more than generous with their time helping me understand the architecture underlying their products, including Bill Brown, John Driver, Michael Hwang, Eric Johnson, Collin Jow, Salil Kulkarni, Erik Lundevall, Bill McLane, Jean-Noel Moyne, Kevin O'Keefe, Denny Page, and Shivajee Samdarshi. My specific thanks to those who corrected my flawed understanding and provided the foundation for the threading diagrams in this book: Mohamed Aariff, Praveen Balaji, Seema Deshmukh, Laurent Domenech, Tejaswini Hiwale, Sabin Ielceanu, Shashank Jahagirdar, Salil Kulkarni, and Pankaj Tolani.

I wish to thank the management team at TIBCO whose support made this book possible: Paul Asmar, Eugene Coleman, Jan Plutzer, Bill Poteat, Murray Rode, and Murat Sonmez.

I would like to thank those who took the time to review the manuscript for this book and provide valuable feedback: Rodrigo Candido de Abreu, Sunil Apte, Abbey Brown, Antonio Bruno, Jose Estefania, Marcel Grauwen, Ben Gundry, Nochum Klein, Lee Kleir, Alexandre Jeong, Michael Roeschter, Peter Schindler, Mohamed Shahat, Mark Shelton, Mohan Sidda, and Nikky Sooriakumar.

Finally, I would like to once again thank my wife, Maria, who makes all things possible for me.

About the Author

 **Dr. Paul C. Brown** is a Principal Software Architect at TIBCO Software Inc., and is the author of *Succeeding with SOA: Realizing Business Value Through Total Architecture* (2007), *Implementing SOA: Total Architecture in Practice* (2008), and *TIBCO® Architecture Fundamentals* (2011), all from Addison-Wesley. He is also a co-author of the SOA Manifesto (soa-manifesto.org). His model-based tool architectures are the foundation of a diverse family of applications that design distributed control systems, process control interfaces, internal combustion engines, and NASA satellite missions. Dr. Brown's extensive design work on enterprise scale information systems led him to develop the total architecture concept: business processes and information systems are so intertwined that they must be architected together. Dr. Brown received his Ph.D. in computer science from Rensselaer Polytechnic Institute and his BSEE from Union College. He is a member of IEEE and ACM.

Part I

Getting Started

Chapter 1

Components, Services, and Architectures

Objectives

When you talk about an architecture, you have to be clear about the scope of that architecture. It might be the architecture of an overall solution or that of a specific service. Complicating this understanding is the relationship that exists between these architectures if the service is a part of the solution. A specification is an architecture that defines this relationship.

This chapter presents an overview of these and other concepts for which details are explored in subsequent chapters. After reading this chapter you should be able to describe the following concepts:

- Architecture views
- The hierarchy of architectures
- Solution architecture

- Service architecture, comprising
  - ○ Service specification architecture
  - ○ Service implementation architecture
- Composite architecture
- Service utilization contract
- Component life cycle

Architecture Views

As was discussed extensively in *TIBCO® Architecture Fundamentals*,[1] there are three views of an architecture that are essential when designing IT solutions: the process model, the architecture pattern, and the process-pattern mapping (Figure 1-1).

Process Model

The process model shows the structure of the work activities in the business process. Figure 1-2 is an example of a simple process for checking the status of an order. The process model also indicates the information (and other artifacts) being passed between activities. Most process models are more complex than the example shown.

The process model includes a model of the information being used in the process. Retrieving the status of an order poses the question as to what the information content of the Order Status Result should be (Figure 1-3). Should an order status include the shipping and billing

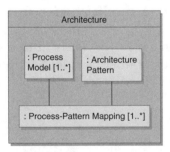

Figure 1-1: *Essential Architecture Views*

---

1. Paul C. Brown, *TIBCO® Architecture Fundamentals*, Boston: Addison-Wesley (2011), pp. 13–33.

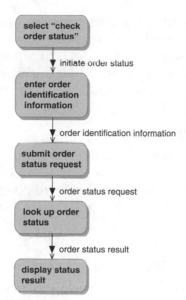

Figure 1-2: *Process Model Example*

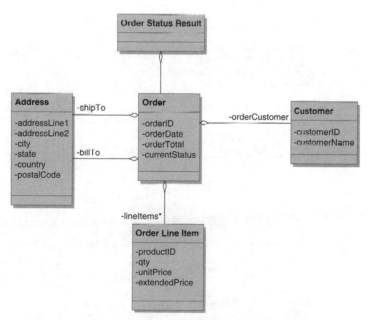

Figure 1-3: *Order Status Result Information Model*

address? Should it include the details of the line items? How much customer information should be included?

The intent of the information model is to capture the concepts, relationships, and attributes involved in the business process while consciously avoiding specifics as to how this information is represented.

Architecture Pattern

The architecture pattern shows the participants in the business process and the communications channels between them (Figure 1-4). The participants are typically a collection of people and systems. The architecture pattern also indicates any constraints that are placed on the participants.

Process-Pattern Mapping

The process-pattern mapping shows how the process is being executed by the participants in the architecture pattern (Figure 1-5). It shows which activities are being performed by which participants. When this

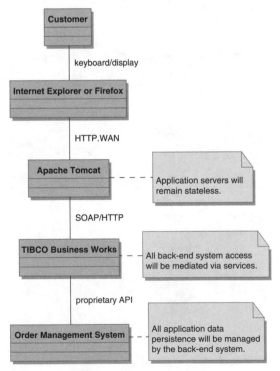

Figure 1-4: *Architecture Pattern Example*

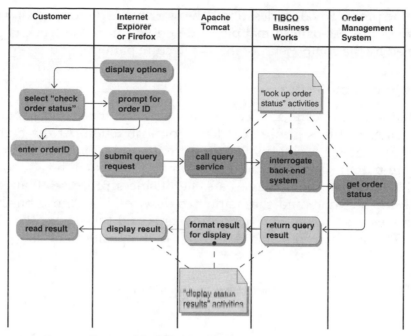

Figure 1-5: *Process-Pattern Mapping Example*

mapping is performed, a single activity in the process model may become distributed across several participants. In the example, looking up the order status is distributed across three participants, as is the display of the order status result.

Many design decisions are made as the process model is mapped onto the architecture pattern. Most of the serious design mistakes occur in this process. For this reason, it is important to document the mapping using Unified Modeling Language (UML) Activity Diagrams or Business Process Modeling Notation (BPMN) diagrams. Creating the diagrams ensures that the design thinking is complete: You can't draw the picture if you haven't decided what happens next. The diagrams are also powerful communications tools for interacting with both the business and technical communities.

A Hierarchy of Architectures

In the abstract, an architecture comprises three major elements: the architecture pattern, describing the components and their relationships; one or more process models, describing the work being performed; and one or more process-pattern mappings, describing how the work is performed by the components of the architecture pattern (Figure 1-6).

Solution Architecture

In defining composite applications and services, this pattern appears a number of times at different levels of abstraction. At the highest level, you have the solution architecture (Figure 1-7). Here the architecture pattern describes the major components (including services) of the solution. The processes are the business processes that comprise the solution, and the mappings describe how those business processes are executed by the components and services of the solution. This is the overall architecture of the composite solution.

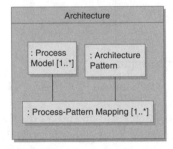

Figure 1-6: *Abstract Architecture Pattern*

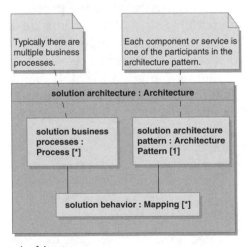

Figure 1-7: *Solution Architecture*

Service or Component Specification Architecture

A composite solution is comprised of a number of components that collaborate to bring the solution to life. Some of these components may be services that are intended to support multiple solutions.

The specification of an individual component or service defines an architecture that is related to but distinct from the solution architectures it supports (Figure 1-8). The processes of this specification architecture are fragments of the solution's business processes. These fragments show the patterns of how the component or service capabilities participate in the solutions they support.

For services, these patterns are abstractions drawn from the multiple business processes (solutions) in which the service is intended to participate. Some of these patterns may be speculative, reflecting intended future usages. In some cases, the specification may precede any actual solution design. In these cases, the clarity of the crystal ball from which the usage patterns are abstracted is crucial: If the pattern doesn't match the eventual solution's needs, the service will not be usable.

The specification's architecture pattern includes the component or service being specified and the components that it interacts with in an observable way (i.e., those components that are not internal). These interacting components include the solution components that interact with this component or service as well as the components it interacts with and depends upon. The specification's mapping details the observable interactions between the component or service being specified and the other observable components.

Service or Component Implementation Architecture

A component or service typically has internal structure—an architecture of its own (Figure 1-9). This architecture is closely related to the specification architecture but contains additional detail. The processes of this architecture are exactly the processes of the specification, that is, the usage scenarios for the components or service. The architecture pattern details the internal structure of the component or service, but also contains the external components with which there are direct interactions. The mapping details how the internal structural elements collaborate to provide the behavior given in the specification.

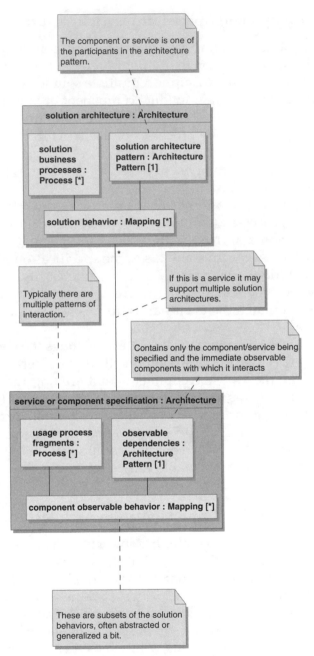

Figure 1-8: *Service or Component Specification Architecture*

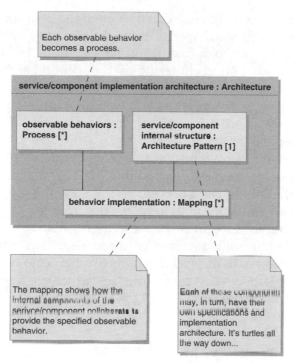

Figure 1-9: *Service or Component Implementation Architecture*

Why Make These Architecture Distinctions?

You may ask yourself why you need to distinguish between these different architectures. The answer is that you don't have to, but it is often convenient to do so, particularly for services.

Solutions Comprising Dedicated Components

If all components are dedicated to the solution, then the solution architecture document can also serve as the specification architecture document for each of the components involved. After all, the specification architecture is just a subset of the solution architecture. However, the portion of the solution architecture that constitutes the component specification must be clear to each team responsible for a component. In complex systems, it may be appropriate to separate each component's specification architecture into a separate document.

Assuming that you have decided to have the solution architecture double as the component specification architectures, you must now consider where the component implementation architectures are defined. If you don't mind cluttering up the solution architecture with some details, you might add the sub-structures for each component, thus incorporating their implementation architectures. However, this is not recommended, particularly if the components are going to be architected by independent teams.

With different teams responsible for different components, it becomes necessary to separate each component's implementation architecture from the solution architecture. In this case, the solution architecture document can continue to play the role of the component specification architecture. In such cases, careful change control over the solution architecture document is required so that component teams are aware of changes to the specifications for their components. From a management perspective, it may be simpler to create a separate specification for each component.

Solutions Comprising Shared Services

The need for separating solution, specification, and implementation architectures becomes more obvious when you consider shared services. To begin with, since the service is intended to be shared, there will likely be multiple solution architectures in which the service will participate. In some cases, the architectures for some of these solutions may not yet exist.

It is this need to consider multiple solution architectures and be able to accommodate solutions that do not yet exist that leads to the creation of a service specification architecture. It abstracts the fragments of solution architectures in which the service is intended to participate.

Once you have a specification architecture, you can consider where the implementation architecture should be documented. Again, you have a choice: It could be an extension of the specification architecture, or it could be a separate document. If the different teams are specifying and implementing the service, then this argues for separate documents. Separate documents also make it less confusing for service consumers to look at the specification and understand the intended utilization. On the other hand, if the same team is doing both the specification and implementation, a case can be made for a single document.

Design Patterns: Reference Architectures

There is yet another situation in which the abstract architecture of Figure 1-6 appears, and that is in documenting a design pattern (Figure 1-10). A design pattern describes a general solution to a common problem. It characterizes the problem and describes, in general terms, a solution. The solution describes the roles and responsibilities of the components comprising the solution. The pattern also spells out the benefits of solving the problem in this particular way.[2]

A design pattern is well represented by an abstracted architecture, commonly referred to as a reference architecture. The process part of the reference architecture defines how the work is organized in the design pattern. The architecture pattern describes the components comprising the solution, and the mapping describes how these components collaborate to perform the work. Design patterns may be applicable at multiple levels in the architecture hierarchy.

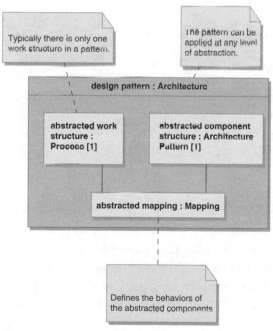

Figure 1-10: *Design Pattern Architecture*

2. Erich Gamma, Richard Helm, Ralph Johnson, and John Vlissides, *Design Patterns: Elements of Reusable Object-Oriented Software*, Reading, MA: Addison-Wesley (1995).

Solution Architecture

A solution is a working answer to a business problem. It comprises one or more business processes that do the work of solving the problem along with the participants (human and system) who execute those processes. A solution architecture describes the overall structure and organization of the solution: its business processes, its architecture pattern, and the mapping of the processes onto that pattern.

Solution Architecture Pattern

When a service is used in a solution, it becomes an element in the solution's architecture pattern. Figure 1-11 shows a solution pattern for a wholesale goods business that utilizes an Account Manager to keep track of customer account balances. The architecture pattern indicates which elements are users of the service and the interface(s) being used. In this example, the Order Manager and Billing Manager are both users of the Account Management Service.

Solution Business Processes

Solutions implement one or more business processes. It is through these business processes that the solution provides value to the enterprise. In the wholesale goods example we have two business processes: Purchase Goods and Settle Account (Figure 1-12).

Each of these business processes involves the execution of a number of activities. Figure 1-13 shows the activities of the Purchase Goods business process.

Solution Process Mapping

To complete the solution, each business process has to be mapped onto the elements of the architecture pattern. When a service is involved, some of the activities in the process are performed by the service. In the Purchase Goods process, the updating of the customer account balance is done by the Account Manager (Figure 1-14). This mapping shows the specific operation involved in the interaction. In defining the mapping, the coordination pattern for each interaction is determined.

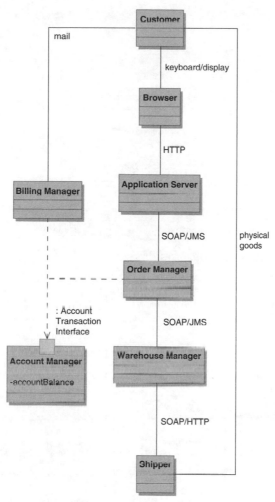

Figure 1-11: *Wholesale Goods Solution Architecture Pattern with a Service*

Figure 1-12: *Solution Business Processes*

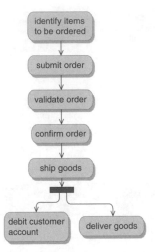

Figure 1-13: *Purchase Goods Business Process*

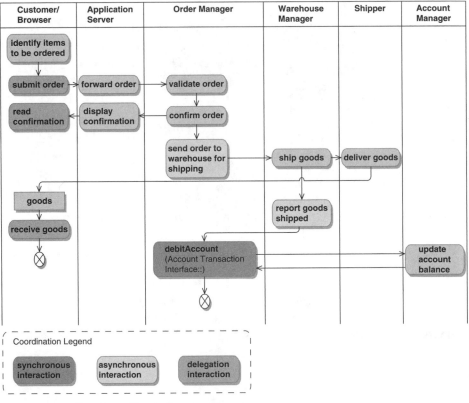

Figure 1-14: *Purchase Goods Process Mapping*

Service Architecture

A service is a component designed to provide conveniently packaged functionality for use in solutions. Its architecture comprises two parts: its specification architecture, which describes how the service fits into a larger design, and its implementation architecture, which describes the internal structure of the service.

The service specification architecture, in turn, has two aspects. One is the characterization of how the service is intended to be used—how it is supposed to interact with the service consumer. The other is the characterization of the service's dependence on other observable components—components that are not part of the service itself. Potential service consumers need to be aware of both aspects. Together, the utilization and dependence form an important part of the service specification.

The service's implementation architecture, with the exception of its observable aspects, is generally not of concern to the service consumer. In this book, when the term *service architecture* is used it means the combination of both the service specification architecture and the implementation architecture.

Service Utilization Pattern

Services are intended to be components of solutions, becoming components of the solution architecture. However, when a service is being conceptualized, it is not unusual for the solution architecture to be incomplete. Furthermore, future solutions that will incorporate the service have yet to be defined. In these circumstances, you cannot use the solution architecture to describe how the service fits into the solution. Yet when you design the service, you must make clear how the service is intended to be used. This is the role of the service utilization pattern, which is expressed as a reference architecture. The pattern represents the service and the fragment of the solution architecture with which it is supposed to interact. As with any reference architecture, it comprises three views: the architecture pattern, process models, and process mappings onto the architecture pattern.

Service Utilization Architecture Pattern

In the architecture pattern, the solution component or components that interact directly with the service are abstracted as a generic Service Consumer(s) (Figure 1-15). The pattern shows the channel of interaction between the service and its consumer along with any of the service's state information that may be visible through its interfaces. The most complete graphical representation of the architecture pattern shows the interface details, but these may be elided and documented elsewhere. This example shows the Account Manager service that maintains a customer's account balance along with the operations it offers to its consumers.

Service Utilization Process Models

Services execute processes to perform their work. Generally one of these processes is initiated each time a service operation is invoked, but this is not a requirement. Since the whole idea of a service is to treat its internal workings as a black box, the process structure often consists of a single activity that accepts an input and produces an output (i.e., the operation is a pure function). But many services are stateful, and their operations read or modify that state. Such is the case for the Account Manager's Credit Account process, which reads the current account balance, adds the amount to be credited, and updates the account balance (Figure 1-16).

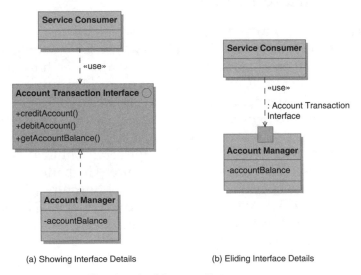

(a) Showing Interface Details   (b) Eliding Interface Details

Figure 1-15: *Service Utilization Architecture Pattern*

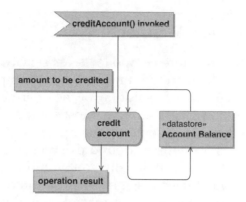

Figure 1-16: *Credit Account Operation Process*

Service Utilization Process Mappings

The service utilization process mappings are typically simple, involving only the service consumer and service provider. The primary information they add to the process is the detail of how the work of this process is coordinated with that of the service provider. The process mapping and the process itself are so similar that the process mapping often serves as the full process representation (Figure 1-17).

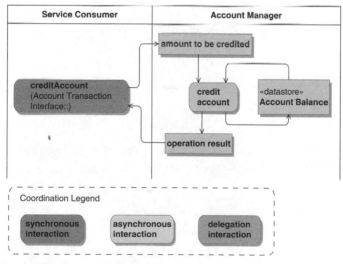

Figure 1-17: *Credit Account Process Mapping*

Composite Service Architecture

In a composite, two or more components (or services) collaborate to collectively provide the required functionality. A composite may be an entire solution, a fragment of a solution, or the internal structure of one of the solution components or services. Most solutions are composites.

Services are often implemented as composites, particularly when the service serves as a wrapper around existing functionality implemented in another component. Ideally you would like to treat the service (or any component) as a black box whose internal details can be ignored. However, the black-box approach is not always appropriate, as will be discussed in Chapter 5. For now, we'll simply examine the architecture of a composite service and ignore the question as to what portion of that architecture properly belongs in the service specification architecture (because it is observable) as opposed to the service implementation architecture (because it is not).

Composite Service Architecture Pattern

Let's suppose that the Account Manager is actually a façade wrapped around a Legacy Accounting System (Figure 1-18). It is important for

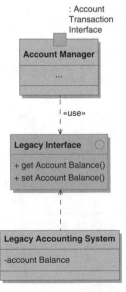

Figure 1-18: *Composite Service Architecture Pattern*

users of the Account Manager to be aware of this, for three important reasons:

1. The availability and performance of Account Manager operations are impacted by the performance and availability of the Legacy Accounting System.

2. The composite's state information may, in fact, be saved in the underlying components.

3. The state changes made to the Legacy Accounting System by the Account Manager may be directly observable by other systems.

Composite Service Process Mapping

Although it is generally not important to understand how the service implements its processes, this is not the case when external components are involved (Figure 1-19). Invocation of the creditAccount() operation not only requires the Legacy Accounting System to be operational, it requires that system to do work and thus has a performance impact on that system. In addition, Account Balance state is being retained by the legacy system, not the Account Manager service. This has implications for fault tolerance design. There is even a flaw in the design as presently shown, which would not be apparent without this

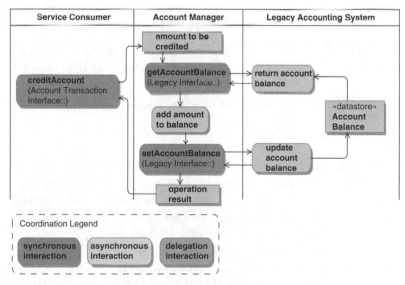

Figure 1-19: *Composite Service Process Mapping*

process mapping: If a third party updates the account balance between the time the Account Manager gets and sets the balance, that third party update will be lost. To avoid this, some other type of coordination (e.g., including both the operations in a transaction) is required.

Service Utilization Contract

Solutions that utilize services have one or more components within them that are service consumers. Each service consumer may place different demands upon the service. The service utilization contract defines the agreement between a single service consumer and the service in terms of what the service will provide that service consumer. This includes

- The organizations responsible for the service consumer and service provider.
- The specifics of the systems and interfaces involved in the various environments (development, test, production).
- The functionality provided to this particular consumer (interfaces and other observable behavior). This may be a reference to portions of the service specification and may only be a subset of the service capabilities.
- Nonfunctional requirements for this particular consumer: throughput, response time, availability, recovery point objective, recovery time objective, and so forth.

Service utilization contracts are discussed in detail in Chapter 6.

Component Life Cycle

When considering life-cycle governance, there is a tendency to view the life cycles of service providers and service consumers as somehow being distinct. They are not. Any component might be a a service provider, a service consumer, or both. Consequently, there is only one life cycle: architect, design, implement, test, deploy, and operate.

Having said that, there is still value in distinguishing the life-cycle governance questions associated with the roles of service provider and service consumer (Figure 1-20). There are different questions associ-

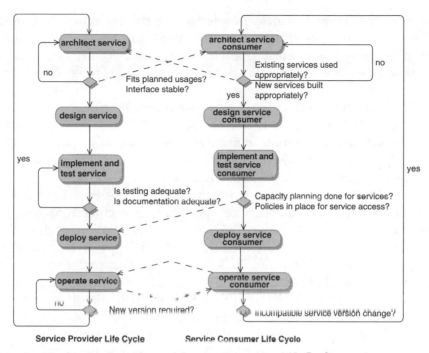

Figure 1-20: *Service Provider and Service Consumer Life Cycles*

ated with each of these roles, and knowing the role(s) the component will play will determine which of the questions are relevant.

Summary

There are three views of an architecture that are essential for successful IT projects: process model, architecture pattern, and process-pattern mapping. The process model describes how the work of the business process is organized and the information (and other artifacts) that are involved. The architecture pattern shows the participants in the process (human and system) along with the communications channels between them and any constraints upon their use. The process-pattern mapping shows how the work is allocated to the participants and the resulting pattern of interactions between the participants.

In discussing the architecture, you must be clear about the scope of your discussion. The term *solution* refers to the combination of business processes that solve business problems and the collection of participants (people and systems) that execute these processes. The architecture of a solution is characterized by three basic architectural views: process models, the architecture pattern, and the mapping of each process onto the architecture pattern.

Although the architecture of a service might be considered to be a fragment of the solution architecture of which it is a part, you often have services that participate in more than one solution, some of which may not yet exist. Consequently, service architectures need to be described independent of solution architectures.

When defining a service architecture, there are two aspects that need to be captured: the service specification architecture and the implementation architecture. The service specification architecture characterizes the manner in which the service is supposed to fit into a solution architecture. It shows the service utilization pattern as a reference architecture that represents the service along with the fragment of the solution that interacts with the service. It also shows the interactions of the service with the observable components upon which it depends. The implementation architecture shows the internal nonobservable architecture of the service. The term *service architecture* refers to the combination of the service specification architecture and its implementation architecture.

Any given component can potentially be both a service provider and a service consumer. There are different governance questions associated with each of these roles. For a composite service, all of these governance questions are relevant. For a detailed discussion of governance, see Chapter 13 of *Succeeding with SOA: Realizing Business Value Through Total Architecture*.[3]

---

3. Paul C. Brown, *Succeeding with SOA: Realizing Business Value Through Total Architecture*, Boston: Addison-Wesley (2007).

Chapter 2

TIBCO® Architecture Fundamentals Review

Objectives

This book builds upon the material presented in *TIBCO® Architecture Fundamentals*.[1] This chapter presents a brief summary of those materials to serve as a refresher. This summary assumes that you are already familiar with this material.

Products Covered in *TIBCO® Architecture Fundamentals*

TIBCO® Architecture Fundamentals provided an overview of the most commonly used TIBCO products. These are summarized in the following sections.

1. Paul C. Brown, *TIBCO® Architecture Fundamentals*, Boston, MA: Addison-Wesley (2011).

TIBCO Enterprise Message Service™

The Enterprise Message Service™ (EMS) product consists of a server and a number of client libraries (Figure 2-1). Optionally, the server can persist messages in either files or a database.

Under normal circumstances, clients use the client library to interact directly with the server. The client library connects directly to the server. By exception, multicast daemons can be used to deliver messages to clients.

There are several options for administering servers. The administration tool provides a command-line interface for configuring a server. The same capabilities are provided by the administrative plugin for the TIBCO Administrator™, which is not to be confused with the TIBCO ActiveMatrix® Administrator. Groups of servers can be administered using TIBCO Enterprise Message Service™ Central Administration.

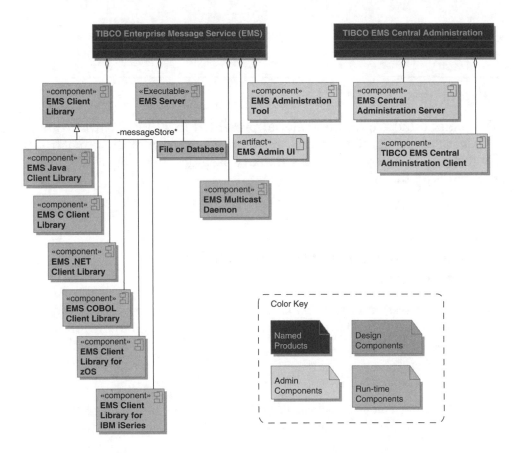

Figure 2-1: *Enterprise Message Service*

TIBCO ActiveMatrix® Product Portfolio

There are a number of products within the ActiveMatrix® product portfolio (Figure 2-2). Four of these are directly relevant to the discussions in this book: TIBCO ActiveMatrix® Service Bus, TIBCO ActiveMatrix® Service Grid, TIBCO ActiveMatrix BusinessWorks™, and the family of ActiveMatrix adapters.

TIBCO ActiveMatrix® Service Bus

The central product of the family is the ActiveMatrix Service Bus (Figure 2-3). The ActiveMatrix node provides the execution environment for all designs based on ActiveMatrix Service Bus. Functional components deployed within a node can be of different implementation types. ActiveMatrix Service Bus provides one implementation type: Mediation. It also provides the ActiveMatrix® Administrator, which itself runs as an implementation type within a special node that is, by default, designated the SystemNode.

Installing ActiveMatrix Service Bus installs Enterprise Message Service as well, but the license for ActiveMatrix Service Bus only allows the message service to be used for internal communications within ActiveMatrix. Any other use of the message service requires an explicit license.

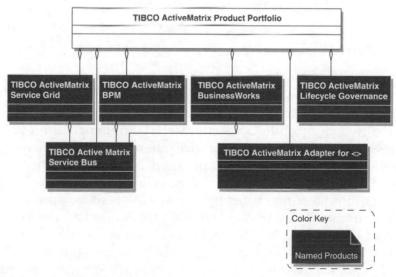

Figure 2-2: *ActiveMatrix Product Portfolio*

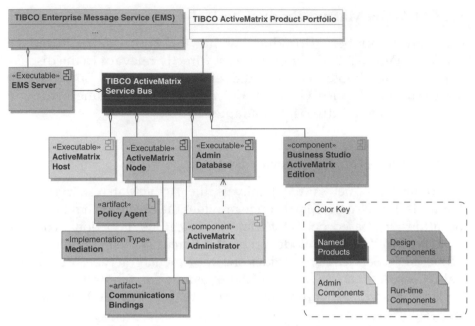

Figure 2-3: *ActiveMatrix Service Bus and Its Components*

ActiveMatrix® Service Grid

ActiveMatrix Service Grid includes all of the ActiveMatrix Service Bus components plus four additional implementation types: Java, C++, Spring, and WebApp (Figure 2-4).

ActiveMatrix BusinessWorks™

The ActiveMatrix BusinessWorks product includes two design and deployment options (Figure 2-5). When deployed in an ActiveMatrix node, the TIBCO ActiveMatrix BusinessWorks™ Service Engine is installed, which provides an ActiveMatrix implementation type for BusinessWorks. Services and service references that are designed using the Service palette can be monitored and wired to other components in the ActiveMatrix Service Bus. When deployed in this manner, other interfaces presented by BusinessWorks work properly, but they are not monitored by the ActiveMatrix Administrator. Typically, the TIBCO Designer™ Add-in for TIBCO Business Studio™ is used for design work, although the stand-alone TIBCO Designer may also be used. Note that the installation of the service engine also installs

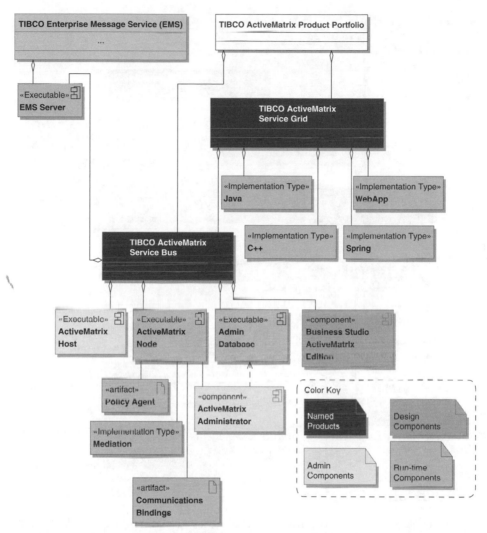

Figure 2-4: *ActiveMatrix Service Grid and Its Components*

ActiveMatrix Service Bus, and these configurations are managed with the ActiveMatrix Administrator.

The alternative, often referred to as TIBCO "Classic," is to deploy ActiveMatrix BusinessWorks processes in stand-alone BusinessWorks engines. In these cases, the stand-alone TIBCO Designer is used to configure the BusinessWorks processes, and the stand-alone TIBCO Administrator (not to be confused with the ActiveMatrix Administrator) is used to administer the environment.

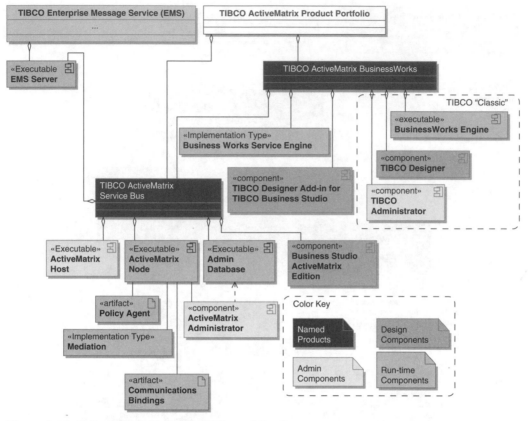

Figure 2-5: *ActiveMatrix BusinessWorks and Its Components*

ActiveMatrix Adapters

As with ActiveMatrix BusinessWorks, there are two design and deployment options for ActiveMatrix adapters (Figure 2-6). When deployed in ActiveMatrix nodes, the adapter service engine is installed in the ActiveMatrix environment, and the TIBCO Business Studio™ is used to configure the adapters. The adapters, however, do not include TIBCO ActiveMatrix Service Bus as part of the product. Thus a separate installation (and license) of either ActiveMatrix Service Bus, Service Grid, or BusinessWorks is required.

Alternatively, adapters can be deployed in stand-alone adapter engines. In these environments the TIBCO Designer is used to configure the adapter and the TIBCO Administrator is used to deploy and

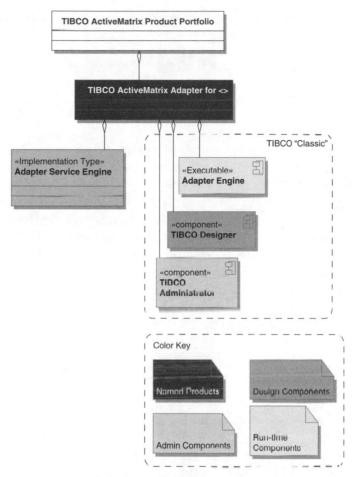

Figure 2-6: *ActiveMatrix Adapters and Their Components*

manage the instances. Note that the adapters whose names do not contain "ActiveMatrix" are all deployed and managed in this way.

ActiveMatrix Deployment Options

ActiveMatrix Service Grid uses the Service Component Architecture (SCA) graphic notation as its design interface. Figure 2-7 shows a simple SCA design consisting of a promoted service named

Figure 2-7: *SCA Design Example*

OrderServiceInterface, a component implementing that service named OrderManager, and a promoted reference named ProductReference that is used by the OrderManager.

The elements of the SCA design (promoted services, components, and promoted references) are each independently deployable. Figure 2-8 shows all three elements of the design being deployed on a single ActiveMatrix node. By default, communications between these elements occurs within the node.

Figure 2-9 shows this same design deployed on three separate nodes. Interactions between the nodes occur via the instance of the EMS server that is private to the ActiveMatrix environment.

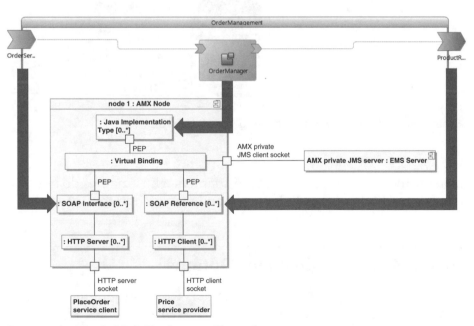

Figure 2-8: *Single-Node Deployment Example*

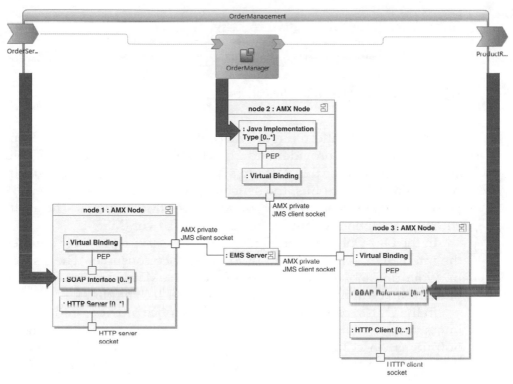

Figure 2-9: *Three-Node Deployment Example*

Design Patterns

There are a number of simple design patterns that provide the foundation for the patterns described in this book. These are summarized in the following sections.

Basic Interaction Patterns

There are four basic interaction (message-exchange) patterns possible between a pair of participants. In the In-Only pattern (Figure 2-10), the service consumer sends an input to the service provider and does not expect a response. In ActiveMatrix Service Bus, this pattern is supported by SOAP over HTTP and JMS and by XML over JMS bindings.

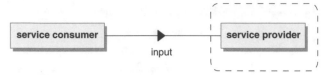

Figure 2-10: *In-Only Architecture Pattern*

In the In-Out pattern (Figure 2-11), the service consumer sends an input to the service provider and expects an output in response. There are two variations of this pattern: synchronous and asynchronous. In ActiveMatrix Service Bus, the synchronous variation is supported by SOAP over HTTP and JMS and by XML over JMS bindings. The asynchronous variation is only supported by XML over JMS.

In the Out-Only pattern (Figure 2-12), the service provider initiates the interaction, sending an input to the service consumer. The service provider does not expect a response. In ActiveMatrix Service Bus, this pattern can be approximated using XML over JMS bindings.

In the Out-In pattern (Figure 2-13), the service provider initiates the interaction, sending an input to the service consumer and expecting an output response. Such interactions are almost always asynchronous. In ActiveMatrix Service Bus, this pattern can be approximated using XML over JMS bindings.

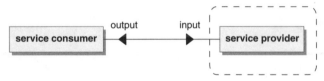

Figure 2-11: *In-Out Architecture Pattern*

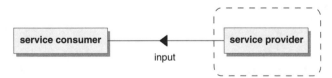

Figure 2-12: *Out-Only Architecture Pattern*

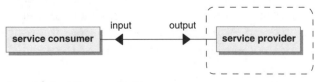

Figure 2-13: *Out-In Architecture Pattern*

Event-Driven Interaction Patterns

Event-driven interactions (Figure 2-14) introduce a third party (the channel) as an intermediary for passing messages from publishers to subscribers. The Enterprise Message Service is designed to play this role.

The Enterprise Message Service supports two message delivery semantics. For queues, each message is delivered to a single subscriber regardless of how many subscribers there are (Figure 2-15). This semantic is useful for load distribution when all of the subscribers perform exactly the same function.

The other message delivery pattern is the topic (Figure 2-16). Here each message is delivered to all of the subscribers. This semantic is useful for broadcasting information to many parties.

Figure 2-14: *Event-Driven Interaction Pattern*

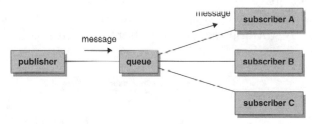

Figure 2-15: *Queue Message Delivery Semantic*

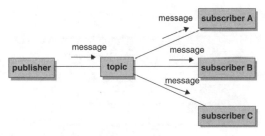

Figure 2-16: *Topic Message Delivery Semantic*

Mediation Patterns

This family of patterns arises when some relatively simple logic needs to be inserted between a service consumer and a service provider. The ActiveMatrix Service Bus Mediation implementation type is designed to play this role.

The simplest mediation pattern is the straight-through pattern (Figure 2-17). Here the mediation is a direct mapping from a proxy interface to the actual service provider interface. In this pattern, the logical interface (portType) must be identical for both parties, although the transports may be different. The service interfaces and references offer points at which policies may be enforced (e.g., to govern access control).

When the service consumer and service provider interfaces are different, content transformation may be required (Figure 2-18). In this pattern, there is a one-to-one relationship between the operations on the proxy interface and the operations of the service provider. Furthermore, the information content of the operations is the same. The only difference is the actual format (structure) of the data.

When there is insufficient information supplied to the proxy operation, it may be necessary to access a service to retrieve augmenting information (Figure 2-19). This information is then used to provide the required service provider input.

Sometimes there are multiple providers of the same service and individual requests need to be routed to the correct service provider. This leads to the routing mediation pattern of Figure 2-20.

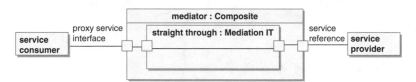

Figure 2-17: *Straight-Through Mediation Pattern*

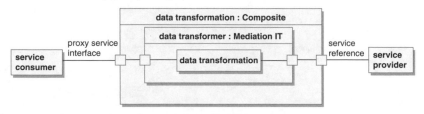

Figure 2-18: *Content Transformation Mediation Pattern*

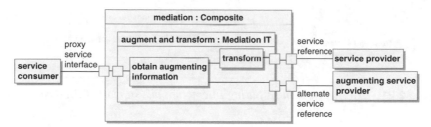

Figure 2-19: *Augmentation and Content Transformation Mediation Pattern*

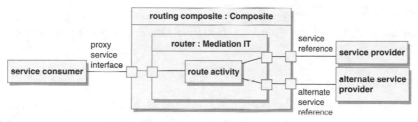

Figure 2-20. *Routing Mediation Pattern*

External System Access Patterns

This family of patterns focuses on the interactions between components hosted in ActiveMatrix Service Bus and external components. These interactions fall into three categories:

1. Interaction via a protocol supported by ActiveMatrix Service Bus
2. Interaction via a TIBCO adapter or ActiveMatrix adapter
3. Interaction via a protocol not supported by ActiveMatrix Service Bus

Interaction via a Supported Protocol

ActiveMatrix Service Bus directly supports a number of protocols including SOAP over HTTP and JMS, XML over JMS, and EJB interactions. There are two variations of direct interaction patterns depending upon which party initiates the interaction. Figure 2-21 shows the case in which the external system (typically a front-end system) initiates the interaction. This is the pattern you find when the ActiveMatrix composite is exposing a web service for use by external components.

Figure 2-22 shows the case in which the ActiveMatrix composite initiates the interaction. This is the pattern you will find when the external system (typically a back-end system) is exposing a web service that is being referenced by the ActiveMatrix composite.

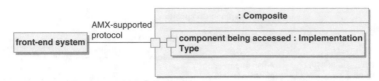

Figure 2-21: *External System Initiating Interaction via Supported Protocol*

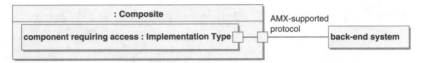

Figure 2-22: *ActiveMatrix Composite Initiating Interaction via Supported Protocol*

Interaction via Adapter

TIBCO adapters and ActiveMatrix adapters are designed to interact with external systems using their native proprietary interfaces. TIBCO adapters are always deployed as stand-alone executables, while Active-Matrix adapters may either be deployed in ActiveMatrix nodes or run as stand-alone executables.

Figure 2-23 shows changes in external systems triggering interactions with ActiveMatrix composites. The adapters are configured to recognize changes (events) in the external systems and initiate the interaction with the ActiveMatrix composite. The adapter-composite interactions occur using the TIBCO adapter protocol.

Figure 2-24 shows the ActiveMatrix composite initiating the interaction via the adapter. The interaction between the composite and the adapter uses the TIBCO adapter protocol.

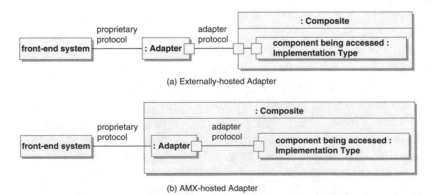

Figure 2-23: *External System Changes Triggering Interaction via Adapter*

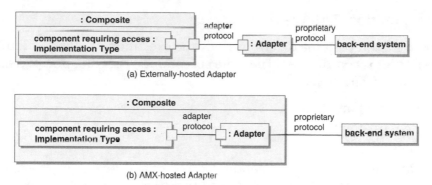

Figure 2-24: *ActiveMatrix Composite Initiating Interaction via Adapter*

Interaction via Non-Supported Protocol

In these patterns the ActiveMatrix component interacts directly with the external system but using a protocol for which there is no ActiveMatrix Service Bus binding. HTTP and JDBC are two examples of this type of protocol. Figure 2-25 shows an external system initiating an interaction with an ActiveMatrix component. This is the pattern that represents an external system interacting with the HTTP interface of an ActiveMatrix WebApp implementation type.

Figure 2-26 shows an ActiveMatrix component initiating an interaction with an external system. This is the pattern that represents an ActiveMatrix component using JDBC to interact with a database.

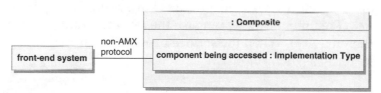

Figure 2-25: *External System Initiating Interaction via Non-Supported Protocol*

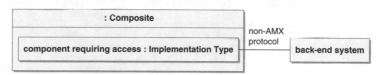

Figure 2-26: *ActiveMatrix Component Initiating Interaction via Non-Supported Protocol*

Coordination Patterns

Coordination patterns determine how the execution of work by multiple parties is coordinated. There are six common coordination patterns (and many variations):

1. Fire and Forget
2. Request-Reply
3. Delegation
4. Delegation with Confirmation
5. Distributed Transaction with Two-Phase Commit
6. Process Coordinator Using Compensating Transactions

The fire-and-forget coordination pattern (Figure 2-27) is the simplest coordination pattern, but it offers no opportunity for either party to detect breakdowns in the process.

To simplify the recognition of coordination patterns in more complex processes, we introduce a color-coding of the initiator's activities. In this pattern, the interaction is asynchronous; that is, the sender is not waiting for a response from the recipient.

The request-reply coordination pattern (Figure 2-28) affords the opportunity for the service consumer to detect breakdowns in the process, but only if a service-level agreement for the response time is established. It also ties up the resources of the service consumer while the work is being performed. Here the synchronous variation of the pattern is shown.

Figure 2-29 shows the asynchronous variation of this pattern. Here the service consumer is not waiting for the response (and is likely doing some other activity). When the service provider completes the work, it sends the reply asynchronously.

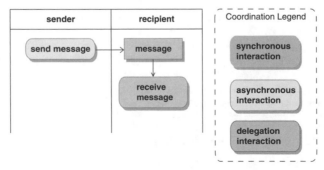

Figure 2-27: *Fire-and-Forget Coordination Pattern*

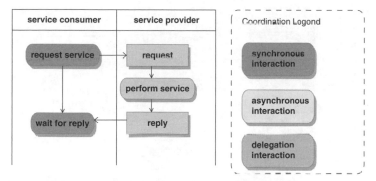

Figure 2-28: *Synchronous Request-Reply Coordination Pattern*

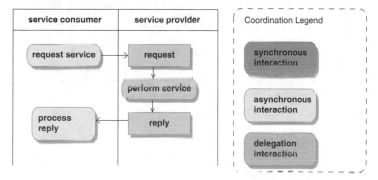

Figure 2-29: *Asynchronous Request-Reply Coordination Pattern*

The delegation pattern (Figure 2-30) involves an initial request-reply interaction with the service provider, but the reply only indicates a promise to do the work at some later time. When this pattern arises, typically the work result is sent to a third party. This pattern ensures a successful hand-off of responsibility, but is not capable of detecting breakdowns in the subsequent performance of the service.

In delegation with confirmation (Figure 2-31), an additional asynchronous interaction with the service consumer informs the consumer that the service has (or has not) been performed. For this to be useful, a service-level agreement must be established for the time frame in which this response is to be expected. It is important to clearly recognize what this confirmation represents. In the example shown, it indicates that the work has been performed and the service result generated. However, since the service result is being sent using a fire-and-forget pattern, the confirmation says nothing about the successful delivery of that result to the third party.

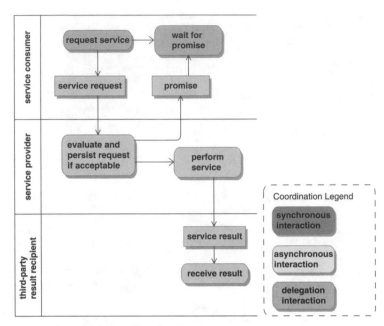

Figure 2-30: *Delegation Coordination Pattern*

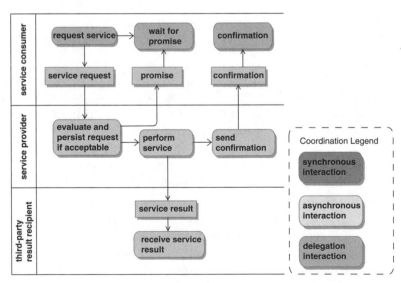

Figure 2-31: *Delegation with Confirmation Coordination Pattern*

Distributed transactions with two-phase commit (Figure 2-32) provide the ability to coordinate the work of multiple parties. However, if any of the parties are unavailable, the application cannot proceed. There is also a fair amount of overhead involved in this type of transaction. Note that the application program is using synchronous request-reply for its interactions with the transaction manager.

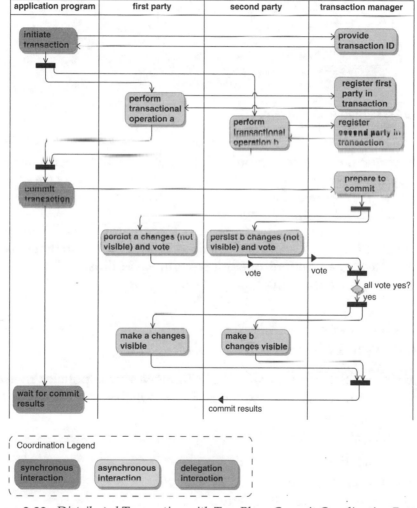

Figure 2-32: *Distributed Transaction with Two-Phase Commit Coordination Pattern*

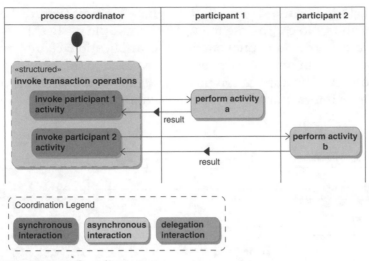

Figure 2-33: *Process Coordinator*

Introducing a process coordinator (Figure 2-33) explicitly assigns the responsibility for managing the overall process. The process coordinator then uses lower-level coordination patterns to initiate participant's work and confirm its success.

A tool commonly used by a process coordinator is the compensating transaction. A compensating transaction is an operation that undoes the net effect of a previous operation. Figure 2-34 illustrates the use of compensating transactions.

ActiveMatrix Service Bus Policies

ActiveMatrix Service Bus provides a framework for policies that are enforced within ActiveMatrix nodes. These policies provide transport-agnostic mechanisms for

- Authentication
- Authorization
- Privacy (encryption)
- Data integrity (digital signatures)
- Tuning (thread management policies)
- Transactions

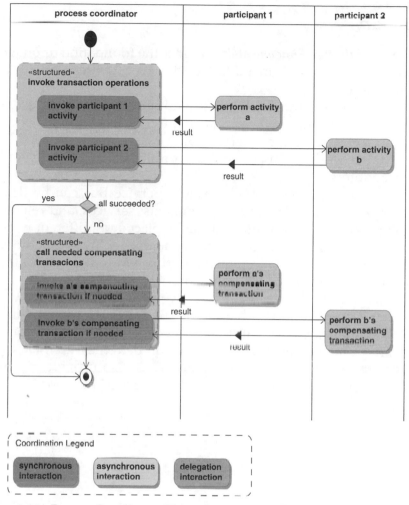

Figure 2-34: *Process Coordinator Using Compensating Transactions*

The framework also provides a means of specifying the policy requirements, which are called policy intents. A policy intent states a requirement for a particular type of policy (e.g., authentication) that will be provided at some later point in the life cycle. The framework automatically provides the governance to ensure that the required policies are, in fact, provided.

Summary

TIBCO® Architecture Fundamentals provides the foundation upon which the contents of this book are built. This chapter provides a brief review of that material.

The solutions in this book utilize a number of products described in *TIBCO® Architecture Fundamentals*. These include Enterprise Message Service, ActiveMatrix Service Bus, ActiveMatrix Service Grid, ActiveMatrix BusinessWorks, and a portfolio of TIBCO and ActiveMatrix adapters.

Designs built upon the ActiveMatrix Service Bus can be flexibly deployed in a number of ways. Components, services, and references are independently deployable and can be placed on different nodes if desired. Communications between elements deployed on different nodes occurs via the instance of the Enterprise Message Service that is private to the deployment environment.

TIBCO® Architecture Fundamentals covered a number of design patterns that serve as building blocks for the patterns described in this book. These include basic interactions between pairs of components, event-driven interaction patterns, mediation patterns, external system access patterns, and coordination patterns. It also provides an overview of the policy framework provided by ActiveMatrix Service Bus.

Chapter 3

TIBCO Products

Objectives

TIBCO® Architecture Fundamentals provided an overview of the core products typically found in solutions based on TIBCO products. These include ActiveMatrix Service Grid, ActiveMatrix Service Bus, ActiveMatrix BusinessWorks, Enterprise Message Service, and the family of ActiveMatrix adapters.

Composite applications and services often involve additional TIBCO products. This chapter provides an overview of a number of commonly used products, including

- TIBCO Hawk®
- The TIBCO® Managed File Transfer product portfolio, including
    - TIBCO® Managed File Transfer Platform Servers for various platforms
    - TIBCO® Managed File Transfer Platform Server Agent
    - TIBCO® Managed File Transfer Internet Agent
    - TIBCO® Managed File Transfer Internet Server
- Mainframe-related products, including
    - TIBCO Substation ES™
    - TIBCO Mainframe Service Tracker™
    - TIBCO ActiveMatrix® Adapter for IBM i

    ○   TIBCO® Adapter for Files z/OS (MVS)

    ○   TIBCO® Adapter for Files (IBM i)

    ○   TIBCO ActiveMatrix BusinessWorks™ Plug-in for Data Conversion

• TIBCO BusinessConnect™

• TIBCO Collaborative Information Manager™

After reading this chapter you should be able to describe the appropriate use of each of these products.

Hawk®

Overview

Hawk comprises a set of components for monitoring the status of components (executing programs) and the services running on them (Figure 3-1). For each non-mainframe machine environment (physical

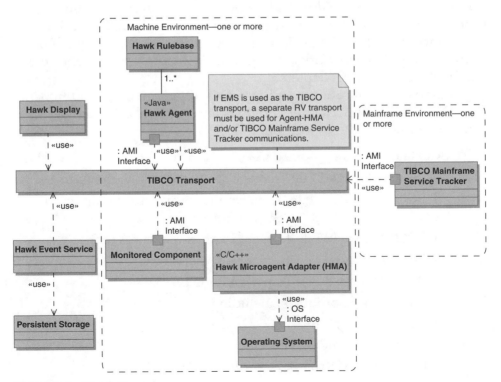

Figure 3-1: *Hawk Overview*

or virtual) in which components are to be monitored, two Hawk executables run: the Hawk Agent and the Hawk Microagent Adapter (HMA). On a mainframe, the TIBCO Mainframe Service Tracker executes.

Hawk Agent

The Hawk Agent is the workhorse. Directed by rulebases, it monitors components (executing programs) in its environment, interacting with those components via an Application Microagent Interface (AMI) provided by the component. Most TIBCO products provide AMI interfaces, and there is a toolkit for adding AMI interfaces to other components. The Hawk Agent communicates with the AMI interface using a TIBCO transport, either Enterprise Message Service or TIBCO Rendezvous®.

The Hawk Agent also provides functionality via an AMI interface of its own. Among other things, this interface provides the ability for agents to send and receive any message via Rendezvous® and Enterprise Message Service.

Hawk Rules

Typically you create Hawk rules using the Rulebase Editor (Figure 3-2), although the rulebase is just an XML file that can be edited directly. The rule name (the highlighted string) specifies the source of the data upon which the rule will operate. The data source specifies the Microagent,

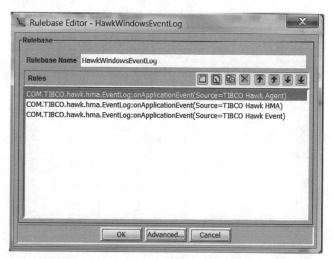

Figure 3-2: *Three Rules in the Hawk Rulebase Editor*

operation, and data element to be used as the source of the data. Both subscription and request-reply operations are supported. Subscription operations immediately trigger the rule when the referenced data changes (i.e., the component containing the Microagent notifies Hawk when the value changes). For request-reply operations, Hawk invokes the operation at regular intervals. For request-reply operations, the interval (in seconds) between invocations of the operation is specified.

Once the rule is created, you define one or more tests to be applied to the data source. Figure 3-3 shows two tests that have already been defined for this rule. Each of these is examining the type of the event that has occurred.

There are many different types of tests that you can define. Figure 3-4 shows the tests that can be defined for this particular data source.

There are some advanced configuration options for the rule as well (Figure 3-5). One of these advanced options is overruling. Overruling provides a mechanism for extending rulebases by adding a new rulebase containing revised logic without having to rewrite the original rulebase. The new rulebase has a rule with the same name as the original but a higher Over Ruling value. When the Hawk Agent loads both rulebases and encounters multiple rules with the same name, it only executes the one with the highest Over Ruling value. Another advanced option is Scheduling. By default, a rule is always applied. Optionally, you can provide a schedule for when the rule should be applied. You can, for example, schedule a rule to be applied only during specified peak hours.

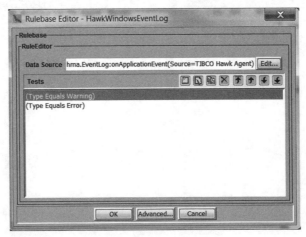

Figure 3-3: *Defined Tests for a Hawk Rule*

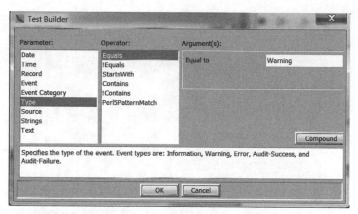

Figure 3-4: *Defining a Test*

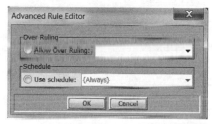

Figure 3-5: *Advanced Rule Configuration*

Finally, once the test is specified, you define the actions to be taken once the test is satisfied (Figure 3-6). Multiple actions can be specified, if required. Types of actions include

- Sending a Hawk alert to the Hawk Display (and other interested listeners).
- Executing an operating system command-line operation.
- Sending a Hawk notification to the Hawk Display (and other interested listeners).
- Invoking a Microagent operation—note that many things can be done with this approach, including sending messages.
- Sending an e-mail.
- Posting a condition, which may be referenced as a data source in another rule in the same rulebase.

The end result is the Hawk rule shown in Listing 3-1.

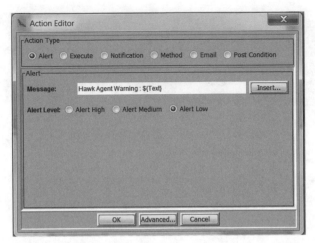

Figure 3-6: *Defining the Actions Taken*

Listing 3-1: *Hawk Rule Example*

```
<rule>
  <name><![CDATA[COM.TIBCO.hawk.hma.EventLog:onApplicationEvent
    (Source=TIBCO Hawk Agent)]]>
  </name>
  <schedule></schedule>
  <overRuling>0</overRuling>
  <dataSource>
    <microAgentName>
      <![CDATA[COM.TIBCO.hawk.hma.EventLog]]>
    </microAgentName>
    <methodName>onApplicationEvent</methodName>
    <dataElement name="Source">
      <dataObject class="java.lang.String" >
        <![CDATA[TIBCO Hawk Agent]]>
      </dataObject>
    </dataElement>
    <interval>0</interval>
  </dataSource>
  <test>
    <name><![CDATA[(Type Equals Warning)]]></name>
    <schedule></schedule>
    <operator class="COM.TIBCO.hawk.config.rbengine.
      rulebase.operators.EqualsObject" >
      <operator class="COM.TIBCO.hawk.config.rbengine.
        rulebase.operators.RuleData" >
        <dataObject class="java.lang.String" >
          <![CDATA[Type]]>
        </dataObject>
```

```
        </operator>
        <dataObject class="java.lang.String" >
          <![CDATA[Warning]]>
        </dataObject>
      </operator>
      <consequenceAction>
        <name>
          <![CDATA[sendAlertLow
            (alertMsg=Hawk Agent Warning : ${Text} )]]>
        </name>
        <schedule></schedule>
        <microAgentName>
          COM.TIBCO.hawk.microagent.RuleBaseEngine
        </microAgentName>
        <methodName>sendAlertMessage</methodName>
        <dataElement name="message">
          <dataObject class=
            "COM.TIBCO.hawk.config.rbengine.rulebase.util.
              AlertLow" >
            <![CDATA[Hawk Agent Warning : ${Text} ]]>
          </dataObject>
        </dataElement>
        <performOnceOnly/>
        <escalationTime>0</escalationTime>
      </consequenceAction>
      <trueConditionPolicy>
        <trueCountThreshold>1</trueCountThreshold>
      </trueConditionPolicy>
      <clearOn>
        <clearTimer>
          <second>900</second>
        </clearTimer>
      </clearOn>
    </test>
    <test>
      ...
    </test>
</rule>
```

Hawk Microagent Adapter (HMA)

Since the Hawk Agent is written in Java, it is unable to directly make the operating system calls required to obtain the status of the environment and interact with the file system. Thus it cannot interact directly with the file system or operating system for either monitoring or executing actions. The Hawk Microagent Adapter (HMA) serves this purpose. It is written in C/C++ and makes the needed operating system calls to provide access to these capabilities via an AMI interface.

The Hawk Microagent Adapter provides the ability to monitor individual operating system processes using the capabilities provided by the operating system itself. In addition, it can monitor the overall operating system, gathering information such as memory and CPU utilization.

Microagent Interfaces

Microagent interfaces present three different kinds of operations: query, update, and subscription. To illustrate, Figure 3-7 shows the operations of the TIBCO Hawk ActiveMatrix Service Monitoring Microagent. This microagent is provided by each ActiveMatrix node and exposes details of that node's operation.

Microagent query operations, usually of the form getXXX(), are request-reply interactions in which the component being monitored (in this case, the node) is asked to return some information. The getBindingInfo() operation, for example, returns the specifics of the bindings being used in the node upon which the operation was invoked. When invoked from the Hawk Display, query operations provide real-time data. These operations can also be invoked by Hawk rules.

Update operations—for example, changeMonitoringConfig(), are request-reply interactions that make stateful changes to the component being monitored. This particular operation changes the monitoring configuration of the specific ActiveMatrix node upon which it is invoked. Update operations can either be invoked from the Hawk display or by Hawk rules.

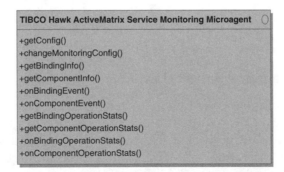

TIBCO Hawk ActiveMatrix Service Monitoring Microagent ◯

+getConfig()
+changeMonitoringConfig()
+getBindingInfo()
+getComponentInfo()
+onBindingEvent()
+onComponentEvent()
+getBindingOperationStats()
+getComponentOperationStats()
+onBindingOperationStats()
+onComponentOperationStats()

Figure 3-7: *TIBCO Hawk ActiveMatrix Service Monitoring Microagent Interface*

Subscription operations, usually of the form on$XXwX$( ), identify an event for which notifications are desired. These operations are used to trigger the execution of Hawk rules and may not be invoked from the Hawk Display.

Hawk Display

The Hawk Display is a user interface that shows the status of all Hawk agents belonging to a particular Hawk domain. The display enables the user to see the agents and rulebases in use and to see which ones are generating alerts. From the display you can drill down into the details and interact with the components using the microagent methods (Figure 3-8).

Hawk Event Service

The Hawk Event Service is a separate executable that provides the ability to log events either to a file or to a database. Events that can be logged include those reported by agents (notifications and alerts) and events surrounding the starting and stopping of agents themselves.

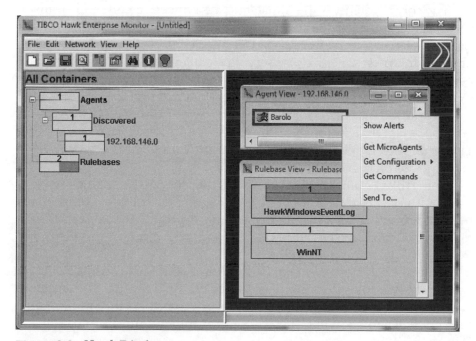

Figure 3-8: *Hawk Display*

The event service can also execute command-line scripts or run executables in the event of the loss of heartbeats from a Hawk agent.

Hawk Adapters

Available as separate products, there are a number of Hawk adapters

- TIBCO Hawk® Adapter for Tivoli
- TIBCO Hawk® Database Adapter
- TIBCO Hawk® JMX Plug-in
- TIBCO Hawk® SNMP Adapter

TIBCO® Managed File Transfer Product Portfolio

The purpose of TIBCO Managed File Transfer Product Portfolio is to move files of any size from the file system on one machine to the file system on another or to an external partner. With the TIBCO Managed File Transfer portfolio of products, there are a number of approaches available (Figure 3-9).

The core capability is the transfer of files between a pair of file transfer servers that are either Platform Servers (TIBCO® Managed File Transfer Platform Server for <platform>) or Internet Servers (TIBCO Managed File Transfer Internet Server). These servers are intended for transferring files between systems within an enterprise. The Internet Server can also exchange files with Internet clients using standard protocols.

Supported platforms for the Platform Server include z/OS, AS/400, AIX, Solaris, HP/UX, Linux, zLinux, and Windows. These servers provide guaranteed delivery facilities for transferring files between different types of platforms.

The TIBCO Managed File Transfer Internet Server enables interactions with parties that do not have Managed File Transfer components installed. It supports a number of standard protocols such as HTTPS, HTTP, FTPS (SSL), SFTP (SSH), FTP, and AS2 along with streaming PGP encryption and decryption.

An option available is the TIBCO Managed File Transfer Platform Server for Windows RocketStream® Accelerator Upgrade. The accelerator utilizes PDP or UDP protocols to improve performance in file transfer between servers when there is significant communications latency (Figure 3-10).

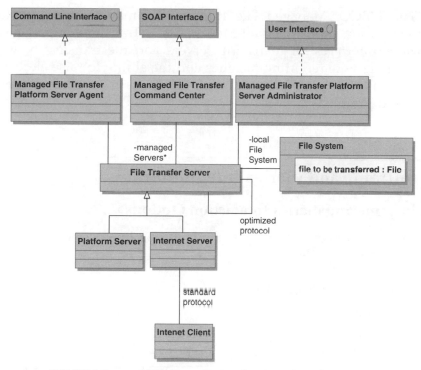

Figure 3-9: *TIBCO Managed File Transfer Product Portfolio Overview*

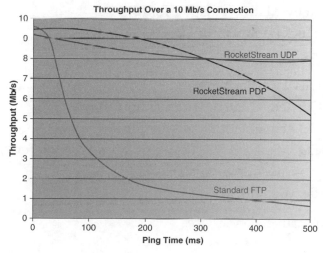

Figure 3-10: *RocketStream Accelerator Performance*

The TIBCO® Managed File Transfer Command Center provides web-based management of all Managed File Transfer components. It provides interfaces for managing servers and file transfers between them, along with reporting facilities and the ability to raise alerts in a number of formats. Command Center interfaces are available for both users and programs.

Mainframe and iSeries Integration

Mainframe and iSeries Interaction Options

There are a number of options available for interacting with main-frames. These include:

- Platform-specific products
  - z/OS
    - Substation ES™
    - TIBCO Mainframe Service Tracker
    - TIBCO ActiveMatrix BusinessWorks™ Plug-in for CICS
    - TIBCO Adapter for Files z/OS (MVS)
  - iSeries
    - ActiveMatrix® Adapter for IBM i
    - TIBCO Adapter for Files (IBM i)

- Generic TIBCO products
  - ActiveMatrix BusinessWorks™ Plug-in for Data Conversion
  - TIBCO ActiveMatrix® Adapter for Database
  - TIBCO ActiveMatrix® Adapter for WebSphere MQ
  - TIBCO® Managed File Transfer Platform Server for z/OS
  - Enterprise Message Service client
  - Rendezvous client

- Platform-native web services

Interaction Intent

In selecting the appropriate mainframe interaction option, it is important to keep in mind the intent of the interaction. Some possible intents are

- Program-to-program interaction
  - Initiated off mainframe
  - Initiated on mainframe

- Data access
  - Off-mainframe access to mainframe data
  - On-mainframe access to off-mainframe data
  - On-mainframe access to mainframe data

- Event Recognition
  - On-mainframe event recognition and annunciation

Table 3-1 summarizes the ability of different mainframe interaction options to satisfy these intents.

Table 3-1: *Satisfying Mainframe Interaction Intents*

Intent	Direction	z/OS Options	IBM i Options
Program-to-program interaction	Initiated off mainframe	Substation ES ActiveMatrix Business-Works™ Plug-in for CICS	TIBCO® ActiveMatrix® Adapter for IBM i
	Initiated on mainframe	Substation ES	TIBCO ActiveMatrix Adapter for IBM i
Data access	Off-mainframe access to mainframe data	ActiveMatrix Business-Works Plug-in for Data Conversion TIBCO Adapter for Files z/OS (MVS)	TIBCO ActiveMatrix Adapter for IBM i TIBCO Adapter for Files (IBM i) ActiveMatrix Business-Works Plug-in for Data Conversion
Event recognition	On-mainframe event recognition and annunciation	TIBCO Adapter for Files z/OS (MVS) (PDS and sequential) Custom application code using messaging	Custom application code using messaging

Substation ES

Substation ES is a z/OS-hosted component that enables program-to-program interaction. It supports interaction both to and from the mainframe, although z/OS programs may have to be modified to initiate interactions.

Figure 3-11 provides an overview of the Substation ES deployment. The substation itself runs on the z/OS mainframe and can initiate or provide access to both CICS and IMS programs. Off-mainframe communications can use either Enterprise Message Service or Rendezvous as a transport. Data in these communications is represented in mainframe format. Managing and monitoring Substation ES can be done from a browser-based UI.

The ActiveMatrix BusinessWorks Plug-in for Data Conversion provides convenient facilities for accessing data in this format. Similar facilities are provided in the Eclipse IDE provided with the product. These tools significantly reduce application development time.

TIBCO Mainframe Service Tracker

The TIBCO Mainframe Service Tracker (Figure 3-11) is a z/OS subsystem that can monitor jobs and job steps as well as SYSLOG messages

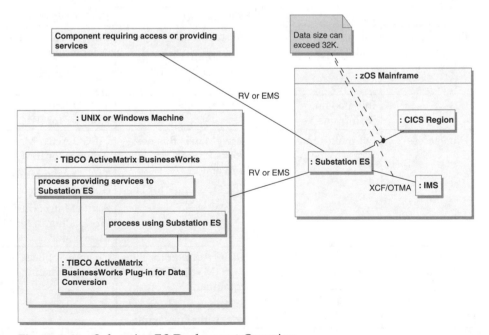

Figure 3-11: *Substation ES Deployment Overview*

and events. It has an event client facility that enables z/OS applications to send Hawk Alerts and Notifications, and a smart client facility that allows applications to subscribe to the job monitoring events.

TIBCO ActiveMatrix BusinessWorks Plug-in for CICS

The ActiveMatrix BusinessWorks Plug-in for CICS enables Active-Matrix BusinessWorks processes to execute CICS transactions (Figure 3-12). There are two parts to the plugin: a component installed on the mainframe and the plug-in installed with BusinessWorks. Also useful in this context is the ActiveMatrix BusinessWorks Plug-in for Data Conversion.

TIBCO Adapter for IBM i

The TIBCO Adapter for IBM i allows bidirectional interactions between UNIX or Windows applications and an i5/OS. It allows an i5/OS application to interact with a UNIX and Windows application via data queues. In the other direction, it allows UNIX and Windows applications to interact with an i5/OS application via data queues, PGM program objects, and spooled files.

The adapter is deployed on a UNIX or Windows machine and interacts with applications using either the Enterprise Message Service or Rendezvous transports (Figure 3-13). The ActiveMatrix BusinessWorks Plug-in for Data Conversion greatly simplifies working with the System i data structures and its use significantly reduces development time.

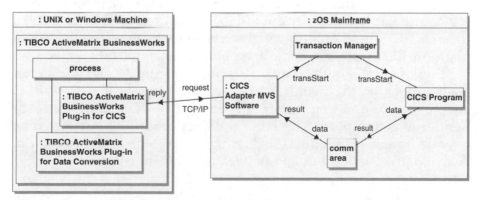

Figure 3-12: *ActiveMatrix BusinessWorks Plug-in for CICS Deployment*

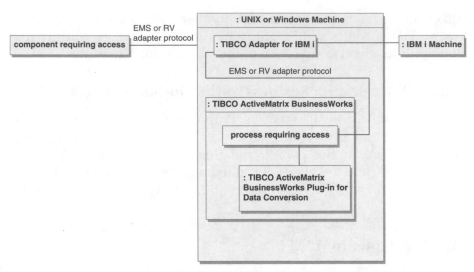

Figure 3-13: *TIBCO Adapter for IBM i Deployment*

Mainframe and iSeries File Adapters

The TIBCO Adapter for Files z/OS (MVS) and TIBCO Adapter for Files (IBM i) provide off-mainframe access to files on their respective platforms. Files are accessible either in their entirety by block transfer (whole file) or by record for record-based processing.

Capabilities on the two platforms are slightly different. On the z/OS platform, applications can write to VSAM, sequential datasets (SEQs), generation dataset groups (GDGs), and partitioned datasets (PDSs). Applications can trigger the publishing of these same file types by sending a message. The adapter can also be configured to poll partitioned datasets (PDSs) and publish the files when they change. For the iSeries platform, the adapter can write and publish sequential (SEQ) files.

Deployment of both adapters is similar (Figure 3-14). The adapter itself resides on the mainframe, providing services via the TIBCO adapter protocol using either the Enterprise Message Service or Rendezvous transports. The TIBCO adapter protocol is supported by a wide range of products including ActiveMatrix Service Grid, ActiveMatrix Service Bus, and ActiveMatrix BusinessWorks.

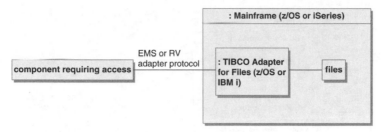

Figure 3-14: *Mainframe File Adapter Deployment*

BusinessConnect™

Many business processes require interactions with business partners. Generally these interactions require prior arrangement to register the partner, establish security credentials, and define both the kinds of interactions that can occur and the mechanisms that will be used.

BusinessConnect facilitates these interactions with business partners. It implements a number of business-to-business (B2B) communications protocols and acts as an intermediary between these protocols and an enterprise's private business processes. The B2B protocols supported include

- EDI (including HIPAA)
- RosettaNet
- SOAP
- EZComm
- ebXML
- cXML
- TIBCO BusinessConnect™ Remote
- TIBCO BusinessConnect™ Trading Community Management

BusinessConnect also implements many commonly required features for B2B interactions including non-repudiation, partner registration, and credential management.

There are several options for deploying BusinessConnect (Figure 3-15). All options include the BusinessConnect Interior Engine, a stand-alone executable that is based upon ActiveMatrix Business-Works. It uses a local database to store the information it uses. Business

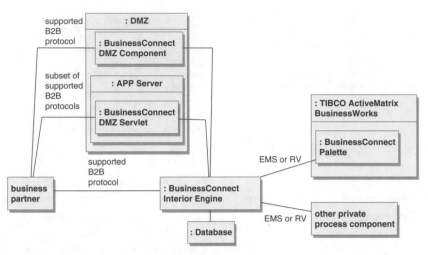

Figure 3-15: *BusinessConnect Deployment*

partners may connect directly with the engine using one of the supported B2B protocols or they may connect through a component running in a demineralized zone (DMZ). The BusinessConnect DMZ Component enables connection via any of the supported B2B protocols. The BusinessConnect DMZ Servlet runs in an application server but only enables connection to a subset of the supported B2B protocols.

The BusinessConnect Interior Engine communicates with the enterprise's private processes using XML messages delivered by either Enterprise Message Service or Rendezvous transports. These messages are in BusinessConnect's aeRvMsg format. The TIBCO BusinessConnect™ Palette for BusinessWorks™ (supplied as a component of the BusinessConnect product) simplifies the use of this protocol.

TIBCO Collaborative Information Manager

The TIBCO Collaborative Information Manager is designed to manage reference data (often referred to as master data) in the enterprise (Figure 3-16). Customer, partner, and product data generally fall into this category. This information is generally distributed across a number of systems, and the product makes it possible to manage this information in a consistent way.

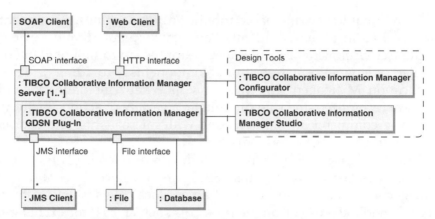

Figure 3-16: *Simplified TIBCO Collaborative Information Manager Deployment*

There are three major roles played by the information manager:

1. Provide a single consistent logical view of reference data and a single point for accessing this information.

2. Maintain the consistency of the data across multiple systems, detecting changes and managing the workflow updating other systems to maintain consistency.

3. When discrepancies cannot be automatically resolved, initiate and manage the human workflow required to investigate and resolve discrepancies.

Views of the managed information are available both through user (Web Client) interfaces and programmatic interfaces (SOAP, JMS, and File). These same interfaces can be used to inform the information manager of data changes in other systems as well as to update the data in those systems.

Summary

There are a number of specialized TIBCO products that are often used in composite applications and services. These include Hawk, TIBCO Managed File Transfer products, a number of mainframe-related products, and BusinessConnect.

Hawk enables the rule-based monitoring of machines, components, and services in an environment. The Hawk Agent running in each machine environment uses rules to monitor the environment. It obtains detailed status information from components providing a Hawk Application Microagent Interface (AMI). When rule-defined conditions are recognized, the rule can initiate a variety of actions including executing command lines, interacting with microagents, and sending Hawk alerts, messages, and e-mails.

TIBCO Managed File Transfer product family controls the movement of files between systems. Files are transferred to and from Managed File Transfer servers that access local file systems. Internet servers enable the use of public protocols such as FTP for exchanging files with systems that do not have TIBCO Managed File Transfer components installed on them. File movement over communications links with high latency can be sped up by using the Rocket Stream Accelerator version of the products.

There are a number of mechanisms available for interacting with mainframes. Each mechanism provides a different assortment of interaction capabilities: program-to-program interaction, data access, and event recognition. For z/OS systems, options include the Substation ES, the ActiveMatrix BusinessWorks Plug-in for CICS, the TIBCO Adapter for Files z/OS (MVS), and the ActiveMatrix Adapter for Database. For the System i platform, options include the TIBCO Adapter for IBM i and the TIBCO Adapter for Files (IBM i).

BusinessConnect enables business-to-business interactions using a variety of protocols. It acts as an intermediary between these protocols and the enterprise's private business processes. It also provides non-repudiation capability, and it manages the registration and credentials for business partners.

TIBCO Collaborative Information Manager provides a consistent view of reference information distributed across multiple systems. It also provides the workflow necessary to maintain the consistency of that data as it gets updated in individual systems.

Chapter 4

Case Study: Nouveau Health Care

Objectives

One of the challenges in writing about architecture and architecture patterns is to pick examples that are rich enough to motivate the discussion and realistic enough to represent real-world challenges while at the same time being simple enough to be readily explained.

The fictional Nouveau Health Care case study was created for this purpose. Its business processes, though simplified when compared with their real-world equivalent, are still complex enough to present most of the common design challenges found in their real-world counterparts. An important aspect of reality is that the processes and their corresponding solution implementations do not operate in isolation— they interact with one another and with other business processes as they would in the real world.

Different aspects of the Nouveau Health Care example are used throughout this architecture book series. This chapter provides a conceptual overview of the company and its business processes and then introduces the Payment Manager and its related business processes, which are used to illustrate many of the points and design principles in this book.

Nouveau Health Care Solution Architecture

Nouveau Health Care is a traditional health care insurance company. It sells health care insurance policies and covers claim payments with the revenue it collects from its premiums. It also administers the processing of claims.

There are factors that add to the complexity of Nouveau's business. In some cases, the employers for whom Nouveau provides the health care benefits also provide the funds for paying the claims: Nouveau simply administers the policies. In other cases the administration of specialized services (vision and dental care) is farmed out to other companies. Both variations present some interesting design challenges.

Nouveau Health Care Business Processes

Our use of Nouveau focuses on four of its business processes (Figure 4-1):

1. Validate Membership and its underlying Validate Membership Service
2. Manage Payments, which manages claim payments to health care service providers
3. Process Claim, and its initiator, Route Claim, which together handle the processing of insurance claims
4. Monitor Claim Processing, a process that monitors the execution of claim processing

The Validate Membership process is used by authorized parties (health care providers, employers, and members) to validate whether or not an individual was covered by the policy on a given date. This business process utilizes an underlying Validate Membership Service, which is also used by the Process Claim business process. Validate Membership is used as an example in the *TIBCO® Architecture Fundamentals* book.

The Manage Payments process manages the payments to health care service providers resulting from health care claims.[1] What makes

---

1. In the real world, the Manage Payments process would also manage payments to members, reimbursing them for claim-related expenses that they have already paid themselves.

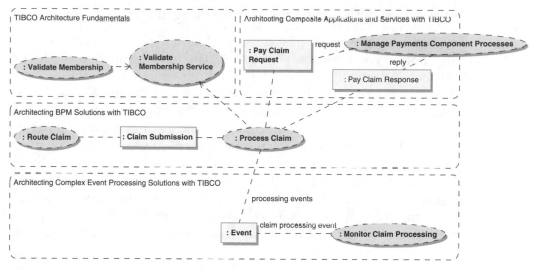

Figure 4-1: *Nouveau Health Care Business Processes*

this process interesting is that, under normal circumstances, payments are made on a periodic basis (e.g., monthly) to health care service providers. This means that the payment manager must keep track of pending payments. By exception, payments to health care service providers for specific claims may be made immediately. Many of the examples in this book are drawn utilizing the Manage Payments processes to illustrate the points being made.

Process Claim and its related Route Claim process actually handle the processing of health care claims. Routing is required because some claims are processed by Nouveau itself while others are processed by partner companies. Process Claim is a consumer of both the Validate Membership Service and the services of the Payment Manager. Process Claim and Route Claim are used as examples in the upcoming book, *Architecting BPM Solutions with TIBCO®*.

Monitor Claim Processing keeps track of the progress of claim processing. The reason that this is necessary is that some claim processing is done by partner companies. Monitoring provides uniform tracking of all health care claims regardless of whether Nouveau or one of its partners is handling the claim. This process is used as an example in the upcoming book, *Architecting Complex Event Processing Solutions with TIBCO®*.

Nouveau Health Care Architecture Pattern

The business processes of Nouveau Health Care are executed by a collection of components (Figure 4-2). The Claim Router provides an interface for the Billing Provider to submit claims. It validates membership with the Membership Service, routes claims to the Claim Processor, and reports status to the Claim Tracker. The Claim Processor (and there may be more than one) adjudicates the claim, validating membership via the Membership Service, requesting claim payment via the Payment Manager, and reporting status to the Claim Tracker. The Payment Manager pays the service providers, getting the account associated with the plan from the Benefits Service, the account associated with the health care service provider from the Provider Service, and using the Banking Service to make the payments. It also reports status to the Claim Tracker.

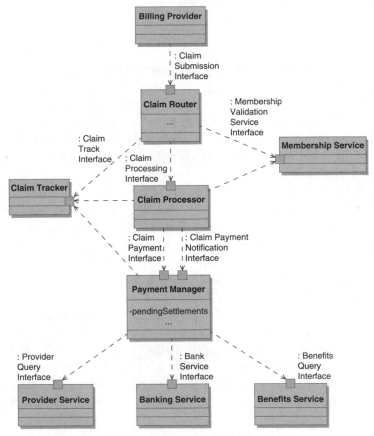

Figure 4-2: *Nouveau Health Care Architecture Pattern*

Nouveau Health Care in Context

Nouveau Health Care is part of a larger environment that includes the health care service providers that submit claims and the partner companies that process some of the claims (Figure 4-3). Here we see that there can be more than one claim processor, which explains the need for the Claim Router.

Processing Claims from Providers

Health care claims can be submitted by either the health care service provider or by the member to whom the service was provided. In the Nouveau Health Care example we focus on the claims submitted by providers and on the payments to those providers.

Figure 4-4 presents an overview of the processing of claims submitted by health care service providers. This sunny-day scenario shows provider interactions via the US quasi-standard HIPAA transactions[2] and shows deferred payments to the provider. The process model shows payer and provider account references, but not the details of the interactions with the Benefits Service and Provider Service required to

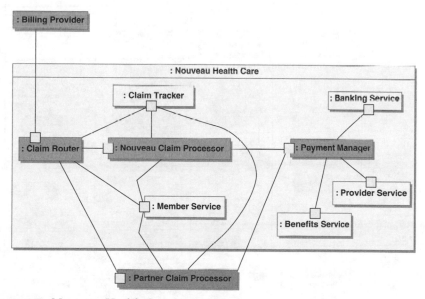

Figure 4-3: *Nouveau Health Care in Context*

---

2. In practice, each HIPAA transaction interface that is implemented by an enterprise is extended to accommodate the specific requirements of that enterprise.

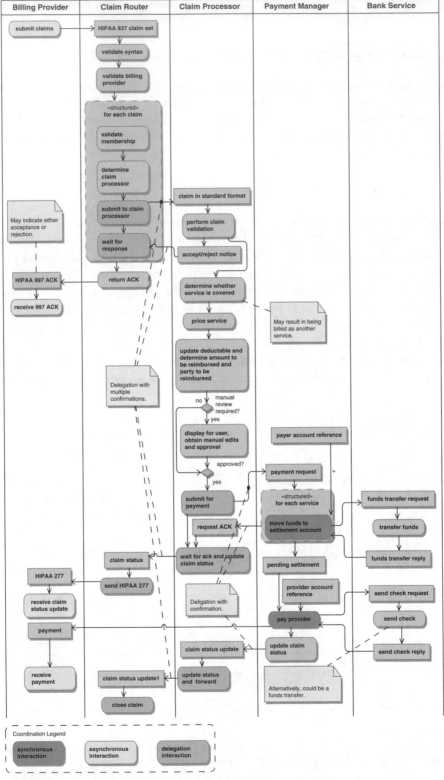

Figure 4-4: *Processing Claims from Providers*

obtain them. Similarly, it shows where membership is validated, but not the interactions with the Member Service that actually does the validation. Finally, for simplicity, all interactions with the Claim Tracker have been omitted.

Payment Manager Service Specification

The Payment Manager is a nontrivial service that will be used as an example throughout this book. Here is a simplified version of its specification to give you an understanding of its intended role in Nouveau Health Care. The full specification is provided online at informit.com/title/9780321802057 and as an appendix to the electronic versions of this book.

The Payment Manager (Figure 4-5) provides services to the Claim Processor for paying health care service providers for their services and (in the event of deferred payments) notifying the Claim Processor that payment has been made. These services are provided via the Claim Payment Interface and the Claim Payment Notification Interface. The Claim Processor here represents a generic component that processes claims. In the planned deployment both the Nouveau Health Care claim processor and external partner claim processors will utilize the Payment Manager.

The Payment Manager is, in turn, a consumer of services provided by the Claim Tracker, the Provider Service, the Banking Service, and the Benefits service via the indicated interfaces.

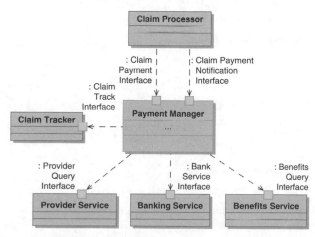

Figure 4-5: *Payment Manager Usage Context*

Payment Manager Specification: Process Overview

On the surface, the payment manager looks simple. It has a simple interface (Figure 4-6).

It also has a seemingly simple relationship to other processes. Process Claim tells it to pay a claim and Manage Payments either sends a check or does an electronic funds transfer (Figure 4-7). But this apparent simplicity is deceiving. To understand this, let's take a look at a health careclaim.

Health Care Claim

Some of the basic concepts involved in a health care claim are shown in Figure 4-8. A claim is a request for reimbursement for services rendered to a member of a health care plan. It contains one or more service

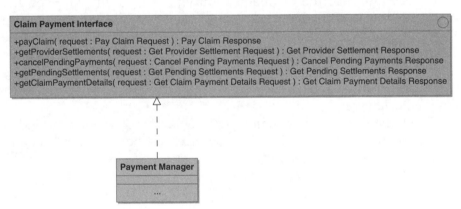

Figure 4-6: *Claim Payment Interface*

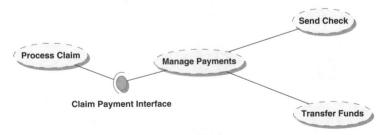

Figure 4-7: *Overview of the Manage Payments Process*

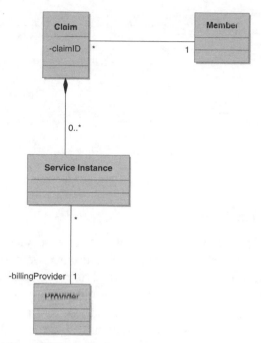

Figure 4-8: *Health Care Claim Basic Concepts*

instances for which reimbursement is required. Associated with each service instance is the health care service provider that is to be reimbursed for that service (the billingProvider). Since different service instances may have different billing providers, a claim payment may result in payments to more than one provider.

Manage Payments Processes

By business rule, under normal circumstances payments are made to health care providers on a periodic (typically monthly) basis. These are referred to as deferred payments. Periodically a process runs to settle (pay) these deferred payments. By exception, claims can be paid immediately. This is generally done as a remedial action for claims that have been excessively delayed in processing for one reason or another.

From this, we see that the Manage Payments process actually consists of three processes (Figure 4-9): Immediate Payment, Deferred Payment, and Settle Deferred Payments.

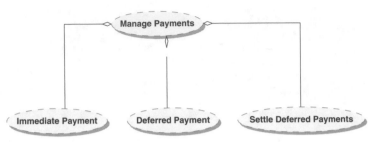

Figure 4-9: *Manage Payments Processes*

Process Coordination

When immediate payment is requested, the service consumer (e.g., Process Claim) requests the payment using the synchronous request-reply coordination pattern (Figure 4-10). The response indicates whether or not the payments were successfully made.

For Deferred Payment (Figure 4-11), the exchange between the service consumer and Payment Manager is the front end of a delegation with confirmation interaction. This portion of the interaction simply returns a promise to make the payments at some point in the future. The back end of the delegation with confirmation interaction is the Settle Deferred Payment process, which is triggered by a timer.

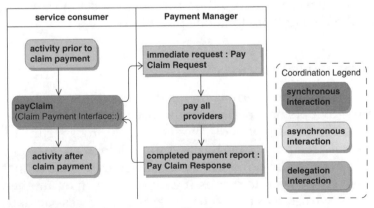

Figure 4-10: *Immediate Payment Coordination*

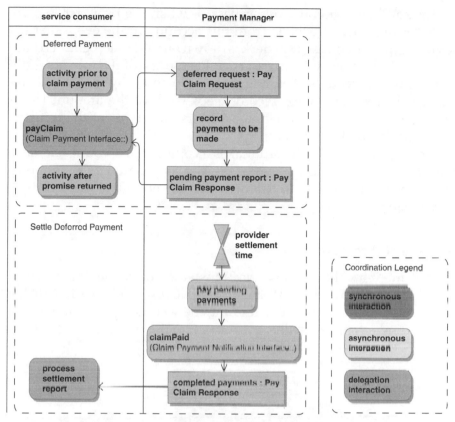

Figure 4-11: *Deferred Payment and Settlement Coordination*

Payment Manager Specification: Domain Model

Accounts and Funds Transfers

There are three types of bank accounts involved in the claims payment process: Payer Accounts, Provider Accounts, and Settlement Accounts. Each insurance policy has an associated Payer Account from which claims against the policy are paid. Each health care service provider being paid through funds transfers has a Provider Account. The Settlement Account is used as an intermediary account. When the Payment Manager is told to pay a claim, funds are moved immediately into the settlement account, regardless of when the provider is paid. Funds for providers are taken from this account. In the event that the provider is paid by check, the check is drawn on the Settlement Account.

For audit reasons, it is necessary to keep track of the movement of funds between accounts. A Funds Transfer Record (Figure 4-12) is created for each transfer. Each record keeps track of the amount transferred, the source and destination accounts, the status of the transfer, and the timing of the transfer.

Each Funds Transfer Record makes a copy of the account reference information at the time the funds transfer is initiated so that subsequent changes to the account information do not affect the record of past transfers.

Settlement Accounts

Each payment involves two Funds Transfer Records: the first captures the movement of funds from the payer account associated with the health care plan to a settlement account; the second captures the movement of funds from the settlement account to the provider account.

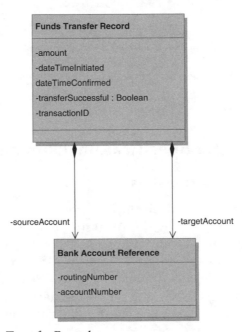

Figure 4-12: *Funds Transfer Record*

By business rule, when the payment manager is told to pay a claim, the related funds are immediately moved from the payer account to the settlement account. The funds remain in the settlement account until the provider is actually paid.

Settlement Concepts

The concepts associated with settling a health care claim are shown in Figure 4-13. Each health care claim has a set of health care service instances, each one of which (if accepted) will eventually be associated

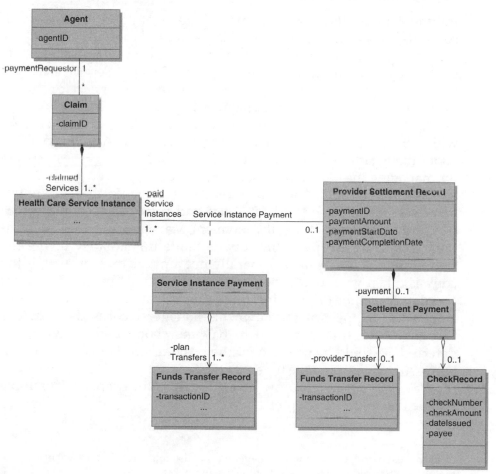

Figure 4-13: *Settlement Concepts*

with a provider settlement. When the Payment Manager is told to pay a claim, it associates the service instance with a Provider Settlement Record, transfers the associated funds to the settlement account, and records the service instance payment in the form of a funds transfer. This records the movement of funds from the individual health care plan to the settlement account. When the health care service provider is actually paid (which may be either immediate or deferred), a Settlement Payment is made. The payment may occur via a direct funds transfer or it may occur via check and be recorded by a Check Record.

Payment Domain Concepts

Putting it all together, we have a partial model of the payment domain concepts shown in Figure 4-14. This model indicates which services serve as systems of record for the various concepts. The issuer is the entity that sells the health care plan. The Benefits Service manages the benefits plan and keeps track of who is paying for services under the plan and what account these payments are taken from. The Provider service keeps track of health care service providers and the means by which they are to be paid. The Claim Service manages information about the health care claims, and the Payment Manager is responsible for managing the payments to service providers.[3]

Note that from the Payment Manager perspective, the account reference information for both the plan and provider accounts comes from other services. When the Payment Manager uses this information, it is using a copy. If the copy is made immediately before the information is used, this is generally not a problem. However, if the copy is taken well in advance, consideration must be given to what should occur if the original information is updated. For example, consider what happens if the Payment Manager records the provider account at the time it is told to pay the claim. If the payment is deferred, it would be possible for the provider to change the account between this time and the time that the account is settled. How would the Payment Manager know about the account change? This topic will be discussed in Chapter 12.

---

3. In the real world, the payment manager would also manage reimbursements to plan members who paid for services out of their own pocket.

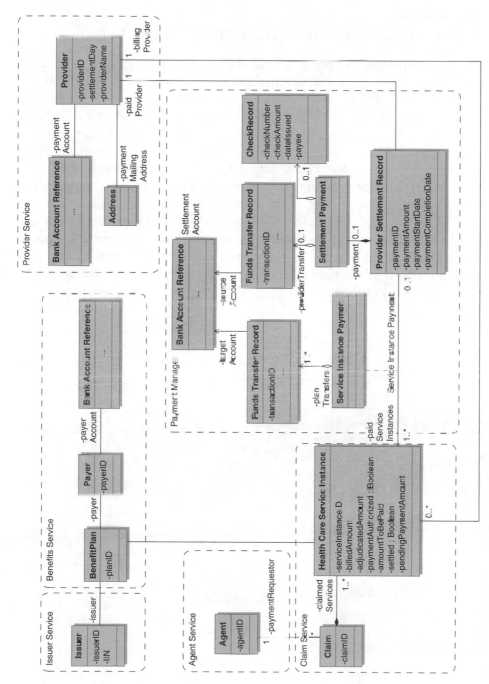

Figure 4-14: *Payment Domain Model (Partial)*

Payment Manager Specification: Interfaces

The Payment Manager has two logical interfaces with respect to claims payment (Figure 4-15). The Claim Payment Interface provides the ability for the Claim Processor to direct the Payment Manager to pay a claim. The Claim Payment Notification Interface supports the deferred payment option and provides the ability for the Payment Manager to inform the Claim Processor that the payment has been completed.[4] The Payment Manager also has some state information visible through these interfaces: the pending settlements. These are planned payments to the health care service providers that have yet to be made.

The logical data structures used by these interfaces are shown in Figure 4-16. The immediatePayment flag in the Claim Payment Request is used to indicate whether the payment is to be made immediately or should be paid in the normal deferred manner. Otherwise the request is identical for both immediate and deferred payments.

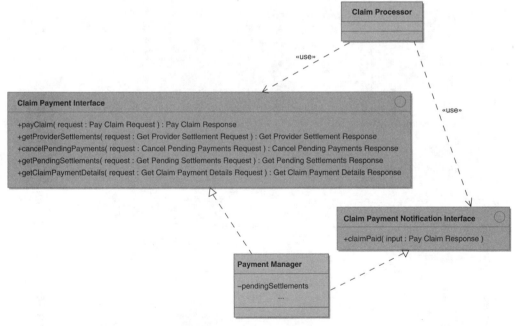

Figure 4-15: *Payment Manager Interfaces*

4. The details of how this interface is implemented can vary considerably depending upon the mechanism chosen for asynchronous interactions. These are discussed in Chapter 10.

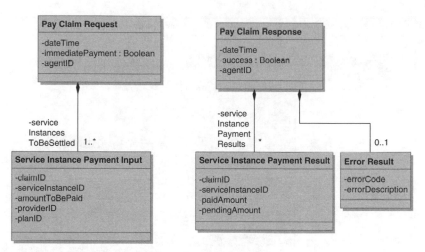

Figure 4-16: *Claim Payment Request and Response*

The Claim Payment Response is used in both interfaces. For immediate payments, the paidAmount in the Service Instance Payment Result will contain the amount actually paid. For deferred payments, this field will be zero and the pendingAmount will indicate the amount that will be paid upon settlement. When this data structure is returned by the Claim Payment Notification Interface, the pendingAmount will be zero and the paidAmount will indicate the amount that was actually paid.

Payment Manager Specification: Processes

Immediate Payment Process

An overview of the process that the Payment Manager uses for immediate payment is shown in Figure 4-17. Upon receipt of the request, the Payment Manager obtains a settlement account. For each service instance the payer account is found, the provider settlement record is obtained, and the funds are transferred from the payer account to the settlement account. Note that, by business rule, failed transfers do not keep other transfers from proceeding. With respect to the Provider Settlement Record, if one has not been created in this instance of the immediate payment process, one is created. Otherwise, the existing

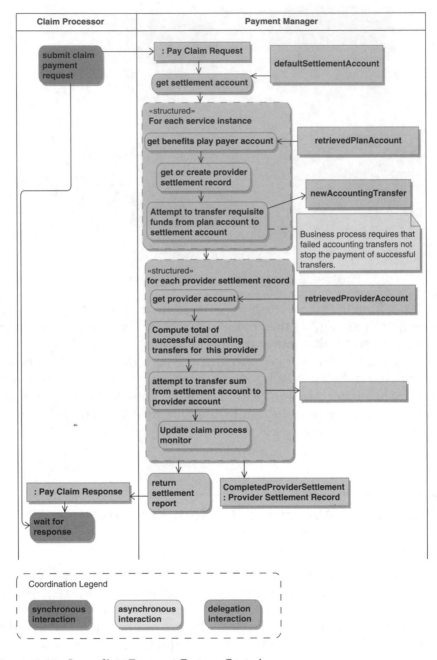

Figure 4-17: *Immediate Payment Process Overview*

record is used. Processing continues until all funds related to this claim have been transferred to the settlement account.

Next, for each Provider Settlement Record, the provider account is obtained. Funds are then transferred to the provider account (there is a slight variation if a check were to be sent instead). Finally, the Provider Settlement Record is updated and the Claim Payment Response is sent back to the service consumer (the Claim Processor).

The details of this process, including the interactions with the Benefits Service, Provider Service, and Banking Service, are shown in Figure 4-18. Note that all interactions with other services are synchronous in this process.

Deferred Payment and Settlement Processes

The Deferred Payment process (Figure 4-19) is the front half of a delegation with confirmation interaction between the Claim Processor and the Payment Manager. Its processing is the same as the first half of the immediate payment process. It transfers funds from the payer account(s) to the settlement account, records these as Plan Transfer Records, and associates each record with the appropriate provider settlement record. If a settlement record already exists (i.e., there are already pending payments for this provider) then it is used. Otherwise a new one is created.

Figure 4-20 (p. 88) shows the deferred payment process mapped onto the architecture pattern of the Payment Manager and indicates the specific interfaces that are used on the underlying services.

The settlement process (Figure 4-21, p. 89) is the confirmation part of the delegation with confirmation interaction that began with the deferred payment process. The process begins with a timer expiration, at which point the settlements to be completed are identified. For each pending settlement, the amount to be transferred is computed and the funds transfer is initiated. In a variation (not shown), a check may be cut instead. The process concludes by updating the Provider Settlement Record and sending a settlement report (a Claim Payment Response) to the Claim Processor.

Figure 4-22 (p. 90) shows the settlement process mapped onto the architecture pattern. It indicates the interface operations being invoked on the Provider Service, Banking Service, and Claim Tracker.

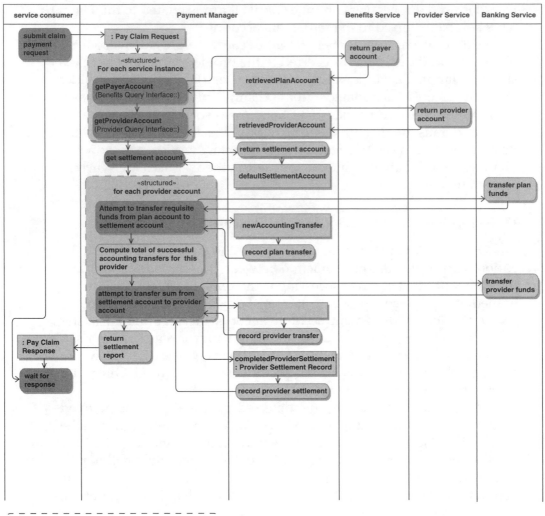

Figure 4-18: *Immediate Payment Process Mapping*

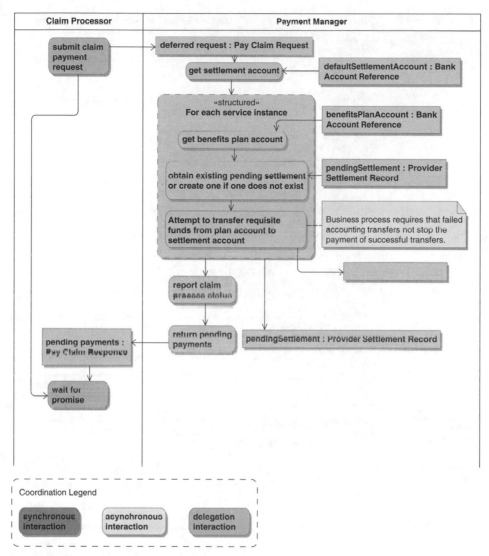

Figure 4-19: *Deferred Payment Process Overview*

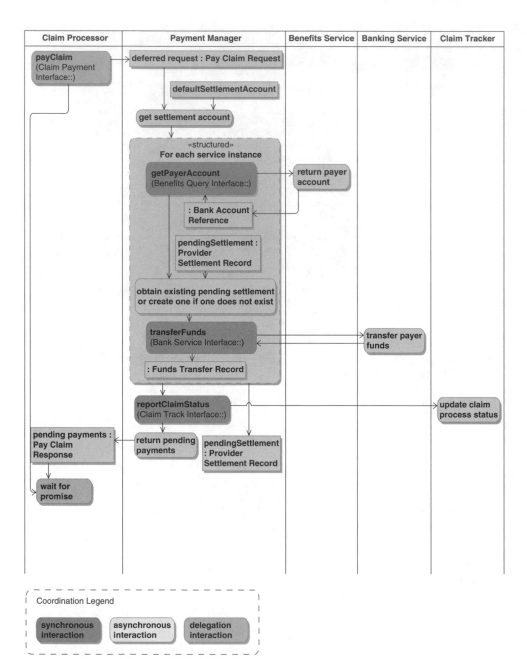

Figure 4-20: *Deferred Payment Process Mapping*

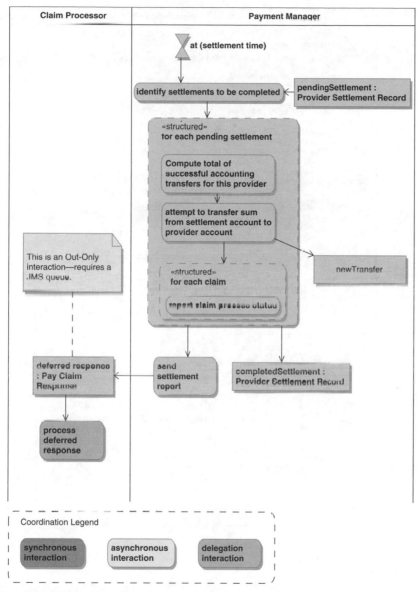

Figure 4-21: *Settlement Process*

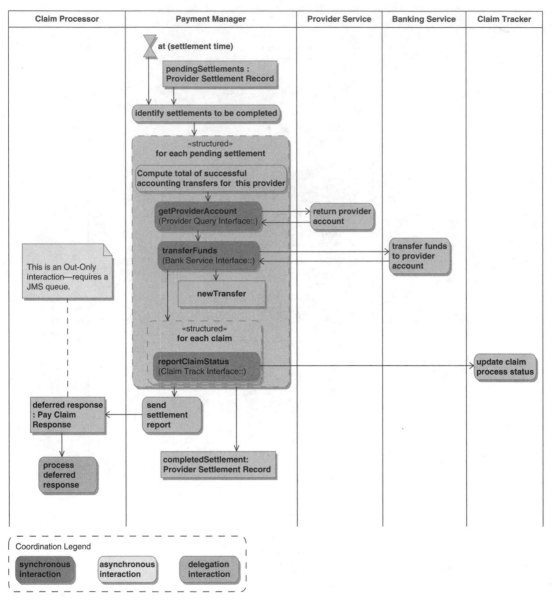

Figure 4-22: *Settlement Process Mapping*

Summary

The fictional Nouveau Health Care example provides a sufficiently rich context for illustrating the major points being made throughout the TIBCO architecture book series. In this book, the Payment Manager is used as an example of a composite application that provides Claim Payment services to the rest of Nouveau Health Care and its business partners.

The Payment Manager illustrates several interesting (and realistic) complexities:

- The processing of one health care claim may involve payments to multiple health care service providers.

- Health care providers are normally paid on a periodic basis (e.g., monthly). By exception, claims can be paid immediately.

- When the Payment Manager is told to pay a claim, it immediately removes the funds from the Payer account associated with the health care benefits plan, regardless of when the provider will actually be paid.

- With respect to the party requesting claim payment, there are two possible coordination patterns: synchronous request-reply (for immediate payment) and delegation with asynchronous confirmation (for deferred payment).

- For audit purposes, the Payment Manager keeps track of all funds transfers.

The Payment Manager has two logical interfaces. The Claim Payment Interface is used to direct the Payment Manager to pay a claim. For deferred payments, the Claim Payment Notification Interface is used by the Payment Manager to notify parties that requested payments have been made.

The architecture pattern for the Payment Manager Specification indicates the services upon which the Payment Manager depends. These include the Benefits Service, the Provider Service, the Banking Service, and the Claim Tracker.

Part II

Designing Services

Chapter 5

Observable Dependencies and Behaviors

Objectives

When you are creating a design as a collection of interacting components (e.g., services), it is useful to be able to ignore the internals of those components and concentrate on their interactions. However, you still need to know something about the component—how it depends upon the environment in which it operates and how it will behave. This chapter is about how to characterize these dependencies and behaviors. As we shall see in the next chapter, this type of characterization forms the core of component and service specifications.

If you are conceptualizing (defining) the component as part of your design, you will be called upon to create this characterization. If you are using an existing component, then you will be the consumer of the characterization. Either way, you need to understand what is required to appropriately characterize the component.

Behavior is the way in which something, in our case a component, responds to a stimulus. To effectively utilize the component in a solution, you need to understand how the component will respond to stimuli provided by the other solution components and what stimuli the component will provide to the rest of the solution.

In this work we will use the term *observable dependency* to refer to the relationship between the component and components in the environment upon which it depends. We will use the term *observable behavior* to refer to the behavior as seen by the rest of the solution—without looking inside the component. After reading this chapter you should be able to describe the concepts of observable dependency and observable behavior and explain how they can be characterized. This will provide the foundation for an ensuing discussion of component and service specifications.

The Black Box Perspective

When you have a solution comprised of collaborating components (services), it is easier to understand the solution if you are able to view each component as a black box and not have to worry about what is inside. To do this, you need to be able to characterize two things: (1) the observable dependencies of the black box—the components in its environment upon which it depends, including their interfaces and behaviors, and (2) the observable behavior of the black box—how it responds to stimuli provided by other solution components and which stimuli it provides to those components. That's what this chapter is about.

There is a strong analogy here to the way in which people learn about things in their environment. When presented with an object they want to learn about, people are inclined to pick it up, turn it at different angles, and experiment with different ways in which they can interact with it. On electronic gadgets they press the keys, flip the switches, and touch the screen, all the while observing both the dependencies and the resultant behavior. They are making observations about the object.

You can think about solution components the same way, only the observations you make are not visual. The other components upon which they rely for proper operation characterize their dependencies, and the stimuli are the invocations of interface operations and other events that trigger component responses. Observations are the responses, such as returned data structures and the invocations of other component's interfaces. What you learn about the component are its dependencies and observable behavior.

Of course, experimenting with a component to learn its dependencies and behaviors is likely to be a time-consuming and error-prone activity. Preferably you would like to have someone tell you how the component will behave and the components upon which it depends for proper operation. Such a characterization of dependency and behavior forms the core of the component's specification.

Facets of Observable Dependencies and Behaviors

So what do you need to know about a component to describe its observable dependencies and behaviors? Some important facets include

- External component dependencies upon the component as characterized by the component's interfaces and operations
- The component's dependencies upon external components, consisting of the identification of these components and the characterization of their interfaces and operations
- Usage scenarios: characterizations of the business processes in which the component is expected to participate and the component's participation in those processes
- Triggered behaviors: the structure of component activities that explain the relationships between the component's triggers, responses, inputs, observable state, and outputs
- Observable state: information retained by the component with a presence that is observable through its interactions
- Coordination: the manner in which the component's activity can be coordinated with that of external components
- Constraints: limitations, particularly on the sequencing of triggers
- Nonfunctional behavior: performance, availability, and so on

Example: Sales Order Service

We will use the example of a Sales Order Service supporting an Order-to-Delivery business process to illustrate the various facets of observable dependencies and behaviors. An overview of the Order-to-Delivery business process is depicted in Figure 5-1. This figure presents a usage scenario for the Sales Order Service, which is one of the participants in

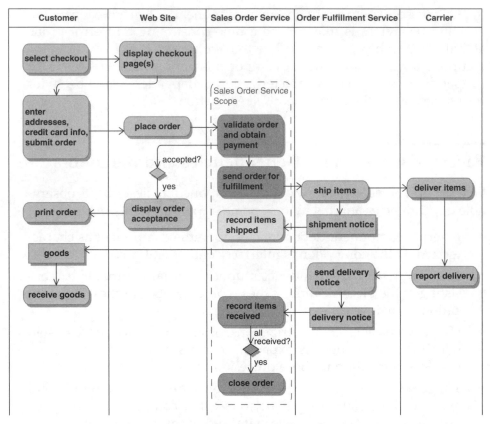

Figure 5-1: *Sales Order Service in the Order-to-Delivery Business Process*

the process. The Sales Order Service manages the full life cycle of an order. Let's examine how it participates in the process and note the relevant observable facets that come into play.

Placing the Order

The Sales Order Service accepts an order from the Web Site via the `placeOrder()` operation of the Sales Order Service Interface (Figure 5-2). The invocation of this operation constitutes a trigger, and the fact that it is invoked by the Web Site indicates a dependency on the interface.

The invocation of the `placeOrder()` operation triggers an associated behavior of the service. This behavior validates the order and obtains payment, in the process deciding whether or not to accept the

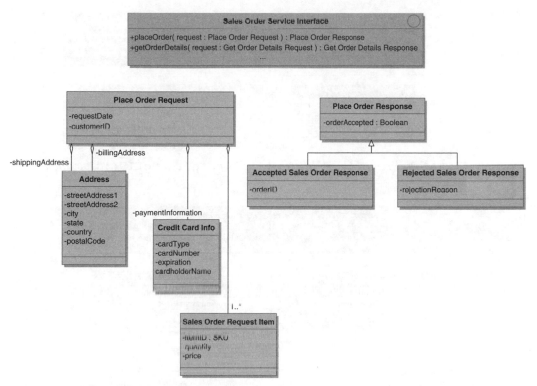

Figure 5-2: *Sales Order Service Interface—*`placeOrder()` *Operation*

order. These activities involve interactions with other components, components that are not part of the service and are thus dependencies. Let's look at the interfaces involved, and later we'll identify the components that provide those interfaces.

The validity of each itemID is established by calling the `validate-ProductID()` operation of the Product Query Interface (Figure 5-3).

The validity of the customerID is established by calling the `get-Customer()` operation of the Customer Query Interface (Figure 5-4).

Payment is obtained by calling the `obtainPayment()` operation on the Credit Interface (Figure 5-5).

At this point the service returns the Place Order Response to the waiting caller of `placeOrder()`. This data structure indicates whether the order was accepted and, if not accepted, the reason why. The data structure exposes the fact that the service is validating the order and obtaining payment, thus making this portion of the behavior observable to the caller of `placeOrder()`.

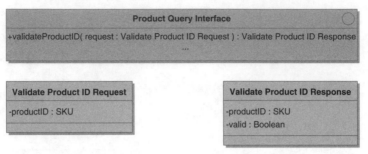

Figure 5-3: *Product Query Interface—*`validateProductID()` *Operation*

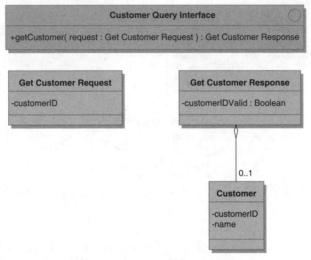

Figure 5-4: *Customer Query Interface—*`getCustomer()` *Operation*

The observable behavior does not end with the return of the Place Order Response data structure. If the order is accepted, the service then sends the order to Order Fulfillment using the `fillOrder()` operation of the Order Fulfillment Interface to accomplish this (Figure 5-6). This is yet another dependency. Note that, as designed, this is an In-Only operation and does not return a response.

At this point the behavior that began with the invocation of the `placeOrder()` operation comes to a conclusion. Putting all the pieces together, the behavior triggered by this invocation is that shown in Figure 5-7. This diagram also indicates components for which there are observable dependencies: Product Service, Customer Service, Credit Service, and Order Fulfillment Service.

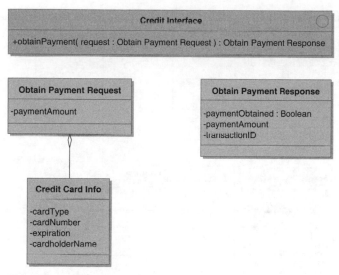

Figure 5-5: *Credit Interface—*`obtainPayment()` *Operation*

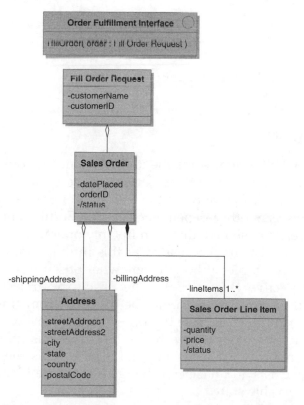

Figure 5-6: *Order Fulfillment Interface—*`fillOrder()` *Operation*

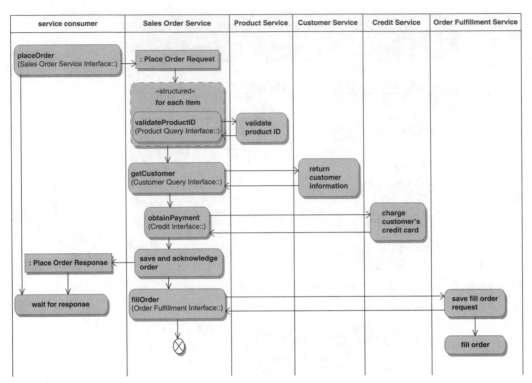

Figure 5-7: *Triggered Behavior for* `placeOrder()`

Order Shipped

When Order Fulfillment ships the items, it sends a copy of the shipment notice to the Sales Order Service. It does this by calling the `orderShipped()` operation of the Sales Order Status Interface (Figure 5-8). This is another dependency: Order Fulfillment depends on this interface. As designed, this is an In-Only operation.

The triggered behavior related to this interaction, the update of order status, is simple, although somewhat obscure from an observability perspective (Figure 5-9). The obscurity arises because the update of the order status cannot be inferred from this interaction alone. It is only the fact that the order status can be retrieved (via other operations), coupled with the fact that this status indicates whether or not the order has shipped, that reveals the fact that the order status exists and has been changed. We have identified an element of observable state.

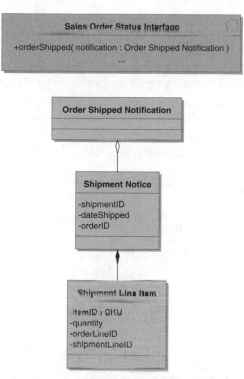

Figure 5-8: *Sales Order Status Interface—*`orderShipped()` *Operation*

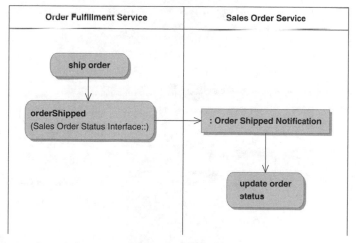

Figure 5-9: `orderShipped()` *Triggered Behavior*

Order Delivered

When the Carrier reports that the shipment has been delivered, Order Fulfillment forwards the delivery notice to the Sales Order Service by calling the `orderDelivered()` operation of the Sales Order Status Interface (Figure 5-10). This is another dependency. Note that this is an In-Only operation and does not return a response.

Figure 5-11 shows the triggered behavior resulting from the invocation of the `orderDelivered()` operation. Once again, the existence of the order status update activity is inferred from information visible through other interface operations.

Observable State Information

Some component operations can reveal that information has been retained within a component. Consider the `getOrder()` operation of the Sales Order Service Interface shown in Figure 5-12. It returns information about the sales order and its line items. In order for the

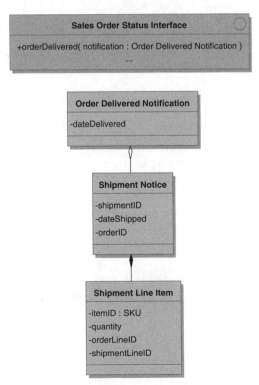

Figure 5-10: *Sales Order Status Interface—*`orderDelivered()` *Operation*

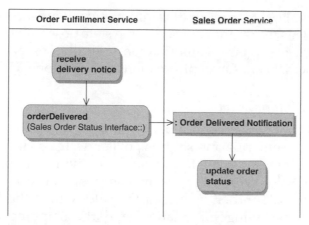

Figure 5-11: `orderDelivered()` *Triggered Behavior*

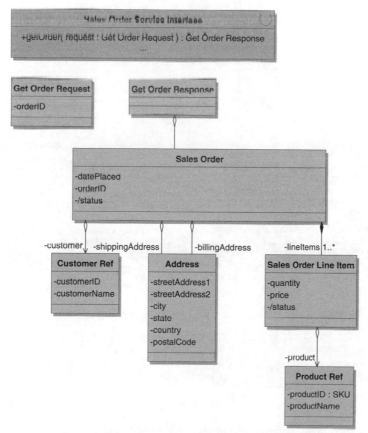

Figure 5-12: *Sales Order Service Interface—*`getOrder()` *Operation*

component to be able to return this information, it must retain it as part of its state. This makes that portion of the state observable.

There are two types of information typically observable through such interfaces: operational information and milestone-level status.

Operational Information

Figure 5-13 shows, at a conceptual level, the operational information involved in the ordering and shipping of goods. It also indicates which components are responsible for managing individual information elements. The Sales Order Service manages operational information related to the sales order, including the Sales Order, the Sales Order Line Items, the billing information, and the shipping and billing addresses. The service is stateful since it retains this information. The fact that the service makes this information (and changes to it) visible at its interfaces makes this state information observable.

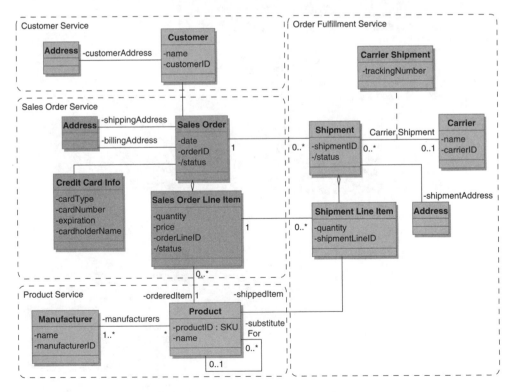

Figure 5-13: *Operational Information in the Order-to-Delivery Process*

When a component retains stateful information, component users need to know the relationship between the interface operations and this stateful information in order to use the operations correctly. Users need to know which operations modify and reveal the state, and the details about which portions of the state are modified or revealed.

Milestone Status

There is another kind of information often visible through service interfaces: milestone-level status. This is usually an abstracted summary of the overall solution state, which includes state information originating outside the component.

For example, the status attribute of the sales order takes on one of a number of values depending upon the overall status of the order (Figure 5-14). Much of the state information being summarized resides outside the scope of the Sales Order Service. Thus, there must be interfaces (and systems implementing or invoking those interfaces) that provide the detailed state information needed to update this summary

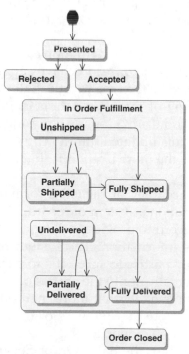

Figure 5-14: *Order Milestone Status*

state information. In this case, these are the `orderShipped()` and `orderDelivered()` operations of the Sales Order Status Interface that are invoked by the Order Fulfillment Service.

Observable State and Cached Information

The Sales Order Service makes use of some state information that it does not directly manage (own): customer information, product information, and information about the related shipments. Other services (components) are the systems of record for this information, but at least some of this information is cached in the Sales Order Service. This situation can raise some interesting design challenges, challenges that when resolved, can impact the observable behavior of the Sales Order Service.

A core design challenge is deciding how to maintain consistency between the cached information as viewed through the Sales Order Service and the same information viewed through its actual system of record. If it is possible (and it almost always is) for inconsistencies to arise, then the component's observable behaviors must indicate the scenarios under which this can arise. Users need to be aware that such inconsistencies are possible and the circumstances under which they can arise.

Let's take a look at how such a situation can arise in the Sales Order Service. If the other systems of record have separate data stores (e.g., databases), then it must be the case that the Sales Order Service retains copies of at least some of the information in its physical data store (Figure 5-15). Since this information is a copy, inconsistencies will arise if the system of record is updated but the copy is not. The more information that is copied, the more likely it is that a discrepancy will arise and be observed.

Maintaining the accuracy of cached information requires interactions with the information's system of record. One common approach is for the system of record to provide facilities to inform interested parties of changes to its information. The system of record provides an interface for interested parties to subscribe to such notifications, and a second interface to actually notify the parties of changes. This approach is often taken when it is likely that more than one party will be interested in the changes. Note that the uses of these interfaces constitute additional observable dependencies.

In the present design, the Sales Order Service has two relationships of this type, one for product information and the other for

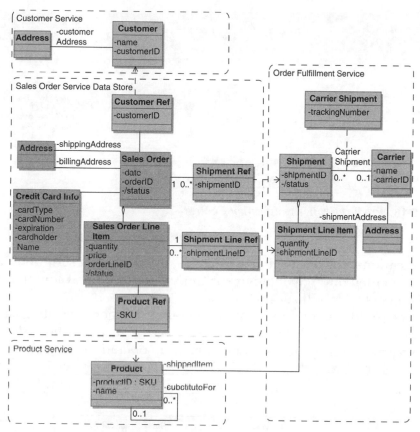

Figure 5-15: *Sales Order Service Data Store*

customer information. Figure 5-16 shows the interfaces provided by the Product Service for this purpose. The Sales Order Service is a user of these interfaces.

Two interesting questions arise with respect to the subscription interface. The first of these relates to the granularity of the subscription: Does the interested party subscribe to changes to particular products, or to all products? The second relates to the timing of the subscription: When does subscription occur? When the component is deployed? When it is started? Does it occur at some other time?

In practice, subscriptions are often realized without implementing subscription interfaces at all. Instead, the design uses a messaging service (e.g., JMS) for the delivery of notifications. The granularity issue is addressed through the choice of the number of destinations (topics or queues) in the design and the determination of which

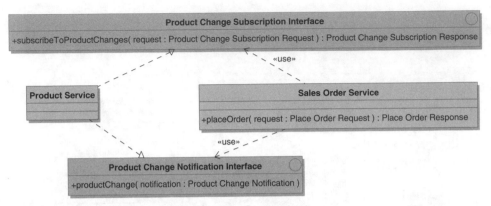

Figure 5-16: *Product Change Notification Context*

notifications will be sent to which destinations. Subscriptions are implemented through deployment-time configuration of components as listeners to specific destinations.

The `productChange()` operation raises another interesting situation from the Sales Order Service's perspective: its invocation triggers activity in the service that is not related to an operation being provided by the Sales Order Service itself (Figure 5-17). It is the arrival of the

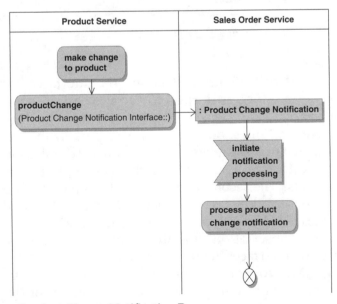

Figure 5-17: *Product Change Notification Process*

notification that triggers the service's activity. This is commonly referred to as an event-driven interaction. As shown, the process depicted in the diagram does not indicate what action should be taken as a result of this notification. However, if the final resolution requires either a change to the observable state of the service (e.g., replacing the item with another item) or an interaction with an external component (such as sending an e-mail notification), these actions constitute changes to the observable behavior that must be documented.

Avoiding Caches: Nested Retrieval

An approach to minimizing inconsistencies is to minimize the amount of cached information in a component. For example, instead of caching a lot of data, the component might only cache an identifier. Then, when the service needs more information about the identified entity, it retrieves it dynamically from the system of record for that entity.

The `placeOrder()` operation described earlier contains two interactions of this type. First, it interacts with the Product Service to validate the productID in the order request. Second, it interacts with the Customer Service for two reasons: to validate the customerID, and to retrieve the customerName, which is a required field for the Fill Order Request (Figure 5-6) data structure used in the `fillOrder()` invocation. Note that only the identifiers for these two entities are retained as part of the Sales Order Service's state.

Characterizing Observable Dependencies and Behaviors

Let's now summarize the information needed to characterize the observable dependencies and behavior of a component.

Context

Context places the component in question into the larger environment in which it must exist and with which it must interact. It defines the dependencies that the component has upon other components. For services, the consumer of the service is often shown only as an abstraction since there may be many service consumers. For components that are not services, the component may require specific interfaces on the consumer and is designed to work only with that consuming component. In such cases the type of the consuming component is explicitly shown.

Dependencies can be readily shown with an abstracted architecture pattern (Figure 5-18). The difference between this and a full architecture pattern is that the actual communications channels have been replaced with the more abstract <<use>> relationship. As the design is refined, these can be replaced with the more concrete communications channels.

This particular diagram indicates another area requiring refinement: The actual mechanisms for subscribing to the Product Change Notification and Customer Change Notification have not been defined, nor is it clear which participant will employ this mechanism to establish the subscriptions. In reality, the implementation of this activity may require manual configuration done at deployment time. The completed component dependency and behavioral description must indicate how this will happen.

Usage Scenarios

The architecture pattern does not indicate how the component (in this case the Sales Order Service) functionally participates in the business processes that comprise the overall solution. For this you need to

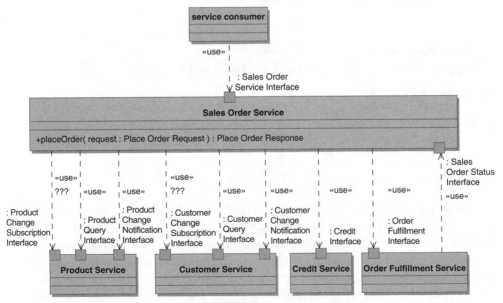

Figure 5-18: *Sales Order Service Context Showing Dependencies*

understand the scenarios that involve the component and show its involvement in the solution's operation. Process-pattern mappings similar to that of Figure 5-1 are well suited for this purpose. For each triggering event of the component, there should be at least one example of a scenario in which the component is expected to participate. If reusability is an issue and the usages are different, there should be a scenario illustrating each type of usage.

To fully characterize the component, more is required than simply the scenario. You need to know how often each scenario occurs, the expected execution time of the scenario, and the required availability of the scenario. It is from this information that the corresponding throughput, response time, and availability characteristics of the component will be derived.

Particularly in the case of services, it is not unusual for some of the scenarios to be speculative, representing potential future usages. Nevertheless, these scenarios need to be documented along with working assumptions about their associated performance and availability characteristics.

From a practical perspective, usage scenarios may only show the fragment of the larger business process in which the component actually participates. However, if the process requires multiple interactions with the component, it is important that the usage scenario span these multiple interactions. If significantly different sequences must be supported, each sequence must be documented.

Triggered Behaviors

The behavior of a component is a description of the sequences of interactions it can have with the components upon which it depends along with the details of those interactions. In most circumstances, this behavior can be readily documented using one or more UML Activity diagrams. The diagrams indicate the behavior's trigger along with the resulting responses, inputs, outputs, and observable state changes.

Figure 5-7 is an example of a triggered behavior. Its trigger is the invocation of the `placeOrder()` process, and its initial input is the Place Order Request. Responses include the calls to `validate-ProductID()`, `getCustomer()`, and `obtainPayment()`; the return of the Place Order Response; and the invocation of the `fillOrder()` operation. The data structures associated with these operations provide details of the interactions. Prior to sending the Place Order Response, the order information is saved and becomes part of the component's observable state.

This, of course, is just one possible behavior for this trigger. Other scenarios are required to describe the expected behavior when one or more of the dependent components becomes unavailable or returns unexpected results.

To fully characterize a component's behavior, a triggered behavior description is required for each possible trigger. Triggering events may include the invocation of interface operations, the receipt of notifications, the expiration of timers, and component life-cycle events such as start, stop, deployment, and un-deployment. In the Sales Order Service example, it is likely that the subscriptions to product and customer change notifications would actually be made via configuration changes implemented as part of the deployment process. Here the deployment would be the event, and one of the participants in the process is the person doing the deployment.

Observable State

The observable state of a component reflects the information or other types of status (such as physical machine state) that can be altered or viewed by interactions among the component and other components. A model of this state information will help the user of the component understand the component's behavior. The model should clearly distinguish between information for which the component is the system of record and information that is a cached copy of information originating in another component.

Figure 5-15 is an example of an observable state model related to the Sales Order Service. It shows the information for which the Sales Order Service is the system of record and the information that it has cached from other components. It also indicates the relationship between the cached information and the system-of-record information from which it is derived.

Some state information can be a derived summary of information that is distributed across a number of components. The status of the Sales Order is such an example. When this type of information is present, the allowed values that it can assume must be modeled (Figure 5-14), and the triggers and triggered behaviors that result in its update must also be captured (Figures 5-9 and 5-11).

Coordination

The work of a component does not occur in isolation, and the performance of this work needs to be coordinated with that of other components in the solution. Consequently, the available coordination approaches are a significant part of the component's observable behavior.

Some coordination patterns are readily captured in the modeling of individual triggered behaviors. For example, in the `placeOrder()` process of Figure 5-7 it is clear that the interaction between the service consumer and the Sales Order Service uses synchronous request-reply coordination.

Other coordination patterns may involve multiple triggering events and therefore multiple triggered behaviors. For example, `place-Order()` sends a `fillOrder()` request to the Order Fulfillment Service, but the responses from the Order Fulfillment Service are returned asynchronously. These interactions involve the Order Fulfillment Services's invocations of the `orderShipped()` (Figure 5-9) and `orderDelivered()` (Figure 5-11) operations. The overall coordination is only apparent when the usage scenario (Figure 5-1) is considered.

Capturing coordination is important because changing coordination patterns involves changes in both components. In the Sales Order Service example, shipment and delivery notices are delivered to the Sales Order Service by calling operations on its Sales Order Status Interface. This makes the design of the Order Fulfillment Service specific to the Sales Order Service.

There is an alternative approach. Consider a situation in which other components in addition to the Sales Order Service need to know about shipments and deliveries. With the present design, accommodating this requirement would necessitate an Order Fulfillment Service change to individually notify each of the additional components.

Alternatively, the Order Fulfillment Service could provide a subscription interface where any component could register to be informed about shipments and deliveries (Figure 5-19). Thus any number of components could subscribe without requiring any design changes in the Order Fulfillment Service. However, to switch to this design the Sales Order Service has to be modified to utilize the new approach to learning about shipments and notifications.

Constraints

Usage scenarios show allowed sequences of interactions with the component, but they do not illustrate sequences that are not allowed. These need to be documented as well.

Consider the Sales Order Service Interface shown in Figure 5-20. This interface has some obvious constraints upon its usage. You can't get, modify, or cancel an order that hasn't been placed. However, there

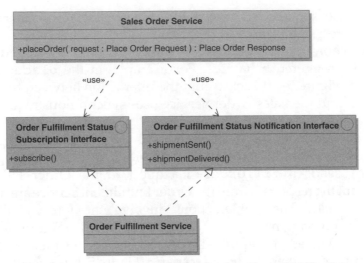

Figure 5-19: *Alternative Design for Shipment and Delivery Notification*

Figure 5-20: *Full Sales Order Service Interface*

may be some less obvious constraints. Depending upon business rules, you may not be able to modify or cancel an order that has already shipped. Users of a component need to understand these constraints.

Nonfunctional Behavior

A component may provide all the functionality required for a usage scenario, but still may not be suitable for nonfunctional reasons. Its throughput capability may be insufficient to support the volume of activity required by the scenario or its response time may be inadequate. The availability of the component may not be sufficient to give the usage scenario its required availability.

Nonfunctional requirements are not arbitrary—they are (or should be) derived from the business requirements. The connection between the business requirements and the individual components is established through the usage scenarios. For example, the business might require that customers be able to place orders at a peak rate of 100 per second. With reference to Figure 5-1, this means that the Sales Order Service must be able to accept order requests at this rate. If the business requires that orders be acknowledged within three seconds, this means that the Sales Order Service must be able to validate orders and obtain payment within three seconds with orders coming in at a rate of 100 per second. Similar reasoning can be used to determine the rate at which shipment and delivery notices will occur and be processed.

This same type of thinking applies to other types of nonfunctional requirements as well. If the business requires that online ordering capability be available 24/7, then this means that the Sales Order Service must be available 24/7. Availability, outage time restrictions, and security requirements must also be connected back to the business requirements via the usage scenarios.

There is another reason for establishing this connection between business requirements and component requirements: It captures the design assumptions that went into specifying the component. When a new utilization for the service comes along, this makes it easy to determine whether the new usage is consistent with the original design assumptions. If it is not, then it is necessary to open the black box and determine whether the actual design is capable of meeting the new requirements.

For all of these reasons, it is important to document the nonfunctional behavior of the component. It is an observable characteristic of the component.

Some Composites May Not Be Suitable for Black Box Characterization

For the black box approach to work, the component must appear to be a coherent whole. For a monolithic self-contained component, that's not a problem. But for a composite, a component comprising other components (Figure 5-21), some conditions must be satisfied for it to be treated as a black box:

- It must (to all appearances) be managed as a single unit.
- It must have a single organization responsible for its operation.
- Access to the constituent parts must be exclusively through the interface(s) of the black box. Note that this does not preclude exposing a sub-component's interface as one of the composite's interfaces.

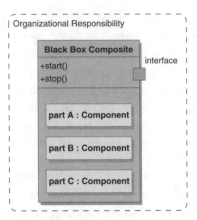

Figure 5-21: *Black Box Perspective*

Key indicators that the composite is not a black box include

- Different organizations are responsible for operating (starting and stopping) different parts of the composite.

- Decisions to start and stop the composite are separate from decisions to start and stop its component parts.

- A component part can be accessed directly via its own interfaces, interfaces that are not declared to be part of the composite's interfaces. This is particularly important when the constituent component is stateful.

An example of a component that should not be treated as a black box is a service (interface) wrapping the functionality of a stateful back-end system that other solution components access directly. In this situation, state changes made via the service interface may be visible through the back-end system's interface, and vice versa. Characterizing the observable behavior of the service will not explain the state changes that are visible through the service interface but did not originate as the result of a service interaction.

Any of these conditions make it important for the user of the composite to be aware of the composite's architectural structure—aware of those components that are independently accessible or managed. Under such circumstances, you can't treat the composite, including its component parts, as a single entity—a black box. Instead, each of the components becomes a black box in its own right. The context and usage scenarios for the "composite" then indicate how these supporting components collaborate with the composite.

Summary

When you want to use a component as part of a solution, you need to understand the behavior of that component so that you can determine whether it is suitable for use in the solution. What you need to know are the aspects of the component's behavior that are observable from outside the component. You treat the component as a black box and focus on its observable behavior.

Understanding observable behavior requires characterizing a number of things, including

- Context: the component's dependencies upon external components and vice versa
- Usage scenarios: characterizations of the business processes in which the component is expected to participate
- Triggered behaviors: structures of activities that explain the relationships among the component's triggers, responses, inputs, observable state, and outputs
- Observable state (information retained from one trigger to the next)
- Coordination: the manner in which the component's activity can be coordinated with that of external components
- Constraints: limitations, particularly on the sequencing of triggers
- Nonfunctional Behavior: performance, availability, and so on

Some composites cannot be safely considered as black boxes. These include components whose constituent parts are operated independently or are accessible by means other than the composite's interfaces.

Chapter 6

Service-Related Documentation

Objectives

In an enterprise that is pursuing a service-oriented architecture, the consumers and providers of services tend to be different groups, often in different organizations. In this situation the quality, availability, and accessibility of service-related documentation has a significant impact on the usage levels of services and on the level of effort required for use. This chapter explores the nature of the documentation required to support service usage.

There are a number of types of documents necessary to support the efficient use of services, including

- A one-line service description
- A brief abstract of the service
- A service specification
- A service utilization contract for each type of service user
- A service architecture document

These document types are described in the following sections. After reading this chapter, you should be able to

- List and describe the purpose of the service-related document types.
- Describe the elements of a service specification.
- Describe the elements of a service utilization contract.
- Describe the elements of a service architecture document.

Service One-Line Description and Abstract

Every service needs a simple one-line description and a short (one or two paragraph) abstract. Their purpose is to support a potential service consumer who is weeding through a number of services and needs to make an initial determination as to which services, if any, are potentially suitable for their needs.

Service One-Line Description

The one-line description presents as brief a summary as possible indicating the intent of the service. An example description for the Nouveau Health Care Payment Manager is

> *The Payment Manager manages both immediate and deferred claim payments to health care service providers.*

The intent of the one-line description is to help someone decide at a glance whether it is worth spending time learning more about the service.

Service Abstract

The service abstract supports a next-level screening of potentially interesting services. It should give a brief overview of what the service does, including significant variations. The description should assume that the reader has no prior knowledge of the service. An example for the Nouveau Health Care Payment Manager is

> *The Payment Manager manages both immediate and deferred claim payments to health care service providers. Under normal circumstances, requested payments are accumulated and paid periodically. The Payment Manager returns an immediate acknowledgment of the payment request, and sends an*

asynchronous notification of payment when the service provider account is settled. The scheduling of claim settlements is configurable on a per-provider basis. Under exceptional conditions, payment to the service provider can be made immediately and the returned acknowledgment indicates payment has been made. As this option places significant additional burden on the service, it should be used sparingly. The same interface is used to initiate both forms of payment.

Although both the one-line description and abstract appear trivial, their positive impact on the efficiency with which potential service consumers can locate services of interest should not be underestimated.

Service Specification Contents

The service specification is a central document to be shared between the service provider and the service consumer. It represents an agreement between the two parties. From the service provider's perspective, it is a *complete* statement of what will be provided and a description of its intended utilization. From the consumer's perspective, it is a user manual that explains what the service is for and how it is intended to be used.

To serve these needs, the specification must clearly state the purpose of the service, describe its context and intended usage scenarios, and detail its interfaces and observable behavior. To accomplish this, the service specification should include the following information:

- One-line description
- Abstract
- Context
- Intended utilization scenarios
- Interface definitions
- References
- Observable state
- Triggered behaviors
- Coordination
- Constraints
- Nonfunctional behavior
- Deployment specifics

One-Line Description

This is the original source of the one-line description that is often published separately from the service specification. This description is the most concise possible statement of the service's purpose and is intended to help the naïve potential user quickly identify services of potential interest.

Abstract

This is the original source of the service abstract that is often published separately from the service specification. The abstract is a short, one-paragraph description of the service's purpose, functionality, and intended usage. Its purpose is to help the naïve potential user further refine their identification of potentially interesting services.

Context

The context describes the architecture pattern into which the service is intended to fit. It shows both the consumer(s) of the service and the observable components whose supporting behavior is required in order for the service to execute properly. It summarizes the observable dependencies.

The context can be shown at different levels of detail. At the highest level of abstraction, the context shows all of the components and identifies the interfaces involved in their interaction. Some additional context information is required to complete the specification, specifically the details of the interface operations and data structures along with the communications channels over which the interactions occur.

However, it is somewhat a matter of choice as to whether this additional information is shown in the context or included in other sections of the specification. In the following example, the interface details are given in the triggered behavior descriptions, and the communications channels are given in the deployment specifics section. Placing the interface details in the triggered behavior descriptions makes the context overview concise and easy to understand. Placing the communications channels in the deployment specifics allows different communications channels to be specified for different environments.

Intended Utilization Scenarios

The utilization scenarios provide a behavioral overview of how the service is intended to fit into the larger business processes. In simple situations in which the service's participation in the business process amounts to the invocation of a single service operation, these scenarios amount to individual use cases for the individual operations. With more complex services, on the other hand, a single business process execution may involve multiple interactions with the service. Such is the case with the Payment Manager used in the following example. In these cases, the utilization scenarios spell out the possible sequences of interactions. In all cases, the utilization scenarios should clearly indicate how the work of the service is coordinated with other work in the business process.

Interface Definitions

This section defines the interfaces provided by the service. It details the operations of each interface and the data structures used by those operations. Although the details for some interfaces can be provided by SOAP WSDL documents, for readability it is prudent to augment such detailed textual representations with graphical representations using UML class diagrams.

References

This section defines the interfaces of other external components that are used by the service. This information is generally taken from the specifications for those components, but it is useful to actually replicate those interface definitions in the present specification. The reason for this becomes clear as the external components begin to evolve: It documents this service's expectations about the definition of the external component's interface, and does so in a manner that is not dependent upon the document version control and retrievability of the other component's specification.

Observable State

Many services are stateful, with some operations of the service altering the state and other operations making that state visible to external components. This section identifies this information.

Services often statefully maintain replicas of information that originate in other components. This section identifies this information and the triggered behavior (if any) involved in maintaining its consistency.

Triggered Behaviors

The triggered behaviors define the service's behavior in response to triggering events along with its dependencies on the behaviors of external components. This section enumerates those triggering events and provides details of the ensuing observable behaviors. These behaviors can include interactions with external components and interactions with the internal observable state maintained by the service.

There are three broad categories of triggers that need to be included: operation invocations, notifications, and time-based events. Operation invocations are obviously identifiable: Any component invoking an operation triggers the behavior. Notifications are generally the result of some form of subscription by the service to notifications originating in external components. Since these notifications may not involve service interfaces (they may be references to the other component's interface), their occurrence as behavior triggers may not be obvious to the service consumer. However, the results of these behaviors (such as updating cached replicas of information in the observable state) may be observable or otherwise impact the observable behaviors of the service. Finally, some activity in the service may be triggered by the passage of time. To the extent that these time-based triggers produce observable results (observable state changes), service consumers need to be aware of them as well.

Coordination

The manner in which the service's activity can be coordinated with that of other components must be clearly understood by the service consumer. To the extent that the intended utilization scenarios document this coordination, simple reference to the scenarios suffices for documentation. Otherwise, this section should document the possible coordination as well as the behavior when coordination fails (e.g., observable behavior upon lack of response in a request-reply interaction).

Constraints

If there are constraints on the use of service operations, these must be documented. In some cases, such as allowed sequences of operations, the utilization scenarios may capture this in sufficient detail. In other cases, particularly involving business rule constraints, these need to be explicitly identified. Service consumers need to understand these restrictions.

Nonfunctional Behavior

This section documents the nonfunctional capabilities of the service. Throughput and corresponding response times for individual service operations should be documented. Required security constraints (authentication, authorization, encryption, non-repudiation) are specified on a per-operation or per-interface basis, as appropriate. Availability, outage constraints, and recovery times may be specified on a per-service, per-interface, or per-operation basis. Whether or not the service guarantees that requests are processed in the order received is another important nonfunctional behavior.

In some cases, the mechanisms used to achieve fault tolerance, high availability, or load distribution may require specific actions on the part of service consumers or the use of external components. A common example is the use of an IP-redirector to distribute HTTP load across a number of service instances. Another common example is the need to configure EMS clients in a specific way to take advantage of EMS fault tolerance and load distribution.

To the extent that the service consumer must be aware of these mechanisms, they must be documented as part of the service specification. In these situations, it is important to clarify whether the performance-related specifications apply to a single instance of the service or to the aggregate capabilities of the multiple instances.

Deployment Specifics

Some observable characteristics of services vary depending upon the deployment environment. SOAP endpoints, for example, will likely be different in development, test, and production environments. Exposed fault-tolerance, high-availability, and load distribution mechanisms may also vary between environments, and these differences need to be documented.

Example Service Specification: Payment Manager

This section presents a sample specification for Nouveau Health Care's Payment Manager. For brevity, some of the sections are intentionally left incomplete.

Service One-Line Description

The Payment Manager manages both immediate and deferred claim payments to health care service providers.

Service Abstract

The Payment Manager manages both immediate and deferred claim payments to health care service providers. Under normal circumstances, requested payments are accumulated and paid periodically. The Payment Manager returns an immediate acknowledgment of the payment request and sends an asynchronous notification of payment when the service provider account is settled. The scheduling of claim settlements is configurable on a per-provider basis. Under exceptional conditions, payment to the service provider can be made immediately and the returned acknowledgment indicates payment has been made. As this option places significant additional burden on the service, it should be used sparingly. The same interface is used to initiate both forms of payment.

Service Context

The usage context for the Payment Manager is shown in Figure 6-1. The service is intended to be used by the Claim Processor, and its operation is dependent upon the Provider Service, Banking Service, and Benefits Service. It also provides inputs to the Claim Tracker to maintain the overall status of claim processing, and thus is dependent upon it as well.

There can be more than one Claim Processor utilizing the Payment Manager. Nouveau Health Care has its own claim processor, but partner company claim processors may also utilize the Payment Manager.

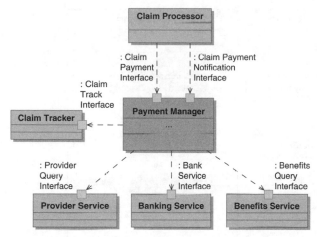

Figure 6-1: *Payment Manager Usage Context*

Intended Utilization Scenarios

There are two intended utilization scenarios for the Payment Manager. The normal scenario is the deferred payment scenario shown in Figure 6-2. In this scenario, the service consumer directs the Payment Manager to pay a claim and receives an acknowledgment that the request has been received. At some later point (configurable for each health care service provider), the pending payments for that provider are paid and the payments are reported back to the service consumer. The scenario follows the delegation with an asynchronous-confirmation coordination pattern.

The second utilization scenario is the immediate payment scenario shown in Figure 6-3. This scenario is expected to represent a small volume of the overall service activity—less than one percent. In this scenario, the service consumer requests immediate payment and receives an acknowledgment that the specified claim payment has been made. This scenario uses a synchronous request-reply coordination pattern.

Both of these scenarios use the same payClaim() interface operation. The difference in behavior is determined by the value of the immediatePayment flag in the Claim Payment Request (Figure 6-4).

Payment Manager Service Interfaces

The Payment Manager presents two interfaces for use by service clients (Figure 6-4). The Claim Payment Interface provides the payClaim()

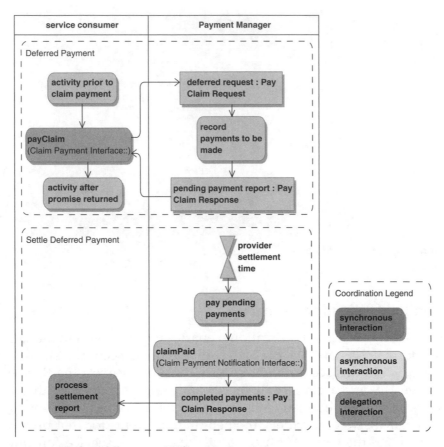

Figure 6-2: *Deferred Payment Utilization Scenario*

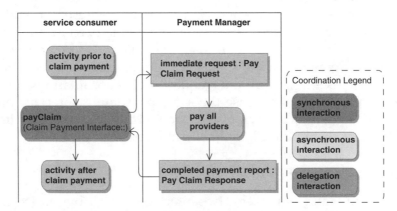

Figure 6-3: *Immediate Payment Utilization Scenario*

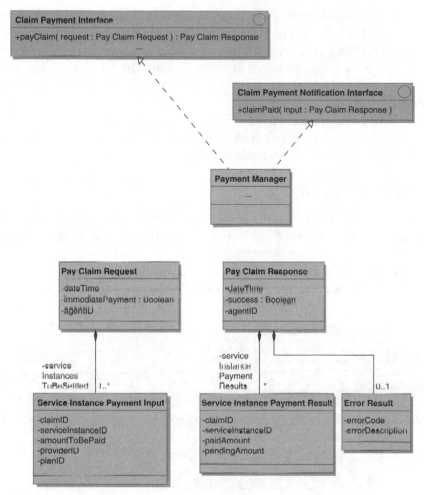

Figure 6-4: *Payment Manager Service Interfaces for Claim Payment*

operation, which is used by claim processors (and other relevant parties) to initiate claim payment. Depending upon the value of the Claim Payment Request's immediatePayment() flag, payment will either be deferred or immediate. For deferred payment, the Claim Payment Response indicates the pending amount for each service instance. For immediate payment, it indicates the amount actually paid. Access to the Claim Payment Interface will be via SOAP over HTTP (for partners) and JMS (for Nouveau Health Care).

The Claim Payment Notification Interface is used by the Payment Manager to notify service clients when deferred payments are actually made to the health care service providers. Such notifications can also occur as part of the recovery process after the failure of an immediate payment request. It is an XML over JMS interface. Subscription to this notification is accomplished at deployment time via JMS subscriptions. The details of this configuration are given in the Deployment Specifics section.

The other operations of the Claim Payment Interface are shown in Figure 6-5. *In the full specification, the data structures associated with these operations would be documented here.*

Referenced Interfaces

Figure 6-6 (taken from the Benefits Service Specification) shows the Benefits Query Interface getPayerAccount() operation used in this process.

Figure 6-7 shows the Bank Service Interface (from the Bank Service Specification) used in this scenario and in the ones that follow.

Figure 6-5: *Claim Payment Interface: Other Operations*

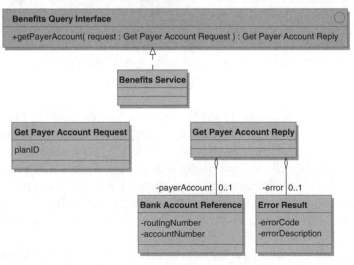

Figure 6-6: *Benefits Query Interface—getPayerAccount()Operation*

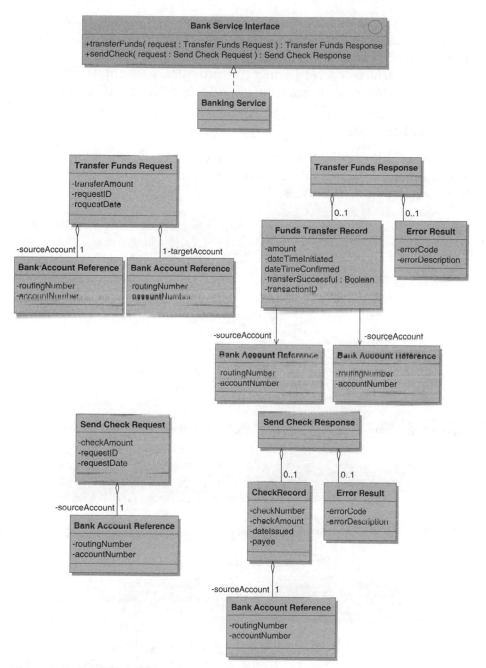

Figure 6-7: *Bank Service Interface*

Figure 6-8 shows the Claim Track Interface reportClaimStatus() operation used in this scenario and in others (taken from the Claim Tracker Specification).

The interface for retrieving the provider account is shown in Figure 6-9. This is taken from the Provider Service specification.

Observable State

The observable state of the Payment Manager is shown in Figure 6-10. The diagram indicates which elements are cached copies of information owned by other services.

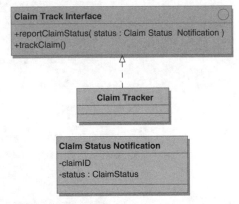

Figure 6-8: *Claim Track Interface—reportClaimStatus() Operation*

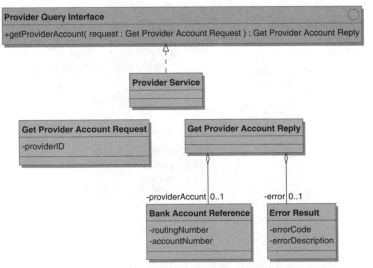

Figure 6-9: *Provider Query Interface—getProviderAccount() Operation*

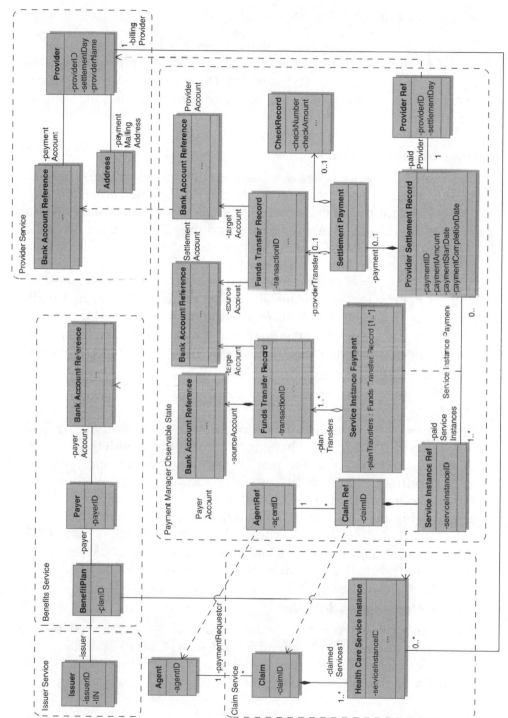

Figure 6-10: *Payment Manager Observable State*

Triggered Behaviors

There are two types of events that trigger behavior in the Payment Manager: the invocation of the payClaim() interface and the arrival of the time for settling deferred payments. There are two major variations in activity for the payClaim() invocation depending upon the value of the immediatePayment() flag.

Deferred Payment Behavior

The deferred payment behavior is shown in Figure 6-11. This behavior is triggered by the invocation of the Claim Payment Interface pay-Claim() operation. The behavior depends upon three services: the Benefits Service, the Banking Service, and the Claim Tracker. Errors in processing are indicated by the success flag being set to false and the presence of an Error Result in the returned data structure. By business rule, service instances that can be processed are completed, so it is possible to have some Service Instance Payment Results returned while others fail. In the event of failures, it is the responsibility of the service consumer (or whatever component is handling error recovery) to re-submit a payment request for the service instances that were not successfully completed.

Settle Deferred Payments Behavior

The behavior for settling deferred payments is shown in Figure 6-12. The behavior is triggered when the time for settling with the provider is reached. At that time the pending settlements are retrieved. For each pending settlement, the provider account is retrieved and the funds are transferred from the settlement account to the provider account (Figure 6-7). Alternatively, if the provider is to be paid with a check, the banking service is directed to draw a check on the settle-ment account (Figure 6-7). This latter scenario variation is not shown in the picture. Finally, the claim status is updated (Figure 6-8).

Immediate Payment Behavior

The immediate payment behavior (Figure 6-13) is triggered by the invocation of the Claim Payment Interface payClaim() operation with the value of immediatePayment set to true. All of the interfaces used by this behavior have already been described.

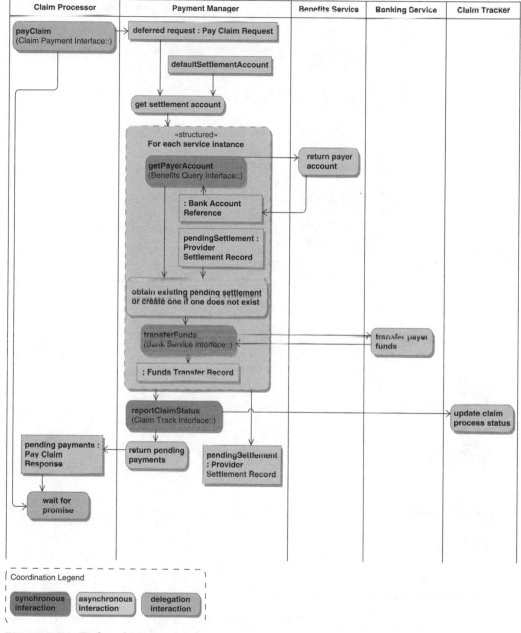

Figure 6-11: *Deferred Payment Behavior*

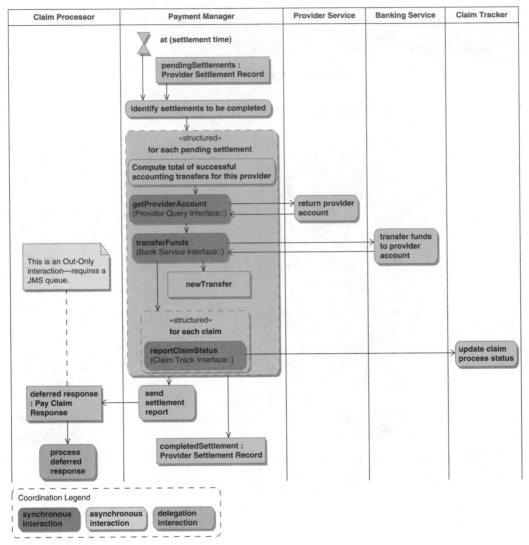

Figure 6-12: *Settle Deferred Payments Behavior*

Coordination

From the service consumer's perspective, there are two coordination patterns available. The normal option, deferred payment, follows the Delegation with Confirmation pattern (Figure 6-2). The immediate payment option (Figure 6-3) is a synchronous request-reply interaction.

Most of the interactions with the back-end systems are synchronous request-reply. These include the Benefits Service, Provider Service,

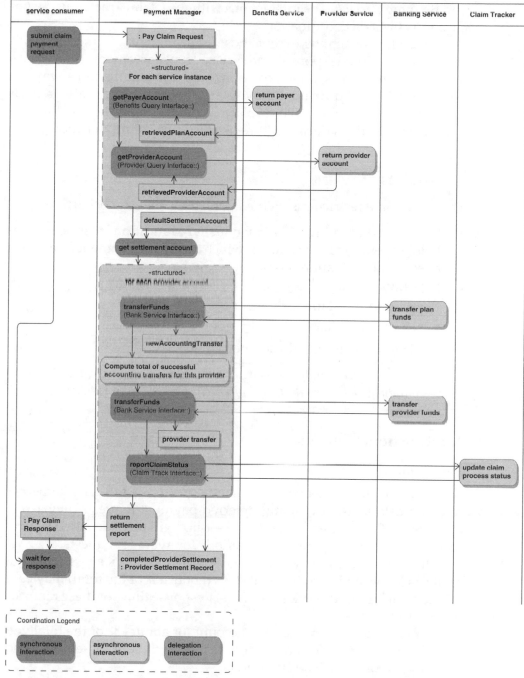

Figure 6-13: *Immediate Payment Behavior*

and Banking Service. The interactions with the Claim Tracker use asynchronous In-Only coordination.

Since all interactions except those with the Claim Tracker return confirmations, and response-time service-level agreements are in place for all these interfaces, breakdowns in these interactions can always be detected. No breakdown detection is available for claim status reporting to the Claim Tracker, which places a premium on the reliability of the communications infrastructure used for this communications.

Constraints

There are some restrictions on the interactions that can occur:

- It is invalid to call the Claim Payment Notification Interface claimPaid() operation for a claim for which the Claim Payment Interface's payClaim() operation has not been invoked.
- It is invalid to call the Claim Payment Interface cancelPendingPayments for a claim for which:
  - payClaim() has not been called
  - The payment has already been made

In a full specification, the triggered behavior mappings would include scenarios to indicate what would happen in each of these circumstances.

Nonfunctional Behavior

Performance

Nouveau Health Care expects to handle up to 4.4 million claims per day. At peak times, payClaim() deferred payment requests may arrive at a rate of 620 requests/second. The service will provide a two-second response time during these peak periods for average requests.

The average claim payment request has three service instances, but requests associated with hospital stays (about 1% of the total) may contain several hundred service instances. Response time for these requests will be 10 seconds.

Immediate payment requests account for about 1% of the total volume. Response time for an average request will be four seconds, and for a large request will be 60 seconds.

There are 1.4 million providers associated with Nouveau. Each provider is typically paid once a month on a working day. Thus the Settle Deferred Payments process runs about 67,000 times a day. Each execution will complete in 4 seconds, and the full batch will be completed in four hours.

At peak, the remaining Claim Payment Interface operations are each invoked 10 times/second and will provide a four-second response time.

Availability within a Data Center

The payClaim() and claimPaid() operations will be available 99.999% of the time on a 24/7 basis. There will be no scheduled outage times for this operation. Maximum outage time per incident is 60 seconds.

The remaining Claim Payment Interface operations will be available 99.999% of the time from 6 AM through 12 AM Eastern time. Maximum outage time per incident is 60 seconds.

Site Disaster Recovery

In the event of a site disaster recovery, the recovery time objective for the Payment Manager is one hour, and the recovery point objective is 60 seconds.

Security

All invocations of the Claim Payment Interface operations require certificate-based authentication and authorization using web service standards. In all cases, WS-Security will be used to encrypt the message body.

Deployment Specifics

Claim Payment Interface operations will be accessible via SOAP over both HTTP and JMS. The endpoints for these operations are SOAP WSDL endpoints. The Claim Payment Notification Interface operation is an XML over JMS communication utilizing JMS queues. There is a separate queue for each agent submitting payClaim requests. The endpoints are as shown in Table 6-1 *(in the completed specification, this table would be filled in)*.

Table 6-1: *Operation Endpoints*

Operation	Development	Test	Production
payClaim			
claimPaid	*One queue per agent submitting claims*		
getProviderSettlement			
cancelPendingPayments			
getPendingSettlements			

Service Usage Contracts

Services typically have more than one consumer. Although the service specification characterizes the full capabilities of a service, it does not indicate how (or whether) those capabilities are dedicated to individual service consumers. This is the role of the service usage contract.

The service usage contract is an agreement between the organization responsible for the service provider and the organization responsible for the service consumer. The process of negotiating this contract is as important as the contract itself. It provides an opportunity to assess and adjust the capacity of the service provider and configure the policies that will govern access control for the service consumer. It also provides an opportunity to add consumer-specific monitoring to determine whether or not the contract is being complied with in practice.

The following sections outline the essential content of a service utilization contract.

Organizations

The service utilization contract specifies the organizations responsible for the service provider and service consumer. It specifies the contact points on both sides that are responsible for the contract itself. These are important during the negotiation of the contract, but also for subsequent modification of the contract should that become necessary.

The organizational contact points related to operations are also identified in the contract. Specifically, contact points related to operations (starting, stopping, deployment, undeployment, access control configuration), first-tier support, and escalation are identified. The contract also specifies the procedures to be used to effect operational changes, interact with support, and escalate issues.

These organizational details may seem obvious and unimportant when both the service consumer and service provider are being developed and managed by the same group of people, but as these responsibilities become distributed among different groups, establishing the contact points and procedures becomes increasingly important. A case in point is the Nouveau Health Care Payment Manager, which provides services not only for Nouveau's in-house claim processing but also for claim processing being performed by Nouveau's business partners.

Service Consumers and Access Mechanisms

The contract indicates the nature and number of service consumers involved along with the access mechanisms that they will use. This may seem unimportant when the service provider presents a single access point (e.g., a WSDL endpoint) that is shared by all consumers, but often for scalability and management reasons the service will present different access points for different service consumers. In the Nouveau Health Care example, the Payment Manager presents a SOAP over JMS interface used for internal service consumers and a SOAP over HTTP interface for its external partners.

In some cases, the service may even present multiple access points for a single class of service consumer. This may be done to support load distribution and/or fault tolerance. To the extent that the service consumer needs to be aware of the multiple access points, they need to be documented in the contract. For example, if the Enterprise Message Service is being used as a JMS transport in a fault-tolerant configuration, the service consumers will need to configure their connections with both members of the fault-tolerant pair (this is discussed in detail in Chapter 16).

Functional Requirements

Most of the time a given service consumer does not utilize all of the capabilities of the service provider. The service utilization contract indicates which of the capabilities will be used by the consumer. The contract indicates which interfaces and operations will be used, but references a particular version of the service specification for details rather than replicating that information.

Nonfunctional Requirements

Performance

For each of the interface operations, the contract specifies the peak rate at which the operation will be invoked and the response time that has been agreed to. This information provides the basis for capacity planning for the service provider.

Availability

For each of the interface operations, the contract specifies the agreed-to availability and maximum outage time.

Site Disaster Recovery

If site disaster recovery is supported for the service, for each of the interface operations, the contract specifies the agreed-to recovery point objective and recovery time objective in the event of a site disaster recovery.

Security

If security is to be enforced, the details specific to the service consumer are detailed.

Deployment

For each of the environments covered by the contract, it specifies the location of the service provider and consumer, the interface transport specifics, and the endpoint details.

Service Architecture

There are a number of parties that must be aware of the internal architecture of the service provider. The organizations responsible for the deployment, operation, and support of the service need to understand how it works. Solution architects need to understand enough about the architecture to be able to understand its limitations and behavior under unusual circumstances. This is particularly important when the architects are evaluating the feasibility of expanding the service's usage beyond the bounds of its present specification. Even the service consumers may need to be at least partially aware of the architecture when load distribution and fault tolerance expose sub-components of the architecture.

The service architecture is documented much as you would any architecture, with emphasis on process models, the architecture pattern of the service, and the process-pattern mapping. In the case of the service, the processes are the intended utilization scenarios and the mappings indicate how those scenarios are executed by the components of the architecture pattern.

Payment Manager Architecture Pattern

The architecture pattern for the Payment Manager is shown in Figure 6-14. At the top level, the payment manager consists of two components: the Payment Manager Composite (an ActiveMatrix composite) and a Database playing the role of an operational data store (ODS).

The composite contains three ActiveMatrix BusinessWorks components: the Claim Payment BW Service, the Settle Deferred Payments BW Process, and the Settlement BW Service. The Claim Payment BW Service implements the Claim Payment Interface and has a Business-Works sub-process for each of the service operations. The Settle Deferred Payments BW Process is triggered on a timer and settles deferred payments. The actual mechanics of settlement are abstracted into the Settlement BW Process since they are used in two places: the Pay Claim BW Process in the event of an immediate payment and Settle Deferred Payments BW Process in the event of a deferred payment. Note that the references made by the Get Pending Settlements BW Process, Get Provider Settlements BW Process, and Cancel Pending Payments BW Process have yet to be defined.

Payment Manager Behavior Implementations

The behaviors that the payment manager exhibits are the triggered behaviors of the service specification.

Payment Manager Behaviors

Immediate Payment Behavior

The design for the Immediate Payment Behavior is shown in Figure 6-15.

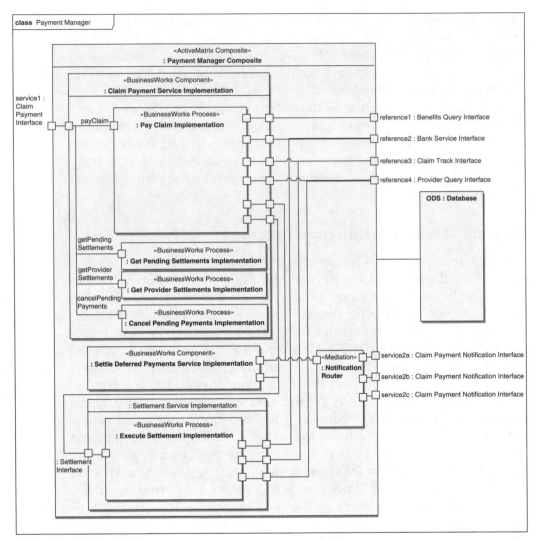

Figure 6-14: *Payment Manager Architecture Pattern*

Deferred Payment Behavior

The design for the Deferred Payment Behavior is shown in Figure 6-16.

Settle Deferred Payments Behavior

The design for the Settle Deferred Payments Behavior is shown in Figure 6-17.

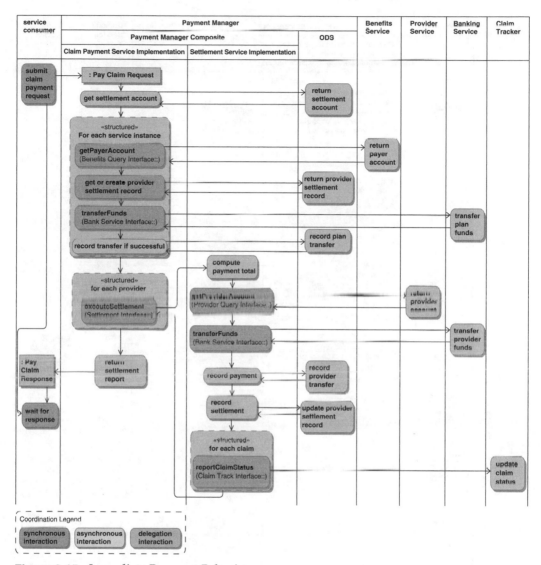

Figure 6-15: *Immediate Payment Behavior*

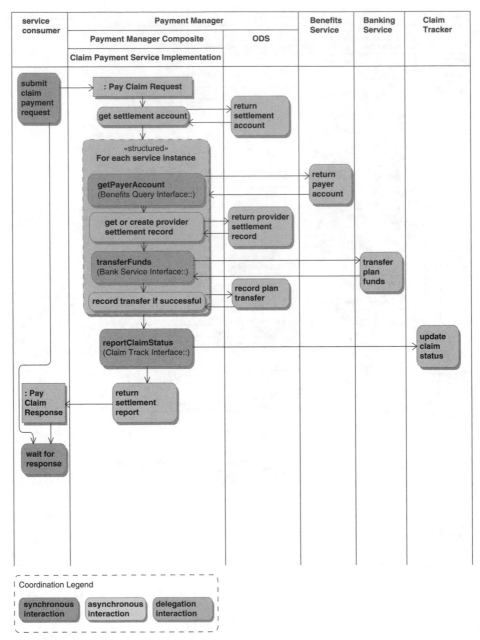

Figure 6-16: *Deferred Payment Behavior*

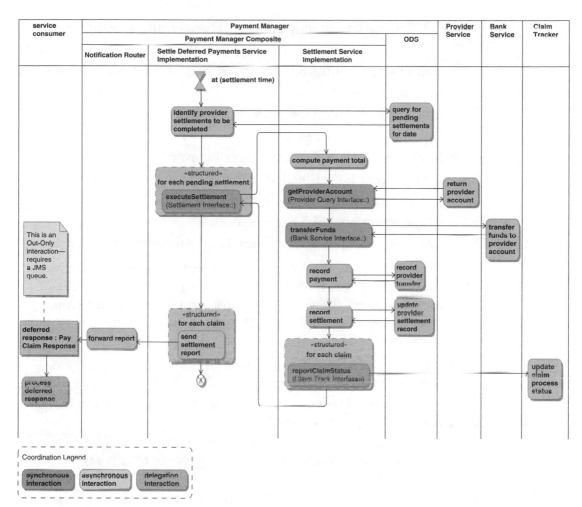

Figure 6-17: *Settle Deferred Payments Behavior*

Summary

A variety of different documents are required to support the effective development and use of services. Some are simple, such as the one-line description and abstract, which are designed to aid a potential service consumer in identifying services of potential interest.

The service specification provides a detailed definition of the service from the perspective of a service consumer. In addition to being the source of the one-line description and abstract, the specification describes:

- The intended service utilization scenarios
- The service interfaces
- The components and interfaces on which it depends
- The observable state of the service
- The behavior resulting from each triggering event
- How service activity is coordinated with that of external components
- The constraints on the use of the service operations
- The nonfunctional capabilities of the service
- Deployment specifics of which the service consumer must be aware

The service specification describes the overall capabilities of the service but does not indicate how those capabilities are allocated to different service consumers. That is the purpose of a service usage contract. Each contract specifies the support that the service will provide for a specific service consumer. It covers

- The relationship between the organization(s) responsible for the service provider and those responsible for the service consumer
- The scope of the service consumers covered by the contract and the mechanisms to be used to access the service
- The specific functional capabilities of the service that will be provided to the service consumer (generally a subset of the overall service capabilities)
- The nonfunctional requirements to be met for this consumer, particularly with respect to performance, availability, and security
- Deployment specifics, such as the access points in the various environments

The service architecture is also of interest to some parties, particularly solution architects who need to evaluate the feasibility of pushing the service beyond its present specification in terms of breakdown detection, performance, availability, and site disaster recovery.

Chapter 7

Versioning

Objectives

Despite your best efforts to conceptualize services so that they can be used without modification, at some point it is inevitable that one will have to be changed. Such changes impact not only the interface definition, but the providers and consumers of the service as well. This makes it necessary to identify the versions of each and track the dependencies between them.

Nowhere is this issue more prominent than in the Open Services Gateway initiative framework (OSGi Framework[1]). This framework provides a standardized approach to defining and integrating components. Significantly, it makes it possible to avoid conflict while incorporating multiple versions of interfaces, service consumers, and service providers.

The OSGi Framework is of interest for two reasons. One is that the deployment model for the ActiveMatrix Service Bus node is based upon the framework. The other is that the best practices for managing versions in the framework, as presented in the OSGi Alliance's Semantic Versioning Technical Whitepaper,[2] are generally applicable best practices for managing versions.

---

1. www.osgi.org/About/Technology#Framework
2. OSGi Alliance, Semantic Versioning Technical Whitepaper, Version 1.0 (May 6, 2010).

This chapter explores the issues raised when versioning services and presents best practices for dealing with these issues. After reading this chapter you should be able to describe the OSGi Alliance's semantic versioning model and the best practices for service versioning.

Dependencies and Compatibility

In a component- or service-based architecture, the interface is the point of contact between the consumer and provider of functionality (Figure 7-1). Both consumer and provider are dependent upon the interface, but in different ways.

The provider must implement all aspects of the interface. Consequently, any change to the interface mandates a change to the provider. Consumers, on the other hand, may only use a portion of the interface. A change to a consumer is only required when the used portion of the interface changes. In particular, additions to the interface do not require any changes to the consumer.

Interface changes that do not require changes to consumers are considered to be *backwards compatible*. Any other change is considered to be *incompatible*.

Packages

In the OSGi Framework, the unit of assembly is a package containing interfaces, consumers, and providers. The package determines which of these are visible outside the package. Packages bring some complexity to representing version dependencies, as the following example illustrates.

Consider the Event Admin and Event Listener interfaces from the OSGi `org.osgi.service.eventadmin` package shown in Figure 7-2. When an Event Destination wants to be notified of events, it provides an instance of the Event Listener interface and then registers that

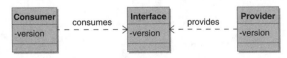

Figure 7-1: *Versioned Elements and Their Dependencies*

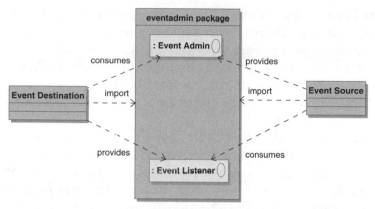

Figure 7-2: *Dependencies and the OSGi eventadmin Package*

instance by using (consuming) the Event Admin interface. The Event Source does the converse. It provides an instance of the Event Admin Interface so that parties can register their event listeners for its events. When events occur, it uses (consumes) the registered event listeners to notify parties that an event has occurred. Both the Event Destination and Event Sources import the same package. Each is a consumer of one interface and a provider of the other.

The approach taken to expressing dependencies on packages must be flexible enough to handle this kind of situation. The OSGi versioning scheme outlined in the following section has this flexibility.

OSGi Versioning

The Version Numbering Scheme

The OSGi Alliance has adopted a convention for expressing versions that provides a foundation for flexibly expressing dependencies. The structure it defines for version numbers is a dot-separated sequence of numbers:

```
<major>.<minor>.<micro>.<qualifier>
```

A `<major>` version number change indicates that the change is not backwards compatible for either consumers or providers. For example, interface version 1.x is incompatible with version 2.x.

A `<minor>` version number change indicates that the change is backwards compatible from a consumer perspective. For example, a consumer designed to work with version 1.1 of an interface will still work properly with version 1.2 of that interface. This implies not only that the original portions of the interface have remained unchanged, but also that the observable behavior associated with those portions of the interface has remained unchanged.

A `<micro>` version number change is one that introduces no backwards-compatibility issues for either the producer or consumer. This is generally a bug fix. If the philosophy of the OSGi approach is strictly adhered to, this should indicate that there are no changes in observable behavior.

The `<qualifier>` is a number that is usually used to indicate a particular build. These numbers often get very large.

The OSGi version numbering scheme not only allows a version to be specified, but indicates the nature of the relationship between that version and other versions. However, the numbering scheme is only a policy. Its usefulness depends upon strict adherence to the policy.

Unfortunately, in practice, major numbers are often used to indicate large-scale changes and minor numbers are smaller-scale changes without any particular regard to indicating compatibility. Releases with minor version number changes are sometimes not backwards compatible. Even worse, micro version number changes sometimes break compatibility as well. This approach limits the usefulness of version numbers in expressing dependencies and should be avoided.

Best Practice: Version Numbering

Adopt the OSGi approach to structuring version numbers. Strictly adhere to the guidelines about indicating compatibility, and make changes in observable behavior the criteria for determining compatibility.

Expressing Dependencies as Ranges

If you want to indicate the dependency of one element upon another, you need to indicate which versions of the other element are acceptable. To make this flexible, the OSGi versioning scheme uses ranges of versions when specifying dependencies.

Ranges are indicated by using a comma-separated pair of versions surrounded by brackets. Two types of bracket symbols are used depending upon whether or not the version number is to be included in the range. The [and] brackets are used to indicate that the version is included, while the (and) brackets indicate that the version is excluded. Thus the range specified by [1.2,2) starts with version 1.2 and includes all versions up to, but not including, version 2. This would be useful to indicate a consumer import policy indicating any version beginning with 1.2 and ranging up to, but not including, version 2 is acceptable.

Versioning and Bug Fixes

One situation that often results in deviations from the ideal versioning policy is the implementation of a bug fix *that results in an incompatible change to observable behavior*. There are a number of cases to be considered:

- The function never worked at all before. In this case, it can be argued that there are no dependencies on the old behavior and therefore the version change can be appropriately denoted as a micro change.

- The function worked, but its behavior was previously inconsistent with the specification. In this case, it can be argued that the old implementation was never correct and the version change can be appropriately denoted as a micro change. *However, for consumers that implemented workarounds that worked with the old behavior but will no longer work with the updated behavior, this constitutes an incompatible change. These components need to be identified and their version dependencies updated to indicate that they cannot use the new version. Thus if the old dependency was expressed as* [1,2) *(note the absence of the minor and micro values), and the new micro version is* 1.0.23, *then the dependency should be changed to* [1.0.0,1.0.23).

- The function worked but the behavior was previously unspecified. From a compatibility perspective, this is an ambiguous situation. Ideally, two things should happen here. One is that the specification should be updated to include the specification of the required behavior. The other is that the major version number should be incremented to reflect incompatible change to behavior.

The alternative is to only update the micro version number and then identify the existing consumers and modify their dependency specification to exclude the now-incompatible version.

- The fix resulted in a change to the service specification. Strictly speaking, this should result in a major version change. *The alternative is to only update the micro version number and then identify the existing consumers and modify their dependency specification to exclude the now-incompatible version.*

Any requirement to update the dependency specification for the consuming component becomes increasingly difficult as the scope of utilization increases. The worst case is public distribution of the component being versioned: There is no way of knowing who the consumers are. Strict adherence to the versioning guidelines completely avoids this problem by indicating clearly when compatibility has been broken. *Without strict adherence, consumers have no choice but to fully re-test after every release to ensure that they are still compatible with the new release.*

WSDL and XML Schema Versioning

Versioning web services is challenging because the standards used to specify WSDLs and XML schemas do not make any provisions for versions. Increasing the challenge is the fact that so many different things can change within a WSDL or schema.

Figure 7-3 shows the major concepts involved in WSDL and XML schema definitions. Any combination of these concepts can be changed: Elements, Types, Messages, Operations, or Interfaces (portTypes). Although you might be tempted then to assign a version number to each definition, you are then faced with representing the dependencies between the definitions, and there is no support for this in the standards. If element X version 1.0 is declared to be of type Y version 1.0 and then the type is changed (now version 1.1), the element must be considered to have changed as well. This means that its version would also have to be updated, but recognizing and doing this is a strictly manual process. This makes versioning individual concept definitions administratively awkward and error prone—that is, impractical.

Alternatively, versions can be tracked at the WSDL or XML schema level, with the version number applying to the entire WSDL or schema. When you are doing this, you are treating the entire WSDL or schema as a package.

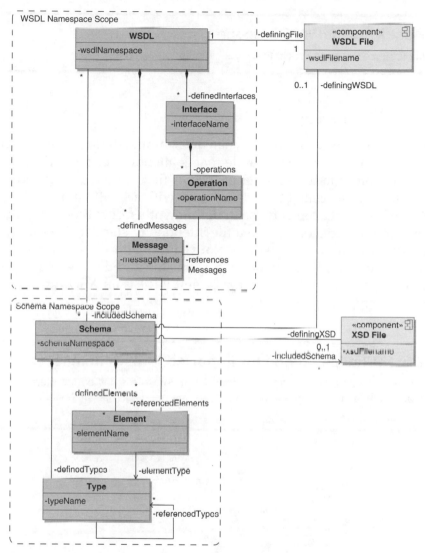

Figure 7-3: *WSDL and XML Schema Concepts*

WSDL Scope

To make versioning at the WSDL level practical, you must limit the content scope of an individual WSDL. The best practice is to limit the scope to a single interface (portType), and WSDL 2.0 makes this a requirement. This will simplify the management of dependencies between the providers and consumers of the specified interface.

Best Practice: WSDL Scope

Limit the content of a WSDL to a single interface (portType).

XML Schema Scope

The considerations are similar when determining the scope of a schema file. The contents of a schema file that is intended for reuse (i.e., incorporation into another schema or WSDL file) should be limited to a small set of interrelated type definitions, with a small number of types intended for inclusion and use in defining other data types. Figure 7-4 shows the contents of a schema file intended to standardize the representation of an address within Nouveau Health Care. Any schema referring to an address would import this file and declare one or more elements to be of type `Address`. Note that it is an XSD type, not an XSD element, being exported.

Best Practice: Scope for Imported XML Schemas

Limit the content of a schema intended for import to a small set of interrelated types with a small number of data types intended for use in defining other schemas.

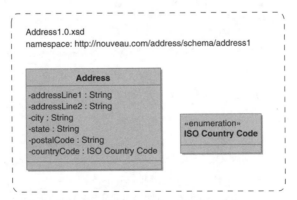

Figure 7-4: *Example Content for Address1.0.xsd File*

Version Number Placement for WSDLs and XML Schemas

The next question is where to put the version numbers. It is good practice to put version numbers in three places:

1. The filenames of WSDLs and schemas
2. The namespace names of WSDLs and schemas
3. The `soapAction` field in a WSDL binding

Although version numbers appear in each of these places, the rules for updating each are a bit different.

Version Numbers in Filenames

The version number in the filename should always be updated, regardless of the nature of the change. The version number in the filename should follow the `<major>.<minor>` OSGi scheme outlined earlier. Note that there is no point in including micro and qualifier values in the filename as this level of change never occurs in an interface definition. The resulting filename format is

`<path>/<filename><major>.<minor>.<fileExtension>`

For the address XSD file, this gives you

`File://C:/nouveau.com/address/schema/address1.0.xsd`

Version Numbers in Namespace Names

The namespace URI, on the other hand, should only contain the major version number. The rationale for not including the minor (compatible change) version number is that the namespace URI is included in the XML data structures being exchanged between the parties. Leaving the namespace URI untouched will allow consumers built to work with older versions of the interface to still interact with backwards-compatible providers implanting the newer versions of the interface. Since the namespace URI is converted into a Java name in many implementations and Java does not allow identifiers to start with numerical digits, the version number should not be separated from the namespace URI—it should be concatenated instead. Thus the namespace URI in Figure 7-4 is

```
http://nouveau.com/address/schema/address1
```

Version Numbers in soapAction Names

In the XML data structure that is exchanged between service consumers and providers, the `soapAction` field indicates the operation to be performed. Since operations are part of interfaces and you are versioning the interfaces, it is good practice to indicate the interface version in the `soapAction` field value. Following the recommended naming practices for the `soapAction` field (discussed in the next chapter), the resulting field name for the `payClaim()` operation of Figure 4-6 with major version 1 of the interface would be

```
http://insurance.nouveau.com/paymentManager/claimPayment1/
  payClaim
```

Best Practice: WSDL and XML Schema Versioning

Place major and minor version numbers in WSDL and schema filenames. Place major version numbers in the namespace URI. Place major version numbers in the interface name in the `soapAction` fields. Update the filename version for all WSDL and schema changes. Update the namespace URI and `soapAction` only when major (incompatible) changes are made.

Backwards-Compatible WSDL and XML Schema Changes

Certain kinds of WSDL and schema changes are backwards compatible *when service consumers and providers are independently deployed* (i.e., not in the same ActiveMatrix composite). The following sections describe some of these changes.

Adding Definitions to a WSDL

Adding message, interface (port type), and operation definitions to a WSDL is always backwards compatible. The service provider must support the new message, interface, or operation, but its absence in the older WSDL being used by existing consumers will not interfere with their ability to use everything defined in the older WSDL. Thus the older consumers will still be able to interoperate with the upgraded service provider. Note that, by best practice, interfaces (portTypes) should not be added to WSDLs.

Deleting Unused Definitions from a WSDL (Conditional)

Deleting unused message, interface (port type), and operation definitions from a WSDL is backwards compatible *if the definitions are truly not used*; that is, there are no clients in existence that actually use the definitions. In such cases, deleting the unused definitions and updating the service provider so that it only supports the remaining definitions will be backwards compatible. Such deletions should only be considered backwards compatible if it can be definitively established that there are no consumers using the deleted definitions.

Adding Definitions to an XML Schema

Adding element and type definitions to a schema is always backwards compatible, whether those definitions are in an XSD file or contained in line in a WSDL.

Deleting Unused Definitions from an XML Schema (Conditional)

Deleting unused element and type definitions from a schema is backwards compatible *if the definitions are truly not used*, meaning that there are no other element and type definitions that reference them and they are not referenced by any WSDL message definitions. In such cases, deleting the unused definitions will be backwards compatible. Such deletions should only be considered backwards compatible if it can be definitively established that there are no consumers using the deleted definitions.

Replacing a SimpleType with an Identical SimpleType

Since the simple type values in the XML file do not reference the type definition that determines their allowed values, replacing a type definition with another that allows exactly the same set of values is a backwards-compatible change. This allows certain types of schema file restructuring.

Consider the case in which one type has been derived from another

```
<xs:simpleType name="AuthorizerId">
  <xs:restriction base="ty:UserID" />
</xs:simpleType>
```

Replacing a reference to the derived type `AuthorizerID`:

```
<xs:element name="authorizer" type="AuthorizerID">
```

with a reference to the base type `UserID`

```
<xs:element name="authorizer" type="UserID">
```

results in a compatible change. Note that this is true regardless of the file in which either type is defined. This technique can be used to remove redundant type definitions impacting either the provider or consumer.

Adding an Optional Field to an XML Schema (Conditional Future)

With the release of the XML schema 1.1 standard,[3] additional types of compatible changes become possible. Under certain conditions, the addition of an optional element to a sequence is backwards compatible. This condition is that the sequence has to end with an XML **any**:

```
<xs:complexType name="InterestRateForTier">
  <xs:sequence>
    <xs:element name="MaxAmountForTier" type="Amount" />
    <xs:element name="InterestRate" type="Rate" />
    <xs:element name="InterestRateConfirmedIndicator"
      type="boolean" />
    <xs:any minOccurs="0" maxOccurs="unbounded"
      processContents="skip" />
  </xs:sequence>
</xs:complexType>
```

If the **any** declaration occurs at the end of the sequence, then the following revised data structure is compatible with the original:

```
<xs:complexType name="InterestRateForTier">
  <xs:sequence>
    <xs:element name="MaxAmountForTier" type="Amount" />
```

---

3. XSD 1.1 became a standard on April 5, 2012.

```
    <xs:element name="InterestRate" type="Rate" />
    <xs:element name="InterestRateConfirmedIndicator"
      type="boolean" />
    <xs:element name="newElement" type="Boolean"
      minOccurs="0" />
    <xs:any minOccurs="0" maxOccurs="unbounded"
      processContents="skip" />
  </xs:sequence>
</xs:complexType>
```

Note that the new element must be declared as optional in order for the data structures to be backwards compatible. Here any data structure created with either definition is acceptable to any other component regardless of which definition that component is using.

Incompatible Changes

In general, any change that cannot be classified as a backwards-compatible change (as defined in the previous section) must be considered an incompatible change for the purpose of versioning. The following sections describe some specific cases that are incompatible, but the sections are not comprehensive in their description of all possible incompatible changes. The working rule is, "When in doubt, consider the change incompatible."

Incompatible Changes in a Schema

The following are all incompatible changes in a schema:

- Adding or removing an element in a complex datatype.
- Changing the name of an element in a complex datatype.
- Changing the datatype of an element when the type is complex. This is because, unlike simple datatypes, the name and namespace of complex datatypes explicitly appear in the XML files.

Incompatible Changes in a WSDL

The following are all incompatible changes in a WSDL:

- Changing the name of the element referenced in a message declaration
- Adding or removing a message from an operation declaration

- Changing the name of a message in an operation declaration
- Changing the name of an operation in a port type (interface) declaration

Once again, a reminder: Any change that cannot be proven to be backwards compatible must be treated as incompatible.

Rules for Versioning WSDLs and Schemas

- If an incompatible change is made to a WSDL or schema, both the filename and the namespace URI are updated with a new `<major>` version number.
- If a compatible change is made to a WSDL or schema, the filename `<minor>` version number is updated but the namespace version number remains unchanged.
- If a WSDL or schema references another schema that has incompatible changes made to it and wishes to use the new schema, it must do the following:
  ○ Update the reference to the file that is being imported to reference the new filename (bear in mind that the version number is in the filename).
  ○ Update the namespace declaration that accompanies the imported file. This declaration repeats the namespace declaration within the imported file (and therefore must contain the correct version number), but it also locally defines the prefix that will be used to indicate the elements and types that were imported from the file.
  ○ If the use of the newly imported elements creates incompatible changes in the current file (WSDL or XSD), then the `<major>` version of the target namespace and the `<major>` version of the filename must also be updated to indicate the incompatibility.
- Version numbers should appear in the SOAP Action field of the SOAP header. This provides the option for having a single endpoint (whether HTTP or JMS) handle requests for all versions of the same service.

Architecture Patterns for Versioning

Services often act as intermediaries between components and back-end systems. Back-end systems often differ in their ability to provide and support multiple versions. This leads to a number of options for evolving the service when its back-end system is upgraded to a new version. The following sections discuss some of these options, all of which are variations on the architecture pattern shown in Figure 7-5.

Accommodating a Compatible Change

If a change to a back-end system can be accommodated with a compatible change to the service interface, the original service can simply be replaced with the new version presenting the new version 1.1 interface (Figure 7-6). The new service interface supports the original clients as well as clients using the full capabilities of the new interface. Necessary changes are made within the service to utilize the new back-end interface, and the back-end system is replaced with the new version. Note that if there are multiple instances of the service, all must be upgraded to the new version before any of the clients are updated.

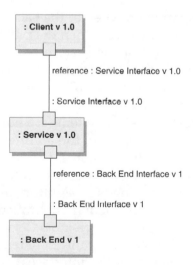

Figure 7-5: *Initial Architecture Pattern*

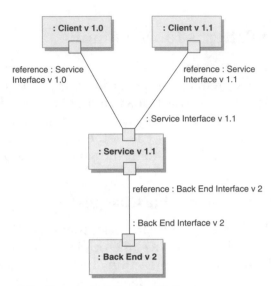

Figure 7-6: *Compatible Change Architecture Pattern*

Incompatible Change Deployment

The situation is a bit more complicated if the back-end system change requires an incompatible change to the service interface. Two different patterns emerge, depending on whether the back end can present both the old and new interfaces. If it can, then the pattern of Figure 7-7 can be used. A new version 2.0 of the service is created to support the incompatibly changed version 2.0 service interface. The back-end system is deployed with both version 2 and version 3 interfaces, and each service utilizes the appropriate interface.

Unfortunately, most back-end systems are not capable of supporting multiple interfaces. In this case, the architecture pattern of Figure 7-8 can be used. Here the version 1.1 service is replaced with a version 1.2 that maps the version 1.1 service interface to the new version 2.0 interface. If the mapping is straightforward, it may be accomplished with an ActiveMatrix Mediation Implementation Type. An alternative would be to make the version 1.2 service access the back end interface version 3.0 directly, but this may require more work than simply mapping between the service interfaces.

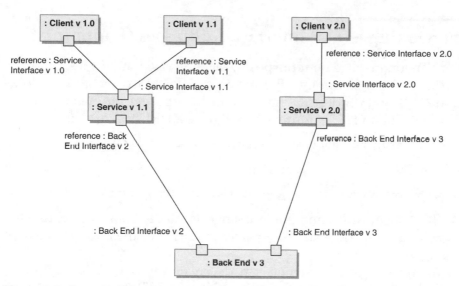

Figure 7-7: *Incompatible Change Architecture Pattern — Back End Supports Multiple Interfaces*

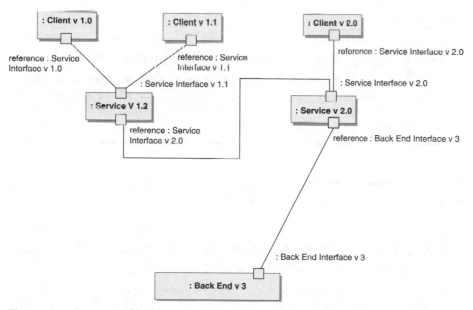

Figure 7-8: *Incompatible Change Architecture Pattern—Back End Supports a Single Interface*

Versioning SOAP Interface Addresses (Endpoints)

For version management purposes, each interface should have its own SOAP address (endpoint). For maximum flexibility, the address location (URI or JMS destination) should incorporate the major version number. For an HTTP address, you'll have a URI structure like

```
http://insurance.nouveau.com/paymentManager/claimPayment1
```

For an EMS destination, you'll have

```
com.nouveau.insurance.paymentManager.claimPayment1
```

If a backwards-compatible change is made, continue to use the same endpoint: The `<major>` version number of the interface has not changed.

If an incompatible change is made, create a new address (endpoint) with the new major version number. For an HTTP address, you'll have

```
http://insurance.nouveau.com/paymentManager/claimPayment2
```

For an EMS destination, you'll have:

```
com.nouveau.insurance.paymentManager.claimPayment2
```

Best Practice: SOAP Address (Endpoint) Versioning

Each interface should have its own address (endpoint) by which it is accessed. The address should include the major version number of the interface. If the interface's major version changes, a new address (endpoint) should be created with the new version number.

Versioning the SOAP Action

The SOAP action name (a URI) should incorporate the interface's major version number. Thus the payClaim operation of the Claim Payment interface would have a SOAP action of

```
http://insurance.nouveau.com/paymentManager/claimPayment1/
   payClaim
```

If the interface's major version changes, the SOAP actions associated with its operations should be updated, as in

```
http://insurance.nouveau.com/paymentManager/claimPayment2/
   payClaim
```

Best Practice: soapAction Versioning

Incorporate the interface and interface major version number into the soap-Action URI. If the interface major version changes, update the SOAP actions for its operations with the new major version number.

How Many Versions Should Be Maintained?

The reason for supporting multiple versions is to ease the transition of service clients from one version to the next. This easing takes the form of allowing the clients some flexibility as to when (not if!) they upgrade to the new version. The intent is to avoid "big bang" upgrades that require simultaneous updates to all (or many) of the clients when a service interface undergoes an incompatible change.

Allowing multiple versions raises the question of how many versions of a particular interface ought to be supported in a given environment (development, test, production, etc.). Recognize that the goal is to minimize artificial client releases—releases that are made solely to accommodate service interface changes that arise *from another client's requirements*. To minimize these artificial releases, you need to understand how often the client would normally be making a release *because of its own changing requirements*. The assumption is that upgrading to the new service interface at this time will be significantly less costly than making an artificial release just to accommodate the service interface change.

Determining the number of versions that must be supported depends upon the rate at which clients (service consumers) typically deploy releases due to their own changing requirements. The numbers will be different for each environment, but the calculations are as follows:

1. Determine the interval at which clients typically deploy changes. For example, there might be a production release opportunity every 30 days, but the average client only updates every other release. This means that there is an average of 60 days between client updates.

2. Multiply this interval by two. If a change to the client is already underway when the service interface needs to change, you don't want to change the client requirements in midstream and force it to

use the new interface. You want to make this a requirement for the subsequent release.

3. Determine the interval at which services normally deploy incompatible changes (compatible changes are not an issue since they never require a client upgrade). In a rapidly evolving environment, this interval might be the same as the production release cycle (30 days in the example we are discussing).

4. Calculate the number of versions that need to be supported by dividing twice the client update interval (120 days in the example) by the service update interval (30 days in the example). For the example, this yields four versions of the service that need to be maintained in each environment.

Putting this all together, you get the following formula:

$$numberDeployedVersions = \frac{2 * clientReleaseInterval}{incompatibleServiceReleaseInterval}$$

The intent is to minimize client churn and allow service changes to be incorporated into the "natural" release cycle of the clients. In other words, you want to avoid making changes to clients solely to accommodate service interface changes. The conclusion concerning the appropriate number of service versions can only be arrived at by examining the overall impact of service changes. Viewing the problem from the narrow perspective of the service provider will likely lead to a lower number of versions (thus reducing the provider's costs) at the expense of additional cost for the service consumers. The number of versions to be supported should reflect an overall optimization of IT costs.

The analysis presented here is simplistic: It does not attempt to analyze the cost of client releases versus the cost of maintaining additional existing versions of a service interface. However, it is hard to imagine a situation in which the cost of maintaining an old version of the service interface exceeds the cost of an otherwise unnecessary release of one or more service clients. In such cases, the conclusions presented by this analysis will result in a net cost savings for the overall solution (clients + services) and a simplification in each release cycle (less of a "big bang").

Summary

Despite all your best efforts, services will eventually need to be changed. When this occurs, it becomes necessary to keep track of the versions of interfaces and the providers and consumers of those interfaces. It also becomes necessary to track the dependencies.

Some changes to interfaces are backwards compatible: Consumers of the old interface are able to use the updated interface. Backwards-compatible changes are primarily additions to the interface that do not affect the portions of the interface already in use. Interface providers must implement all features of the interface. Consequently, any change to the interface requires a change to the provider. Some provider changes, on the other hand, do not require interface changes.

The OSGi Alliance provides a standardized way of denoting versions that indicates whether or not the change is backwards compatible. The structure of these version numbers is

```
<major>.<minor>.<micro> <qualifier>
```

A major change is one that is not compatible for either consumers or providers. A minor change is one that is backwards compatible from a consumer perspective. A micro change is one that introduces no compatibility issues for either the producer or consumer. The qualifier is usually used to indicate a particular build.

In indicating a dependency, it is useful to denote ranges of versions. This is done by giving a pair of version numbers and surrounding the pair with brackets that indicate whether or not the specified version is included in the range. The [and] brackets are used to indicate that the version is included in the range, and (and) are used to indicate that the version is excluded from the range.

Updating versions for bug fixes can be complex. If the bug fix does not introduce a change to observable behavior, incrementing the <micro> number suffices. However, if the observable behavior changes, either the old behavior was different from the specified behavior or the behavior was previously unspecified. In either case, clients consuming the interface will no longer operate properly after the change is made, so the <major> number should be incremented. The alternative is to locate all service consumers and update their dependencies to indicate that they will not operate properly with the new version. This only works if you are able to identify all of the current service consumers.

WSDLs and schemas require versioning. The best practice is to include the `<major>.<minor>` version structure in the filename and the `<major>` structure in the namespace URI.

The addresses (endpoints) through which interfaces are accessed require versioning. The URI should contain the `<major>` version of the interface.

When incompatible changes are made to services, it is important to retain earlier versions for a period of time to avoid unnecessary releases of consuming components. The number of versions that ought to be retained depends upon the typical release cycles of service consumers and service providers.

Chapter 8

Naming Standards

Objectives

This chapter provides guidance for an enterprise architect defining the standardized structure of names for web services and other IT elements in the enterprise. It explores the issues and best practices involved in defining and managing enterprise naming standards. The topic is of particular importance because the structuring of the names and the challenges involved in maintaining the consistency in naming WSDL and XML schema namespaces, services, ports, operations, and other artifacts in the web services space have a significant impact on the complexity of managing an SOA environment.

Although the discussion and examples are focused largely on web services (i.e., services defined with a WSDL), the basic naming principles also apply to schemas, JMS destination names, uniform resource identifiers (URIs) and uniform resource locators (URLs). Several of the important names in a WSDL are required to be URIs.

There are many possible approaches to designing names for use in SOA environments. This chapter sets forth one concise set of best-practice concepts for designing names that can be readily tailored to the needs of your enterprise. In explaining the concepts, particular emphasis is placed on explaining the rationale behind the approach so that the refinements that will inevitably be required in practice can be designed with the same principles.

After reading this chapter you should be able to

- Describe the principles guiding name structure design.
- Apply the principles to the ideal design of names for WSDL and schema artifacts.
- Describe the choices available for addressing real-world complications in name structure design.

Using This Chapter

The intent of this chapter is to provide guidance in the formulation of naming standards. It begins with a discussion of the concepts and general principles for structuring names. These principles represent a rationale for structuring names that should, as a rule, always be adhered to.

But principles are not enough: There are circumstances under which the principles alone will not provide a unique solution. As these cases arise in this chapter, guidelines are provided to indicate reasonable ways of addressing the situation and guidance for selecting an appropriate approach.

Next, some complicating realities are discussed. Practical constraints imposed by the implementation technology constrain the structures of names. Organizational issues of various types introduce complications that require guidelines for resolution. The existence of multiple environments (development, test, production) and the need for flexible deployment (for fault tolerance, high availability, site disaster recovery, or simply administrative convenience) add wrinkles of their own. Versioning must also be taken into consideration.

The chapter concludes with some practical guidance for creating SOA naming standards.

Concepts

Abstract Services

Any discussion of service naming standards has to begin by putting a stake in the ground in terms of defining what a service is. Here you run into a difference of abstraction between the working definitions used in the broader SOA community and those provided specifically by web services (i.e., defined by the WSDL schemas).

Thomas Erl provides the following statement that is generally representative of the broader SOA community perspective: "Each [abstract] service is assigned its own distinct functional context and is comprised of a set of capabilities related to this context. Those capabilities suitable for invocation by external consumer programs are commonly expressed via a published service [interface] contract (much like a traditional API)."[1]

The structure of the concepts in this statement is shown in Figure 8-1. Here the term *Interface Contract* is used to reinforce the fact that the concept being represented is an interface. This also emphasizes that an Abstract Service may have multiple interfaces. This concept structure provides a useful framework for exploring the structure of names.

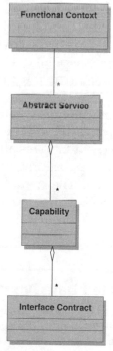

Figure 8-1: *Abstract Service Concepts*

---

1. Thomas Erl, *SOA: Principles of Service Design*, Upper Saddle River, NJ: Prentice Hall (2008), p. 39.

WSDL Interface Definitions

The Web Services Description Language (WSDL) is designed to define service interfaces. A WSDL file contains two different kinds of definitions: abstract definitions (often referred to as types or meta-data) and concrete definitions (Figure 8-2). The abstract definitions specify the types of portTypes (interfaces), operations, messages, and message parts. The message parts, in turn, reference schema data types (see the sidebar on incorporating schema data types). The concrete specifications define the instances of services, ports (endpoints), and their bindings to protocols. WSDL and schema definitions each occur in a context uniquely identified by their respective namespace URIs.

Two of the names are particularly important: the address of the port (endpoint) and the soapAction of the operation binding. Their importance stems from the fact that these are the two primary names used in the communications between the service consumer and provider when SOAP bindings are being used. The address specifies the place to which messages are being sent, and the soapAction is the sole indication of the operation that is being invoked. It is from these two pieces of information that the recipient determines the abstract definitions (meta-data) that characterize the message structure and the operation to be performed.

The WSDL part definitions reference data types from a schema definition. It is a best practice for each message part to have its own dedicated schema type associated with it. This allows each data structure to be specific to the operation it supports and avoids unnecessary updates if these data types are shared. The namespace URI for this schema should be the same as the WSDL namespace URI except for their respective endings (schema or WSDL). The use of different endings is primarily for human readability.

Best Practice: Dedicated Data Types for Message Parts

Use a different dedicated data type for each message part, and define these data types in a schema dedicated to the WSDL. The namespace for the schema and WSDL should be the same except for their respective endings (schema or WSDL).

The dedicated data types for message parts may well contain elements having data types that belong to a common data model. Those

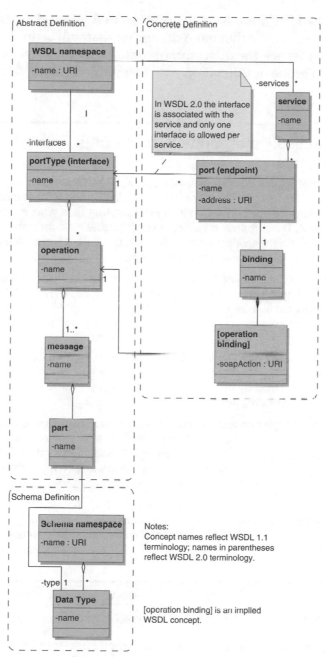

Figure 8-2: *Simplified WSDL Concepts*

data types, which are designed to be shared, should be defined in their own schema, one that has a definition that will be in its own XSD file. The namespace for the common data model XSD should reflect the intended scope of utilization of the contained data types (more on this later).

Best Practice: Incorporate Schema Data Types, Not Elements

Definitions that occur in an XML Schema Definition (XSD) are often incorporated into other schema and WSDL definitions. Both WSDL and XSD standards provide two options for doing this. One is to incorporate a data type, in which case the WSDL or XSD incorporating the type defines a local element of that type. The other is to incorporate an element definition and use it as-is—including its name. The best practice is to incorporate the data type.

The rationale behind this best practice is that the name of an element reflects the role that the element plays in the context in which it is being used. The author of the shared schema has no way of knowing how those definitions are going to be employed and therefore may not be in a position to choose appropriate element names. Furthermore, new usages may require new names.

Consider the concept of an address, a likely candidate for a shared schema definition. If the shared schema defines an Address data type, then it is easy for one consuming data structure to define a homeAddress element and another to define a workAddress element.

This approach is open ended: You do not need to know all of the usages ahead of time to create the correct element names. You can later create other data structures that define a shippingAddress or billingAddress, or any other address role you can imagine. The flexibility occurs because these roles are defined in the new data structures—not the shared schema.

The alternative, creating the elements in the shared schema, not only requires a change to the shared schema each time a new role is added (which requires a new element with that role name), but these shared schema changes impact all of the other consumers of the shared schema. For this reason, the best practice is to incorporate data types, not elements.

Relating Abstract and WSDL-Defined Services

The correspondence between Erl's abstract concepts and the WSDL definitions is shown in Figure 8-3. The functional context corresponds to a functional area that may contain many WSDL-defined service interfaces. The subdivisions of the functional context, the abstract

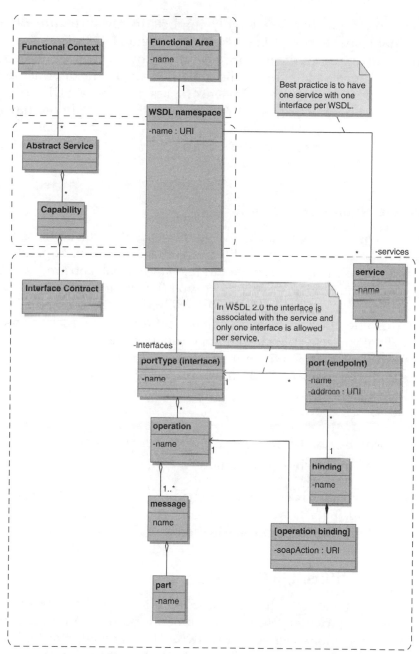

Figure 8-3: *Correspondence between Abstract Services and WSDL Definitions*

service and capability, are largely implicit in the structure of the WSDL namespace (this will be discussed in detail later). The interface contract encompasses the interface definition but, as was discussed in Chapter 6, there is a lot more to the contract than just the interface definition. The interface contract may encompass multiple WSDLs, particularly if the best practice recommendation (Chapter 7) of only having one interface per WSDL is followed. *In the ensuing discussion, unless explicitly stated otherwise, the term* service *is a reference to the abstract service concept, not the WSDL definition.*

Why Are Names Important?

When you use a service, that service and its operations need to be readily identifiable and distinguishable from other services and operations. This is accomplished by giving a unique name to each abstract service and, within the service, to each port type (interface) and operation of that service. Unique names are also required for the messages, data structures, and other artifacts used in the definition of the service interface. When you use JMS destinations (queues and topics), it is also important to distinguish them from other destinations. This gives you the flexibility to move these destinations to other EMS servers.

There are two significant challenges that you will encounter when creating names:

1. Ensuring that each name is reasonably descriptive
2. Ensuring that each name is unique

Naming standards establish how names are structured and organized and how (by whom) uniqueness is guaranteed, and thus determine how both challenges are addressed.

Names Are Difficult to Change

Unfortunately, once established, names tend to become deeply embedded in service providers, service consumers, and the components that mediate interactions between the two. Thus changing established names is expensive—often prohibitively so. You are going to be stuck with the names you choose for a long time, so it is worth an investment of time in considering the standards that govern their structure.

Name Structures Define Search Strategies

In SOA, the structure of a name not only identifies the item being named, but often indicates how to find the item. When people are looking for an artifact, they often begin with only a vague notion of what they are looking for. While indexes and keyword associations can be of use, the structure of the name implicitly defines a search strategy for locating items. Consider, for example, the Nouveau Health Care Payment Manager's Claim Payment Interface. Its WSDL might have the URL

```
http://insurance.nouveau.com/finance/paymentManager/
  claimPayment/wsdl/claimPayment.wsdl
```

This name not only uniquely identifies the WSDL file, it tells us where to find it: Go to the machine designated by `insurance.nouveau.com` (at the default port 80), look in the `finance/paymentManager/claimPayment/wsdl` directory, and obtain the file `ClaimPayment.wsdl`.

Name Structures Define Routing Strategies

Although it is not formally a part of the web services paradigm, ports (endpoints) often make use of names in directing service requests to the actual service provider. The component (and often the machine) that accepts service requests is often different than the component actually servicing those requests. Appropriate naming can aid the receiving component in routing requests to the provider.

For example, the port (endpoint) address (the address to which service requests are directed) is designated by a URI, which is a form of name. Consider the address of the claim payment interface for Nouveau Health Care, given as

```
https://insurance.nouveau.com:443/finance/paymentManager/
  claimPayment
```

Also consider the address of the claim submission interface, given as

```
https://insurance.nouveau.com:443/claims/claimRouter/
  claimSubmission
```

The actual component to which both kinds of requests are directed is designated by the first part of the address URI, namely the domain name and port (not to be confused with the WSDL concept of port):

```
https://insurance.nouveau.com:443
```

This indicates that requests are received on port 443 of the machine designated by `insurance.nouveau.com`. From there, if the requests are to be serviced by another component, they must be routed to the actual service provider. The presence of the URI path structure in the address below the Internet domain name and port number makes it possible to route requests arriving at port 443 based on this path. Alternately, this information can be ignored and all requests can be routed to a common destination that provides support for all web services sharing the domain name and port.

In contrast, both addresses could have been given as

```
https://insurance.nouveau.com:443
```

In this case, since the path is absent, there is no information that can be used to route requests.

Using the structure of the address is, of course, not the only way to route. Other information such as the `soapAction`, the structure of the WSDL namespace URI, and the port/operation naming structure underneath it can also be used for routing. Regardless of which names are being used, the structure of these names and the consistency with which that structure is used can greatly simplify the routing of service requests.

What Needs a Name?

In an SOA environment there are many things that require names. These include

- WSDL-related names:
  - The WSDL itself (the `name` attribute in the top-level `<definitions>` tag).
  - The WSDL filename.
  - The `targetNamespace` defined by the WSDL (also in the top-level `<definitions>` tag). This name is a URI, and is the logical prefix for the name of each entity defined in the WSDL.
  - The entities defined by the WSDL: services, port types (interface), operations, messages, bindings, and ports (endpoints).
  - The `soapAction`.
  - The `schemaLocation` of each imported XSD file.
  - The `address` of each service port (endpoint).

- Schema-related names:
    - The XSD filename (if the schema is not embedded in a WSDL).
    - The `targetNamespace` defined by the schema (either embedded in the WSDL or a stand-alone XSD). This name is a URI and is the logical prefix for the name of each entity defined in the schema.
    - The entities defined by the schema: types, elements, and attributes.
    - The `schemaLocation` of each imported XSD file.
- JMS-related names:
    - Static destination (topic or queue) names
    - EMS server names
- SCA-related names
    - Composite names
    - Component type names
    - Service names

Some of these items are actual artifacts, such as files. Others are simply logical names for definitions (port types, messages, elements, etc.) or groups of definitions (namespace URIs). All of them will have to be dealt with by the producers and consumers of services. These names, and the standards for defining them, are the focus of this chapter.

Structured Name Design Principles

Use a General-to-Specific Structure

Structured names (think www.nouveau.com) are trees. The root of the tree represents the entire tree. Each node below represents a subtree rooted at that node. The root of the Internet (the parent of com) is not explicitly named, but the next tier down in the Internet naming system (referred to as top-level domains) consists of nodes such as .com, .net, .org, and .edu. Within each of those domains there are subdomains whose names are meaningful only in the context of the parent domain. Thus for uniqueness you refer to nouveau.com rather than just nouveau (which has different meanings in .com, .net, .org, etc.).

Because of the inherent tree structure, it is important that the logic of the structure you define be organized around a true hierarchy. The outline of such a hierarchy for services derives from the description of a service presented in the concepts discussion earlier. From the abstract concept discussion we have

```
<functionalContext><abstractService><abstractInterface>
```

This is a general-to-specific structure. A functional context may contain more than one service, and each service can contain more than one interface. Conversely, services are specific to a particular functional context, and each interface is specific to a particular service.

Ideally, the actual hierarchy is represented by a uniform sequence of fields in a left-to-right, most-general-to-most-specific fashion. This is the pattern you see in the naming of Java classes:

```
com.nouveau.insurance.finance.paymentManager.claimPayment.
  payClaim
```

Here `com.nouveau.insurance.finance` represents the functional context. The abstract service is the `paymentManager`. The abstract interface is represented by `claimPayment.payClaim`, the interface and operation used for paying a claim. Note that there is hierarchical structure both within the functional context and within the interface.

Unfortunately, many names in the SOA world are required to be URIs or URLs. These include namespace names and WSDL/SOAP `address` and `soapAction` fields. The structuring scheme for URIs does not strictly adhere to a uniform principle. Each URI or URL actually contains two name hierarchies, each with different construction rules. Consider the earlier example:

```
http://insurance.nouveau.com/finance/paymentManager/
  claimPayment/wsdl/claimPayment.wsdl
```

There are three parts to this string involving two different name structures:

1. `http://`, the first part, represents a protocol to be used to access the artifact. From a name structure perspective, we can ignore this.
2. `insurance.nouveau.com`, the second part, is an *Internet domain name* that designates a machine on the Internet. In the Internet domain name, hierarchy is read right to left.

3. `/finance/paymentManager/claimPayment/wsdl/claimPayment.wsdl`, the third part, is called the path. It represents a name hierarchy local to the machine designated by the Internet domain name. The path name hierarchy is read left to right.

What makes the use of two different name hierarchies and their differences in right-to-left and left-to-right reading unambiguous is the use of two different field separators. The Internet domain namespace fields are separated by a period (.), while the local namespace fields are separated by a forward slash (/). The occurrence of the first slash to the right of the Internet domain name is the clue that you have switched naming hierarchies.

If you wanted to make this namespace uniform, reading entirely left to right, you would have to switch the order of the Internet namespace elements:

```
com.nouveau.insurance.finance.paymentManager.claimPayment.wsdl.
   claimPayment.wsdl
```

This is, of course, the kind of structure used for naming Java classes.

Best Practice: General-to-Specific Structure

When the structure of names is not already constrained, establish a uniform left-to-right, general-to-specific hierarchical structure for names following the pattern

```
<functionalContext><abstractService><abstractInterface>
```

When the structure of names is partially constrained (e.g., URLs and URIs), apply this principle to the lower-level structure of the names (i.e., the path in the URL or URI).

Employ Hierarchical Naming Authorities

Names, to be useful, must be unique. Uniqueness requires that some authority keep track of which names have been assigned so that newly issued names can be assured to be different. Unfortunately, having a single authority to keep track of all names is impractical, particularly for names with global scope.

The systems that have evolved (in numerous places) to address this issue involve the use of hierarchical authorities. This strategy involves two elements. The first is a standardized syntactic structure for defining names as sequences of fields. The Internet domain name structure (e.g., `insurance.nouveau.com`) is one example.

The other element is a policy that establishes authorities for maintaining the uniqueness of individual fields at different levels of the hierarchy. For example, in the Internet domain name structure, the authority for the top-level domain names (`.com`, `.net`, `.org`, etc.) is ICANN (the Internet Corporation for Assigned Names and Numbers). For each of the assigned top-level domain names, ICANN also identifies an authority for maintaining the uniqueness of the next-level names. For the generic top-level domains (`.com`, `.net`, `.org`, etc.) ICANN itself is the naming authority. For sponsored top-level domains (`.edu`, `.gov`, `.mil`) this authority has been delegated to other entities—one for each sponsored domain. For example, the `.edu` domain is administered by EDUCAUSE, the `.gov` domain by the General Services Administration of the US Government, and the .mil domain by the US Department of Defense Network Information Center.

Each naming authority does two things:

- It directly manages the field level for which it is responsible.
- It establishes the policy for managing the lower-level fields.

It is in this latter point that the hierarchical authority gains its flexibility: A naming authority can delegate the responsibility for managing subordinate namespaces. For our fictional domain, ICANN would not only establish `nouveau.com` as a domain name, it would delegate the authority for managing the lower levels of the hierarchy to Nouveau Health Care Inc. Nouveau Health Care directly manages the next level of names (such as `www.nouveau.com` and `insurance.nouveau.com`) and (if desired) delegates the responsibility of managing the next level of namespace.

This idea can, and should, be extended within the enterprise. Rather than having a centralized authority for managing all names, the central authority establishes a policy for the structure of names, directly manages the top field(s) of this namespace, and delegates the authority for managing the lower-level fields.

Best Practice: Hierarchical Naming Authorities

Do not fully centralize the management of names in the enterprise. Instead, set up a central authority to (a) establish a generic structure for names, (b) assign the values for the top-level branches of the namespace, and (c) designate appropriate authorities to manage the lower-level structure of individual branches.

Base Naming on Stable Concepts

Because of the difficulty in changing both the structure of names and the individual names that have been chosen, it is prudent to base the namespace structure and individual names on concepts that remain stable over time, with the exception of enterprise identifiers.

Domain Concepts

The concepts that are most likely to remain stable over time are those that generically occur in any discussion of the business. In a discussion of the shipping industry, you would tend to use general terms like package, shipment, track, rate, shipper, recipient, and location. In banking, you would use general terms like customer, account, deposit, withdrawal, payment, and transaction.

What you want to avoid are terms that are likely to change over time, particularly those with branded terminology. Thus you would want to use the generic term "claim" instead of "expressClaim" or "account" instead of "premierAccount." In doing so, you hedge your bets against mergers, acquisitions, and changes in marketing.

Business Processes

The same rule applies when naming operations associated with business processes. You want to stick with generic names that will remain stable over time. Thus the operation for tracking a claim is called simply "track," while the marketing-branded process may be called "Nouveau Track." An idealized (and somewhat simplified) operation name for tracking a Nouveau Health Care claim might be something like

```
com.nouveau.insurance.claims.claimTracker.claimTrack.trackClaim
```

Here the `claimTracker` service presents a `claimTrack` interface with a `trackClaim` operation.

The Exception to the Rule: Enterprise Identifiers

Names, in the context of the world-wide web, must be unique. To guarantee the global uniqueness of names issued by your enterprise, you need to qualify the name with something that identifies the enterprise issuing the name. The most common approach is to base this on the Internet domain name that has been assigned to your enterprise.

This, of course, violates the notion of naming being based on stable concepts—your enterprise could change its name at any time. Mergers and acquisitions are constantly changing this landscape. Despite this potential for change, the use of the enterprise name as a name prefix is necessary. In the examples we have been using so far, ideally structured names in Nouveau Health Care would be prefixed by `com.nouveau`. Note that the order of the fields in this idealized name structure is reversed from the Internet domain names.

The use of the name prefix not only guarantees the global uniqueness of names, but also serves as a hedge against mergers and acquisitions. Without introducing the enterprise-specific prefix, the IT consolidation after a merger or acquisition is liable to create name conflicts. It is likely that two health care insurance providers would both have names like `claimProcessing.claimSubmission.submitClaim`. Adding the prefix averts a conflict with these names as used by the different companies.

Best Practice: Base Naming on Stable Concepts

Base the namespace structure and individual names on concepts that remain stable over time, with the exception of enterprise identifiers.

Avoid Acronyms and Abbreviations

It is good practice to make the names in individual fields of the naming structure as readable and obvious as possible. This argues against using acronyms unless they are widely used across an entire industry and are universally understood. Some common functional abbreviations that might be considered acceptable (at least in English) include

- HR—Human Resources
- MKTG—Marketing
- MFG—Manufacturing
- FIN—Finance

Best Practice: Avoid Acronyms

Avoid using acronyms and abbreviations unless they are universally understood across an industry.

Distinguish Types from Instances

It is not unusual in a WSDL or schema to define a type and then use that type to define an element. For example, you might define a datatype to represent an account balance and then create an instance of that type (an element) as a field in an account to show the current balance. Even if the structure of the defining language allows the same name to be used for both the type and the field name, doing so can be very confusing to a human reader.

Consequently it is a good idea to adopt a standard way of distinguishing type names from instance names. Some examples of such conventions include

- Using leading capitals to indicate types and leading lowercase to indicate instances. Thus the type for the account balance would have the name `AccountBalance`, and the instance field in the account (the element name) would have the name `accountBalance`.

- Appending a distinguishing term to the end of the type name. Thus the type for the account balance would have the name `Account-BalanceType`, and the instance field in the account would have the name `accountBalance`.

It is not unusual to combine the two strategies, as was done in the second example. Note that it is likely that you already have similar standards in place for writing code. If so, you should examine those standards to determine whether they are applicable here as well. If those standards are applicable, you should adopt the existing standard rather than inventing a new one—this will avoid confusion when people are developing code that references WSDL and schema definitions.

Best Practice: Distinguish Types from Instances

Adopt a standard way of distinguishing type names from instance names.

Plan for Multi-Word Fields

It is often useful to be able to use more than one word when constructing a name. This can be accommodated by adopting a convention for capitalizing names that ensures that the resulting multi-word names are readily readable. Two common conventions that satisfy this criterion are

- Non-leading capitals: Each word in a field other than the first begins with a capital letter, such as `ClaimService` (for a type) or `claimService` (for an instance). The leading capital should be determined by whether the field references a type or an instance (see previous section).

- All letters are capitalized, and an underscore (_) or other separator is used between words, for example, `CLAIM_SERVICE`. This convention pretty much requires that an additional term be used to distinguish types from instances (see previous section).

One convention to be avoided is the use of all capitals with no special characters allowed (e.g., no underscores). Such a convention leads to names like `CLAIMSERVICE`, which is not only hard to read but also may lead to ambiguities.

Best Practice: Plan for Multi-Word Fields

Adopt a convention for capitalizing names that ensures that the resulting multi-word names are readily readable.

Use a Distinct WSDL Namespace URI for Each Interface

To avoid naming conflicts among the messages, ports, and operations of different interfaces, each interface should have its own namespace URI. Equally important, using distinct namespace URIs makes it possible to independently version the interfaces. This will facilitate the graceful evolution of interfaces in the environment.

Best Practice: Use a Unique WSDL Namespace URI for Each Interface

Define each interface in a separate WSDL, and use a unique namespace URI for each WSDL.

Incorporate Interface Major Version Numbers

In keeping with the versioning best practices outlined in Chapter 7, wherever the interface name is incorporated into certain naming structures, the interface's `<major>` version number should be appended to the interface name in those structures. This affects the following items:

- WSDL namespace URLs

- Schema namespace URLs when the schema is dedicated to a specific WSDL (see the section, "Schema Types Specific to an Interface and an Operation" later in this chapter)

- WSDL filenames (also include the interface's `<minor>` version number, as per versioning best practices)

- Schema filenames when the schema is dedicated to the specific WSDL (also include the interface's `<minor>` version number in the filename, as per versioning best practices)

- SOAP addresses (endpoints)

- SOAP action names

For simplicity, the version numbers are omitted from the examples in the following sections.

Applying Naming Principles

Idealized Name Structures

Given the structured name design principles laid out above, an idealized form of structure for naming service operations might have the following structure:

```
<functionalContext><abstractService><interfaceName>
   <operationName>²
```

---

2. In a WSDL the scope of an operation name is the portType (WSDL 1.1) or interface (WSDL 2.0).

For the data types involved in defining the service, you might use one or more of the following structures depending upon the intended scope of utilization for the data type:

```
<functionalContext><abstractService><interfaceName>
  <operationName><datatypeName>
<functionalContext><abstractService><interfaceName>
  <datatypeName>
<functionalContext><abstractService><conceptPackage>
  <datatypeName>
<functionalContext><conceptPackage><datatypeName>
```

The `<conceptPackage>` is explained later in the section on schema shared data types. Similar idealized structures would apply for the messages, elements, and other artifacts involved in defining the service.

Such idealized structures are rarely are seen in their entirety as single strings, with the possible exception of fully qualified Java class names. In most SOA applications, the name structure is fragmented in two different ways:

1. The leading part of the complete name structure appears as the namespace of the WSDL or schema, while the remainder of the structure appears as the name of the artifact being defined within the namespace.
2. Within the namespace URI of the WSDL or schema, part of the name appears as an Internet domain name while the rest appears as the path.

The following sections explore the practical use of these idealized name structures and show how they can be used to guide and standardize the definitions of names. These will be illustrated using the Nouveau Health Care example. Each topic area will first present an idealized name structure and then discuss its practical implementation.

Functional Context

A fact of life is that enterprises frequently acquire or merge with other enterprises. To avoid name conflicts in the ensuing IT consolidation, it is good practice to make the first field in the functional context be an enterprise-specific qualifier, giving

```
<enterpriseID><functionalArea>
```

In practice, the `enterpriseID` is almost always defined using an Internet domain name. For example,

```
nouveau.com
```

Most often the enterprise ID occurs in the context of a URL or URI and has the form

```
http://nouveau.com
```

Many businesses have more than one line of business, with each line of business essentially operating as a separate company (particularly from an IT perspective). When this occurs, it is good practice to include the line of business as part of the <functionalContext>. This helps avoid name conflicts among similar functional areas (e.g., sales, human resources, finance) in the different lines of business of the same company. The result is

```
<functionalContext> ::= <enterpriseID><lineOfBusiness>
   <functionalArea>
```

Consider Nouveau Health Care and the possibility that it might have two very different lines of business. One is an insurance provider, and the other is an online pharmacy. The idealized enterprise identifiers for Nouveau would then be

```
com.nouveau.insurance
com.nouveau.pharmacy
```

In transforming the idealized form into the form needed for a URL or URI, you have two choices, depending upon whether or not you want the line-of-business name to be part of the Internet domain name or the path. If you want it to be part of the Internet domain name, you end up with

```
http://insurance.nouveau.com
http://pharmacy.nouveau.com
```

If you want the line of business to be part of the path, you end up with

```
http://nouveau.com/insurance
http://nouveau.com/pharmacy
```

This, in practice, may not be an arbitrary choice: Making the line of business part of the Internet domain name allows distinct machines to be used as targets for the different lines of business; making the line of business part of the path forces a single machine to be used as the entry point for both lines of business. There may be organizational and management issues involved. These are discussed later in this chapter in the Complicating Realities section.

To deal with this type of situation, many enterprises employ network appliances that can make seamless conversions between these two formats. Although this adds flexibility, it requires network configuration—yet another administrative task.

Best Practice: Global Uniqueness

Include an enterprise-specific qualifier to the functional context. If the enterprise has independent lines of business, include the line of business in the functional context as well.

A Notational Convention for Internet Domain Names

This question of how much of the idealized name will become part of the Internet domain name occurs so often that we will adopt a convention for indicating the answer: The portion of the idealized structure that will become the Internet domain name will be outlined with a border. Using this convention, the example of the line-of-business name being part of the Internet domain name would be idealized as

```
<enterpriseID><lineOfBusiness><functionalArea>
```

The example of the line-of-business name being part of the path would be idealized as

```
<enterpriseID><lineOfBusiness><functionalArea>
```

WSDL and XSD Namespace URIs

The idealized structure for a WSDL namespace URI has the form

```
<functionalContext><abstractService><abstractInterface>wsdl
  <wsdlName>
```

Expanding the functional context, we have

```
<enterpriseID><lineOfBusiness><functionalArea><abstractService>
  <abstractInterface>wsdl<wsdlName>
```

It is common practice to make the actual name structure a URI. For the Payment Manager service's Claim Payment interface WSDL and including the major version number in the name, this gives

```
http://insurance.nouveau.com/finance/paymentManager/
  claimPayment/wsdl/claimPayment1
```

The idealized structure for a schema namespace URI has the form

```
<functionalContext><abstractService><abstractInterface>schema
  <schemaName>
```

Expanding the functional context, we have

```
<enterpriseID><lineOfBusiness><functionalArea><abstractService>
<abstractInterface>schema<schemaName>
```

It is common practice to make the actual name structure a URI. For the Claim Payment schema associated with the Claim Payment WSDL and including the schema major version number, this gives

```
http://insurance.nouveau.com/finance/paymentManager/
  claimPayment/schema/claimPayment1
```

Best Practice: WSDL and Schema Namespace URIs

Include the full functional context, abstract service name, abstract interface name, and WSDL or schema name in the WSDL and schema namespace URIs. Insert wsdl or schema prior to the WSDL or schema name to differentiate WSDL and schema namespaces.

WSDL and XSD Filenames

It is a good practice is to use the WSDL or schema namespace structure as the basis for defining the structure of the filename (i.e., the path to the file). The idea is to make the fully qualified filename a URL (or at least a URI). Making it a URL tells you where to locate the file. With this approach, the idealized structure for a filename is

```
<enterpriseID><lineOfBusiness><functionalArea><abstractService
  <abstractInterface>wsdl<filename>
<enterpriseID><lineOfBusiness><functionalArea><abstractService
  <abstractInterface>schema<filename>
```

In the implementation, there are a couple of options depending on how the systems hosting the files are physically organized. One uses a single machine as the access point for all files:

```
<enterpriseID><lineOfBusiness><functionalArea><abstractService>
  <interface><filename>
```

Preferable is an approach that uses a different machine per line of business:

```
<enterpriseID><lineOfBusiness><functionalArea><abstractService>
  <interface><filename>
```

This yields the following type of URL:

```
http://insurance.nouveau.com/finance/paymentManager/
claimPayment/wsdl/ClaimPayment.wsdl
```

In some situations, the file will be present in a file system. In such cases, the full structure of the name should be preserved in the folder hierarchy of the file system. For example, you might have

```
file://<rootPath>/com/nouveau/insurance/finance/paymentManager/
  claimPayment/wsdl/claimPayment.wsdl
```

This, however, can lead to deep folder structures in which there is only a single folder in each of the upper-level folders. When converted to Java class structures, it also leads to a Java class for each level. In such cases, the upper part of the structure can be collapsed into a single folder name:

```
file://<rootPath>/com.nouveau.insurance.finance/paymentManager/
  claimPayment/wsdl/claimPayment.wsdl
```

Best Practice: WSDL and Schema Filenames

Include the full functional context, abstract service name, interface name, and `wsdl` or `schema` in the WSDL and schema filenames.

WSDL Names

To ensure the uniqueness of the WSDL name and to make it clear which WSDL it is, it is a good practice to make the WSDL name the same as the fully qualified filename, which should be a URI or URL.

```
http://insurance.nouveau.com/finance/paymentManager/
  claimPayment/wsdl/claimPayment.wsdl
```

Schema Locations

The schema location, by definition, is a URI and is ideally a URL. If the above naming practice for schema filenames is followed, then the fully qualified filename is the schema location.

```
http://insurance.nouveau.com/finance/paymentManager/
  claimPayment/schema/claimPayment.xsd
```

WSDL-Specific Schema Location

Each WSDL requires a schema that defines the types used in its message definitions. The WSDL standard provides two options for supplying the schema: importing a schema file or placing the schema definitions in-line within the WSDL file. The latter approach is preferred. This is because an `import` statement in the WSDL requires retrieving the file, which requires access to that file. In many environments, providing access to these files is impractical. For this reason it is a best practice to place the WSDL schema definitions directly in the WSDL file rather than using an `import` statement.

Best Practice: WSDL-Specific Schema Location

Place WSDL schema definitions in the WSDL file.

WSDL Message Names

When defining WSDL messages, there are two different namespaces involved, one for the message itself and the other for the schema that defines the element type used in the message. While technically the two namespace URIs are allowed to be the same, it creates a very confusing situation when looking at the WSDL. For this reason, it is good practice to include WSDL or schema as the last field in the namespace URIs to keep them distinct, which is the earlier-recommended best practice.

The messages themselves are defined within the WSDL namespace. Typically each message is intended to play a particular role with respect to a specific operation, so it is good practice to include the `<operationName>` as part of the message name. This gives you the following idealized structure for the fully qualified message name:

```
<enterpriseID><lineOfBusiness><functionalArea><abstractService>
  <interfaceName><operationName><messageName>
```

There is a wrinkle in turning this idealized structure. The name given to the message in the WSDL file is defined directly in the context of the WSDL namespace, not under the operation. Thus if two operations have the same message name (such as `requestMessage` or `responseMessage`), there will be a conflict. To avoid this, you simply concatenate the operation name with the message name to give the implementation, for example, `PayClaimRequestMessage`. For the claim payment operation, this gives us the following message definitions in the WSDL.

```
<message name = "PayClaimRequestMessage">
  <part name = "request" type = "ns:PayClaimRequest"/>
</message>
<message name = "PayClaimResponseMessage">
  <part name = "response" type = "ns:PayClaimResponse"/>
</message> <message name="processShipmentRequest">
```

Each message has parts, and each part has a name that is also defined in the WSDL namespace. Since the scope of the part name is local to the message definition, the actual name is not particularly important.

Each part requires a type definition. The type refers to a datatype that is defined in the schema namespace referenced by the WSDL.

Port Type, Service, and Binding Names

An idealized structure for these names has the form

```
<functionalContext><abstractService><interfaceName>
  <portTypeName>
<functionalContext><abstractService><interfaceName>
  <serviceName>
<functionalContext><abstractService><interfaceName>
  <bindingName>
```

Note that, following the best practice recommendations, there is some redundancy here. The best practice is to have a WSDL for each interface and to include the interface name in the WSDL namespace URI. The `portType` is actually the interface, so appending it to the namespace name is redundant. However, since the `portType` is actually defined within this namespace, this is the structure you actually get. A similar situation arises for the service and binding names.

Using the `portType` name as an example and expanding the functional context, you have

```
<enterpriseID><lineOfBusiness><functionalArea><abstractService>
  <interfaceName><portTypeName>
```

In practice, this idealized structure never appears as a single string in the WSDL. Instead, it is divided into two parts. The first part of the structure is represented by the target namespace in the WSDL. By the best practice recommendation, this includes everything up to and including the interface name.

The second part is the `portType` name, which is declared within the scope of the namespace. The names of the `service` and `binding` are similarly declared within the namespace. Here are some example fragments from the `claimPayment.wsdl` file:

```
<definitions
  xmlns:tns=http://insurance.nouveau.com/finance/
    paymentManager/claimPayment/wsdl/claimPayment1
  targetNamespace="http://insurance.nouveau.com/finance/
    paymentManager/claimPayment/wsdl/claimPayment1
  xmlns:ns="http://insurance.nouveau.com/finance/
    paymentManager/claimPayment/schema/claimPayment1">

...

  <portType name="ClaimPayment">
    <operation name="payClaim">
      <input message="tns:PayClaimRequestMessage"
        name="input"/>
      <output message="tns:PayClaimResponseMessage"
        name="output"/>
    </operation>

    ...

  </portType>

  <service name="ClaimPaymentService">
    <port name="ClaimPaymentPort"
      binding="tns:ClaimPaymentPortBinding">
      <soap:address location="http://insurance.nouveau.com:5555/
        com.nouveau.insurance.finance.paymentManager.
        claimPayment.endpoint1"/>
    </port>
  </service>
  <binding name="ClaimPaymentPortBinding" type="tns:ClaimPayment">
    <soap:binding style="document" transport="http://
      schemas.xmlsoap.org/soap/http"/>
    <operation name="payClaim">
      <soap:operation style="document" soapAction="/
        com.nouveau.insurance.finance.paymentManager.
        claimPayment1.payClaim"/>
      <input>
        <soap:body use="literal" parts="request"/>
      </input>
        <output>
```

```
        <soap:body use="literal" parts="response"/>
      </output>
    </operation>
  </binding>
</definitions>
```

There is a nuance here worth pointing out: portTypes are not directly associated with services. Instead, a declaration known as a *binding* provides details of the portType's implementation, and then that binding is used in defining a port (an actual interface instance or endpoint) on the service. The port has its own name. For clarity, it is good practice to choose names for ports and portTypes that distinguish between the two.

Operation Names

An idealized structure for operation names has the form

```
<functionalContext><abstractService><interfaceName>
  <operationName>
```

Expanding the functional context, you have

```
<enterpriseID><lineOfBusiness><functionalArea><abstractService>
  <interfaceName><operationName>
```

In practice, this idealized structure never appears as a single string in the WSDL. Instead, it is divided into two parts. The first part of the structure is represented by the target namespace in the WSDL. By the best practice recommendation, this includes everything up to and including the interface name. The second part is the `operation` name, which is declared within the scope of the portType (interface).

SOAP Address Location

The SOAP address location is a URI that indicates the connection point (physical destination) to which operation requests are directed. Depending upon the policy you choose for separating the traffic directed to different services, you should use one of the following idealized structures for this URI:

```
<enterpriseID><lineOfBusiness><functionalArea>
<enterpriseID><lineOfBusiness><functionalArea><abstractService>
<enterpriseID><lineOfBusiness><functionalArea><abstractService>
  <interfaceName>
```

The choice between these is not arbitrary. If the first form is used, all requests for a given functional area will be sent to the same location.

The second form offers at least the possibility that requests for different services may be directed to different components, and the third can distinguish based on the interface.

This difference may have significant performance implications for the subsequent implementation, particularly if one interface provides real-time operations involving small data structures and quick response while another provides batch operations involving huge data structures and asynchronous responses. Performance considerations drive you toward separating this traffic, but separation requires sufficient information in the location.

Another consideration is that, for many implementation technologies, the use of a detailed path allows the convenient routing of requests for different services and interfaces.

WSDL 2.0 allows multiple endpoints for an interface, giving yet another possibility:

```
<enterpriseID><lineOfBusiness><functionalArea><abstractService>
  <interfaceName><endpointName>
```

It is generally a good idea to include too much rather than too little information in the location. It is relatively easy to ignore the lower-level details, but you cannot synthesize information that is not present.

For JMS bindings, the idealized structure translates in a very straightforward way into JMS destination names:

```
enterpriseID.lineOfBusiness.functionalArea
enterpriseID.lineOfBusiness.functionalArea.serviceName
enterpriseID.lineOfBusiness.functionalArea.serviceName.
  interfaceName
enterpriseID.lineOfBusiness.functionalArea.serviceName.
  interfaceName.endpointName[3]
```

With HTTP bindings a further implementation consideration, relevant to locations, is the choice of a socket number. The structure of a URL is determined by the transport that has been selected. For http (and https) transports, the syntax is

```
http://<hostIdentifier>:<socketNumber>/<path>
```

This raises the question as to which parts of the idealized namespace should map to the <hostIdentifier> and which parts should map

---

3. A fully qualified destination name provides maximum flexibility in assigning destinations to JMS servers.

to the `<path>`. Answering this question requires the recognition that the combination `<hostIdentifier>:<portNumber>` denotes a physical destination, while the `<path>` is used logically at that destination to further distinguish between requests. There are architectural trade-offs involved in this decision, with considerations that go beyond the scope of this book (e.g., how many sockets should there be versus what load can each socket reasonably handle).

For the purposes of the discussion here, consider the socketNumber to be part of the Internet domain name. Assuming you want to include the structural detail down to the interface level, this gives you the following possibilities for the idealized structure of the location URL:

```
<enterpriseID><lineOfBusiness><functionalArea><abstractService>
  <interfaceName>
<enterpriseID><lineOfBusiness><functionalArea><abstractService>
  <interfaceName>
<enterpriseID><lineOfBusiness><functionalArea><abstractService>
  <interfaceName>
<enterpriseID><lineOfBusiness><functionalArea><abstractService>
  <interfaceName>
<enterpriseID><lineOfBusiness><functionalArea><abstractService>
  <interfaceName>
```

The first indicates that a single socket will handle all of the service requests for the entire enterprise. This requires centralized management of the port and a common technology touch point for all services. Generally, the technology employed here uses the `<path>` to redirect different requests to different sockets. The second results in a single socket for each line of business, which again may employ technology to redirect requests to different sockets. The third and fourth choices generally reflect the actual structure of the implementations to which requests of the first or second type are redirected. If you have multiple endpoints per interface, you will need to append an `<endpoint>` field to each of these possibilities.

Best Practice: Location Names

Include the full functional context, abstract service, and interface in the location name.

`soapAction` Names

The `soapAction` name is nearly identical to the fully qualified operation name as described earlier, with the major version number appended to the interface name. An idealized structure for `soapAction` names has the form

```
<functionalContext><abstractService><interfaceName+major>
  <operationName>
```

Expanding the functional context, you have:

```
<enterpriseID><lineOfBusiness><functionalArea><abstractService>
  <interfaceName+major><operationName>
```

This approach provides the maximum flexibility in defining endpoints. Using this approach, all requests for all operations could be sent to a single endpoint (location) without ambiguity: The `soapAction` uniquely identifies the required operation.

Best Practice: SOAP Action Names

The SOAP action name should be the fully qualified operation name with the major version number appended to the interface name.

Schema Types Specific to an Interface and an Operation

As mentioned in the previous section, schema types are often created that are dedicated to a single operation. The ideal structure for an operation-specific message type name would be

```
<enterpriseID><lineOfBusiness><functionalArea><abstractService>
  <interfaceName><operationName><typeName>
```

This leads to idealized names like

```
com.nouveau.insurance.finance.paymentManager.claimPayment.
  payClaim.Request
com.nouveau.insurance.finance.paymentManager.claimPayment.
  payClaim.Response
```

In reducing this idealized structure to an implementation you encounter a limitation of the schema definition language: It does not support hierarchical names within the namespace. Specifically, the `Request` and `Response` cannot be scoped within the `payClaim` operation name—they have to be declared directly within the namespace. Thus if other operations have `Request` and `Response` data types (as they likely would), then you'll have a name conflict. The solution to this problem is to concatenate the operation name and the ideal message name, giving type names like `PayClaimRequest` and `PayClaimResponse`.

These definitions would occur (following the earlier recommended best practice) within the schema namespace:

```
http://insurace.nouveau.com/finance/paymentManager/
    claimPaymentInterface/schema/claimPaymentInterface1
```

Schema Shared Data Types (Common Data Model Types)

Even though the types that represent entire messages are often specialized for the operations they support, the subordinate data types that they reference many times can be shared between messages. If these shared data types are specific to the interface, then they can remain in the interface's namespace. But if they are of more general intent, they belong in namespaces of their own.

You might, for example, want to define the standard representation for an address as shown in Figure 8-4. You might want to standardize the use of this data type across all of Nouveau Health Care. To do so, you use the namespace in which the type is defined to indicate the intended scope of utilization.

Types like Address Type often have other closely-related types, such as the ISO Country Code. To keep related concepts grouped together yet separated from other concepts, it is a good practice to define a namespace for the concept and its related elements, which shall be termed a

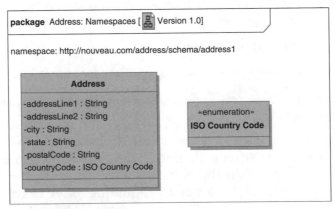

Figure 8-4: *Address Type*

concept package. In this example, the concept package is named `Address` and, in keeping with the versioning best practices, has the version major number appended.

The portion of the namespace that precedes the package name is determined by the intended scope of utilization. This gives the following possibilities for the fully qualified type name:

```
<enterpriseID><conceptPackage>schema<schemaName>
<enterpriseID><lineOfBusiness><conceptPackage>
  schema<schemaName>
<enterpriseID><lineOfBusiness><functionalArea><conceptPackage>
  schema<schemaName>
<enterpriseID><lineOfBusiness><functionalArea><abstractService>
  <conceptPackage>schema<schemaName>
<enterpriseID><lineOfBusiness><functionalArea><abstractService>
  <abstractInterfaceName><conceptPackage>schema<schemaName>
```

Schema names should be versioned in the same manner as interfaces, with <major> and <minor> version numbers. Wherever the <schemaName> name appears in a name structure, its major version should be appended. This includes the namespace URI for the schema and the XSD filename. Note that the XSD filename also includes the minor version number.

Complicating Realities

Technology Constraints

Reality often constrains the ideal approach. This is particularly true with names. Ideally, names have no restrictions with respect to either the number of fields or the length of any individual field. Unfortunately, this does not hold true in practice. The various technologies being employed have both theoretical restrictions and practical limitations.

Internet domain names limit the number of fields in a name to 127 and allow each field to contain up to 63 octets (bytes). The whole domain name (including "." separators) is limited to 253 octets. In practice, some domain registries may have shorter limits.

The JMS standard places no limitations on names, but vendor implementations often do. For example, Enterprise Messages Service destinations can have up to 64 fields. Individual fields cannot exceed 127 characters. Destination names are limited to a total length of 249 characters.

Whatever naming standards are established, they must obviously take into consideration the constraints of the chosen supporting technologies.

There is a practical limitation to consider as well. By default, every byte (octet) of every name must be transmitted with every message. Thus it is a good practice to avoid excessive length in names, while at the same time preserving the readability of the name.

Naming Authorities

Every position in a naming hierarchy requires an authority for its administration. As discussed earlier, each naming authority (a) directly manages the field level for which it is responsible, and (b) establishes the policy for managing the lower-level fields.

The ability to delegate the management of the lower-level structures is part of the power of hierarchical name structures. At the enterprise level, the authority must

- Assign names to represent each of the lines of business.
- Identify who in each line of business will manage the lower-level structures below the line-of-business field.
- Assign names to represent each enterprise-level service.
- Identify who will manage the lower-level structure for each enterprise service.
- Assign names to represent each enterprise-level concept package
- Identify who will manage the lower-level structure for each enterprise concept package.

Within each line of business, the responsibilities are similar: assigning names for line-of-business services, functional areas, and concept packages, and identifying who will manage the lower-level structures for each.

Complex Organizational Structures

Functional Organizations

If a line-of-business organization is functionally complete (i.e., horizontally integrated), then all of the services and concepts required to operate the line of business are part of that organization. The naming structure we have been discussing reflects the line-of-business's singular line of authority over all the services and concepts relevant to the organization.

Many organizations, however, are structured functionally rather than by line of business. An organization might have functional groups for marketing, sales, logistics, finance, engineering, manufacturing, and so forth. If such an organization provides capabilities uniformly across multiple lines of business, the top-level structure may be more appropriately based on function rather than line of business:

```
<enterpriseID><functionalArea>
```

Mixed Functional and Line-of-Business Organizations

Some organizations combine these two approaches. A line-of-business organization may well have a functional substructure under each line of business. In such cases, the structure of the functional context must be expanded. This gives a functional context of

```
<enterpriseID><lineOfBusiness><functionalArea>
```

Less frequently it may be appropriate to reverse the hierarchy:

```
<enterpriseID><functionalArea><lineOfBusiness>
```

The challenge here is that there are, in reality, two hierarchies: the functional hierarchy and the line-of-business hierarchy. Yet the representational technologies (WSDL and schema) only allow for one hierarchy, so the two must be combined into a single functional context. This forces one to be somewhat arbitrarily chosen to dominate the other.

Regardless of how the hierarchies are combined, some caution is in order: Enterprises tend to reorganize. Since you are going to be living with the namespace structure even after the reorganization, it is important to choose a structure and names for both functions and lines of business that will remain stable over time. Bear in mind that a single organization may actually serve more than one functional purpose (e.g., sales and marketing could be in one parent organization) or serve more than one line-of-business purpose (e.g., a division that handles multiple lines of business). In such cases, each individual purpose should have a distinct name in the namespace. This makes the namespace structure relatively stable with respect to reorganization.

Geographic Distribution

Another challenge you are liable to encounter is geographic distribution. This is particularly true for multinational enterprises, where the operations in different countries or regions tend to be conducted by legally distinct entities. This adds yet a third hierarchy to the ways that the enterprise can be viewed (Figure 8-5).

The presence of yet a third hierarchy further complicates the functional context. One possible structure that could emerge is

```
<enterpriseID><geographicRegion><lineOfBusiness><functionalArea>
```

This is but one of six possible combinations, and that does not even count the possibilities of leaving one or more of these hierarchies out of the structure entirely. Altogether, there are 15 possibilities. So how do you select the one for your enterprise?

There are two factors that should drive your thinking. The first one focuses on organizational realities. In this you need to consider the following:

- What does the current organizational structure look like (i.e., what is the actual organizational hierarchy today)?
- What are the realistic prospects for cooperation between organizations?
- Is there a place in the parent organization for a working group to manage namespaces that cross organizational boundaries?
- Is there sufficient authority for such a working group to effectively manage such a namespace (i.e., will the other organizations listen)?

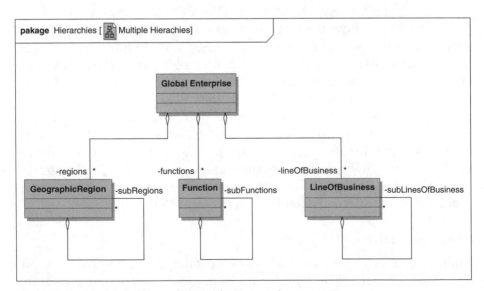

Figure 8-5: *Multiple Hierarchies in the Enterprise*

If the prospects look dim for cooperation between organizational units, then you have little choice other than to adopt a namespace structure that treats the organizations as being independent (see naming authorities earlier).

The other factor to consider is the intended future direction for the enterprise in terms of sharing data, resources, services, and business processes across the organization. If there is an effort underway to increase sharing (which presupposes that there is a reasonable prospect for cooperation between organizations), then the hierarchy you choose should be one that makes the most sense with respect to the chosen direction.

Environments: Values for Address Location Variables

Each service will, in its lifetime, exist in a number of environments, ranging from development through several test environments and, finally, one or more production environments. Thus it becomes necessary to distinguish among the different instances of the service when accessing the service.

The logical place to make this distinction would be in the address location in the WSDL. Unfortunately, the structure of the WSDL does not make provisions for designating different addresses for different environments. Even worse, changing the WSDL to indicate the different environment requires changes to both the consumer and the provider. From a change management and versioning perspective, since the WSDL is the service interface definition, edits to the WSDL could potentially change anything. Therefore, editing the WSDL invalidates whatever testing has been performed and thus defeats the purpose of the WSDL as a specification.

To work around this limitation, most service consumer and service provider implementation technologies allow the address (endpoint) to be provided by a variable whose value is set at deployment time. With this approach, environments must be distinguished within the values provided for the address. These addresses (the provided values) need to be distinct from one another while remaining descriptive of their purpose so that they can be accurately and appropriately set at deployment time.

Referring back to the earlier discussion of addresses, a portion of the idealized address structure maps to the `hostIdentifier`. This is the level at which development, test, and production environments should be distinguished from one another. Using the scheme described earlier, you have the following possibilities (the portions in the box correspond to the host identifier):

```
<enterpriseID><environment><lineOfBusiness><functionalArea>
   <abstractService><interface>
<enterpriseID><lineOfBusiness><environment><functionalArea>
   <abstractService><interface>
<enterpriseID><lineOfBusiness><abstractService><environment>
   <functionalArea><interface>
<enterpriseID><lineOfBusiness><abstractService><functionalArea>
   <interface><environment>
<enterpriseID><lineOfBusiness><abstractService><functionalArea>
   <interface><environment>
```

For HTTP bindings, manifestation of the <environment> can take one of two forms: It can be the hostIdentifier itself or the socket on the host. *It is generally not a good practice to use the same hostIdentifier and socket for multiple environments. It is generally not a good practice to share a hostIdentifier between a production environment and any other environment.*

For JMS bindings, the manifestation of the <environment> can also take one of two forms: It can be the hostIdentifier and socket for the JMS server itself or it can be included directly in the queue name. *It is generally not a good practice to share a JMS server between a production environment and any other environment.*

Deployment Flexibility for HA and DR

An address (at least in the http[s] type of addressing) identifies a specific machine to which requests are to be sent. Should this machine move (for fault tolerance, site disaster recovery, or simply administrative convenience), all the interfaces accessed through that machine would become unavailable. One way around this is to use virtual IP addresses or hostnames, allowing the networking infrastructure to reroute requests to another machine. Another approach is to make the address actually an http query with a response that is the real address. Amazon e-commerce web services, for example, use this approach:

```
<soap:address location="https://ecs.amazonaws.com/onca/
   soap?Service=AWSECommerceService"/>
```

Abstracting the logical structure here, the <hostIdentifier>/<path> part of the location actually identifies the server to which the query is being submitted, while the value of the Service parameter indicates the desired service. This approach facilitates the flexible rehosting of the actual service providers over time.

For greatest flexibility, it is recommended that the full path name of the interface be used as the argument for this type of query. Thus if one query service is being used to support the entire enterprise, the value for the query would have the structure

```
<lineOfBusiness><abstractService><interfaceName>
```

If the query service supports just a line of business, then the query value would be

```
<abstractService><interfaceName>
```

It is not good practice to use the same query service for different environments.

SOAP over JMS utilizes JNDI lookups in a similar manner. The same considerations apply.

Developing Your Standard

To begin with, you need to identify the organization that will have overall responsibility for the naming standards in your enterprise. If you are in the early stages of adopting SOA, you may not be in a position to mandate that a particular naming structure be followed. Nevertheless, there is no reason that you cannot adopt a structure that can be appropriately generalized to meet the needs of the larger enterprise as outlined in this chapter.

The enterprise-level authority has several responsibilities. One is to define an overall strategy for

- WSDL and schema namespace URIs, including versioning
- Location names, including:
  - Versioning
  - Directing requests to the appropriate environment
  - Using indirection (http query or JNDI lookup) for addresses

Another responsibility is to identify which organizations will be responsible for managing the lower levels of the naming structure. If the enterprise is large, this will likely mean identifying an organization in each line of business that is responsible for names used in that line of business. Each of those organizations, in turn, will have to determine how much of the naming structure it will directly manage and how much management responsibility it will delegate to other organizations.

Summary

In the complex world of IT, how things are named has a significant influence on the usability of components when building solutions. Clear, descriptive names make it possible for you to identify things without having to look them up. The structure of the name also helps to avoid ambiguity and name conflicts.

There are a number of general principles that should guide the creation of names. Names should have a hierarchical structure. That hierarchical structure should follow a general-to-specific organization. The names chosen should remain stable over time. With the exception of enterprise identifiers, the names used to identify organizations and systems should be avoided and generic names used instead. The use of acronyms should be avoided unless they are universally understood. Type and instance names should be clearly distinguishable. Conventions should be adopted to ensure that multi-word fields are easily readable. For ease in managing versions, each interface should have its own WSDL with its own namespace.

A good idealized name structure has the form

```
<functionalContext><abstractService><abstractInterface>
```

The functional context commonly expands as follows, with the presence of the `<enterpriseID>` avoiding naming conflicts in the event of mergers and acquisitions:

```
<functionalContext> :== <enterpriseID><lineOfBusiness>
  <functionalArea>
```

The `<abstractService>` may encompass multiple interfaces, each with its own WSDL. For service operations, the `<abstractInterface>` commonly expands to

```
<abstractInterface> :== <interfaceName><operationName>
```

Ideally, WSDL namespaces, WSDL filenames, and SOAP addresses (endpoints) should have the idealized form

```
<enterpriseID><lineOfBusiness><functionalArea><abstractService>
  <interfaceName>
```

SOAP action names should have this form with the operation name appended at the end. Schema namespaces and filenames should use the portion of this structure that describes the intended scope of utilization of the schema.

Technology constraints on the length of individual fields and the overall length of identifiers must be taken into consideration when defining names. The enterprise should establish a policy defining the hierarchical structure of names to be used and identifying the organization responsible for establishing the values of the top-level fields and the organizations responsible for ensuring the uniqueness of subordinate field values.

Chapter 9

Data Structures

Objectives

Data is ubiquitous in solutions. The problem is that it comes in many representations, and each represents merely a fragment of the overall set of information being used in the solution. Using these representations requires that you understand how they relate to one another. This chapter will explore how a high-level domain model can be used to understand these relationships. It explores design issues that arise in defining the XML representations that are typically used in the communications between components. Finally, it explores the impact of versioning considerations on data structure design.

After reading this chapter, you should be able to

- Explain the relationship between domain models and database and data structure schemas.
- Explain the alternatives for data structure design and make application-appropriate selections.
- Explain the versioning considerations for data structures and select an appropriate versioning approach.

Domain Models

When dealing with data, it is easy to become quickly embroiled in the gory details of detailed data structures. In so doing, you get so focused on the minutia that you lose sight of the big picture, yet getting the big picture right is the key factor in making data structures that are usable.

The key to understanding the data big picture is the domain model (Figure 9-1). A domain model focuses on the major concepts and relationships that appear in the solution space. It is a representation of what can be found (or could happen) in the real world, not what is representable in the existing systems, databases, and communications. By focusing on the real world, the model strives for a representation that will remain relatively stable over time. As such, it serves as a stable foundation from which real data structures can be derived.

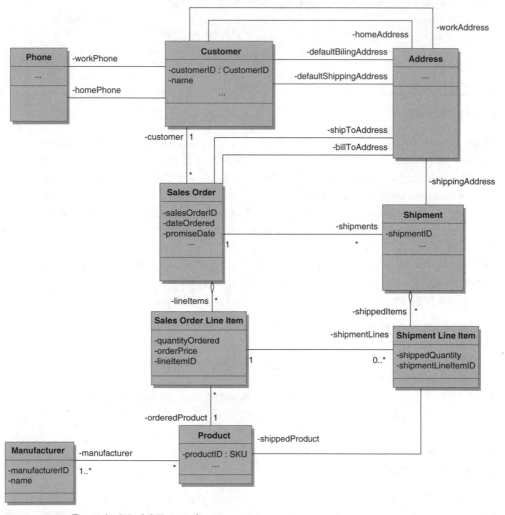

Figure 9-1: *Domain Model Example*

The domain model does not get bogged down in detail. For each concept you'll generally have only a few attributes—things like identifiers and key values that drive decision making. For relationships, you want to identify the roles that the concepts play with respect to one another (these are the labels on the association ends) and the multiplicity of the relationship.

Relationship multiplicity is extremely important because when you build data structures you pour concrete all over the multiplicity assumptions. If you implement a one-to-many relationship in a database and later discover that what you really wanted was a many-to-many relationship, it is a gut-wrenching change not only for the database itself, but for every component that uses that relationship in the database.

In modeling relationships, you want to focus on what could happen in the real world. In the model shown in Figure 9-1, each Order Shipment is associated with a single Sales Order. This means that you can't do consolidated shipments of multiple orders. Is that a valid assumption for your business? You'll probably have to go to the business to find out. If the business thinks that's a valid assumption, that's okay, but just make them aware that if they change their mind it is going to be a very expensive change. If there is any realistic possibility that consolidated shipments could occur, model the association as a many to many. Then it's just a policy decision.

There are a number of similar questions to be asked of this model. Can there be more than one manufacturer for a given product? How many home and work phones can a customer have? How many home and work addresses? Sorting these questions out at this level will save a lot of time and money later.

Domain models provide a basis for understanding the information content of the many data structures you encounter in a solution. The fact that the domain model reflects what can happen in the real world enables you to understand the limitations of solution data structures that perhaps are not as complete in their representations. The big-picture focus (i.e., absence of mind-numbing detail) of the models makes it easy for business people to understand and validate the model. Domain models also serve as a guide when designing database and message schema.

Domain models are relatively simple to maintain. New concepts and relationships can be readily added as projects explore new areas. It is not only practical but a best practice to establish and share a domain model that is comprehensive within a functional area. These models can be exchanged (if not integrated) across functional areas when those areas need to interact.

For more information on data modeling, see Blaha and Rumbaugh's *Object-Oriented Modeling and Design with UML, Second Edition*.[1]

Best Practice: Domain Models

Create and share a common domain model within each functional area. Exchange domain models between functional areas when interactions require sharing information between them.

Information Models

Information models, in contrast with domain models, strive for completeness in their representations (Figure 9-2). They have the same general structure as domain models, but contain more detail. Information models, however, are still abstractions and generally do not specify details like the data types of attributes. Still more information is needed in order to create concrete data structures.

The reason for pointing out the difference between domain models and information models is that it is nearly impossible to keep a large-scale information model completely up to date. Businesses are constantly identifying new data fragments that prove useful or defining new and useful ways of summarizing or viewing data. The `/order-Total` and `/orderStatus` fields of the `Sales Order` concept are examples of such derived information.

For this reason, information models tend to be modest in scope. A best practice is to limit the scope of an information model to the concepts and relationships required to support the design of specific data structures (database and XML schema), components, or solutions. The purpose of the information model is to provide an easy-to-understand overview of the information content of those data structures, particularly the database schema.

---

1. Michael Blaha and James Rumbaugh, *Object-Oriented Modeling and Design with UML, Second Edition*, Upper Saddle River, NJ: Prentice Hall (2005).

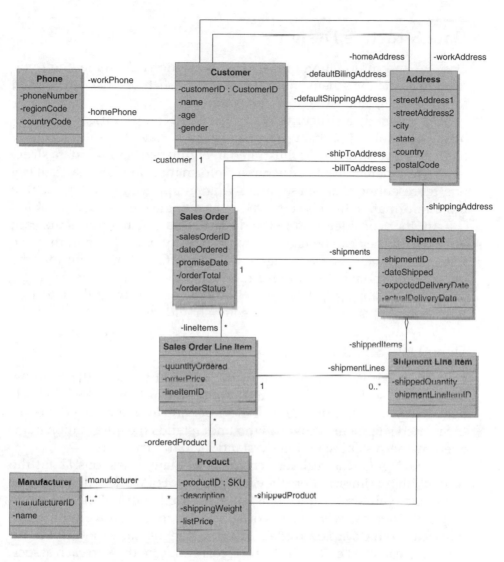

Figure 9-2: *Information Model Example*

Best Practice: Information Model Scope

Limit the scope of an information model to the concepts and relationships required to support the design of specific schemas, components, or solutions.

Data Structure Design

Domain and information models are abstractions. At some point you need to create the schema for concrete data structures that can be used for the sharing and storage of information.

Designing data structures is an exercise in compromises and trade-offs. The information being represented in a data structure generally has a network structure as illustrated in Figure 9-2, yet XML data structures are inherently tree structured. Information models, particularly one representing a database underlying an application, often include more information than is conveyed in any single message.

Another consideration in the design of data structures is the ease with which they can be used, which generally boils down to the ease with which they can be navigated. Assume for the moment that the information model of Figure 9-2 represents the database underlying a sales order management system. Now ask yourself what the information content of an order status message should be.

Deep Data Structures

One approach is to simply return the relevant parts of the complex information set being saved by the application, as in Figure 9-3.[2] This is a relatively complete depiction of the order and even includes details of the related shipments. Anyone who understands the information managed by the system would understand the data structure.

Even though the recipient can answer many questions about the order with this information, they will have a lot of work to do to answer some relatively simple questions, such as whether or not the order had shipped. To know whether the order has shipped, you would have to navigate from `Complex Order Status` (the message root) to `Sales Order` to each `Sales Order Line Item` and from there to each associated `Shipment Line Item`, total the `shippedQuantity`, and then determine whether it equaled the `quantityOrdered`. Finally, to arrive at your answer, you would need to summarize these results across all the line items.

In reality, it would be even worse. This is a network data structure, and it would have to be converted into a tree structure to send it as an

---

2. The derived `Sales Order` field of `/orderStatus` has intentionally been omitted from this example to make the point.

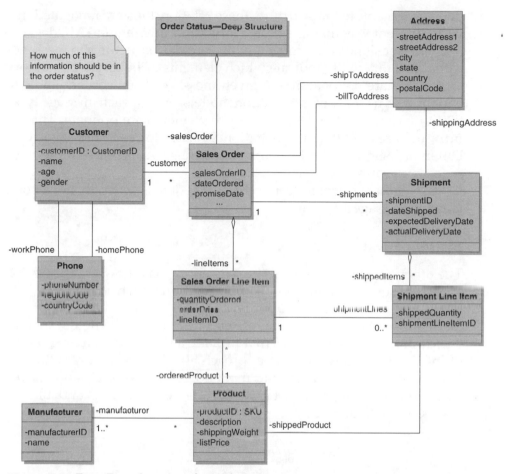

Figure 9-3: *Deep Data Structure for Order Status*

XML message. This means that some of the relationships would have to be represented in different ways than others. The relationship between `Sales Order` and `Sales Order Line Item` and that between `Order Shipment` and `Shipment Line Item` represent themselves very well as nested XML structures. However, this creates a situation in which the relationships between `Sales Order` and `Order Shipment` and that between `Sales Order Line Item` and `Shipment Line Item` must be represented in some other way. To represent these you have to play games like assigning an XML `ID` to each `Shipment Order` (you can't use the `shipmentID` field!) and including a list of `IDREFS` in the `Sales Order` to represent the related `shipments`. Although this does manage to capture the structure, these relationships are navigated in a very different way than the nested structures inherent in XML design.

Another significant problem with deep data structures in messages is that it is difficult to indicate which elements or fields are mandatory and which are optional in any given message. Thus you are liable to end up with a family of information models, one for each message type, that differ only in the details of which elements are optional. This, in turn, requires a different navigation strategy for each message type. Different logic will also be required for constructing each of the message type representations.

For all these reasons, deeply structured data is generally not a good idea for message schemas.

Flattened Data Structures

The other extreme is to flatten the data entirely as shown in Figure 9-4. There are some advantages here. Simple values such as the `orderID`, `customerName`, and `dateOrdered` are readily available without any navigation. These data structures tend to also include fields, such as `/orderStatus`, with values that provide a summary of a broader set of information. However, this approach also loses structural information, such as the understanding that addresses have a common structure, and there happen to be two addresses, shipping and billing, associated with the order.

Figure 9-4: *Flattened Data Structure*

Another problem with flattened data structures is that lists of things (order items, for example) are difficult to represent in flattened format. To represent them, a convention needs to be established regarding the prefix for identifying each member of the list, as in `item1`, `item2`, `item3`, etc. Using the data structure requires understanding the convention as well as the schema. Some activities, like counting the number of elements in the list, require some unpleasantly complicated computations as well.

For these reasons, flattened data structures are to be avoided in messages.

Shallow Data Structures

A working compromise between the deep and flattened data structure is the shallow data structure (Figure 9-5). Given that you understand the commonly required information when an order status is requested, you can organize that information for simple access. This means that you place commonly requested information in the top level of the data structure. If that information is a single field, just give the field the required value. If the information is a structure, include the structure.

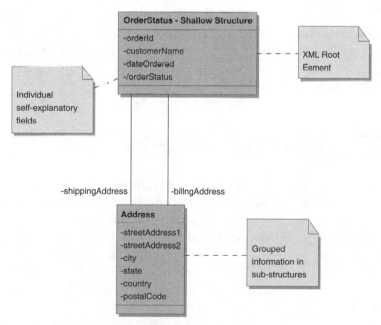

Figure 9-5: *Simple Order Status Information Model*

This data structure contains a subset of the information represented in the database's information model, and the origins of the information are clear. At the same time, the data structure is easier to understand, easier to construct, and easier to navigate. Shallow data structures have the advantage of simplicity.

A good practice is to use a shallow data structure for message schemas, and furthermore to give each message its own unique top-level data type. This makes it easy to indicate which elements of the top-level data type are required and which are optional. It also limits the scope of impact when you need to add or remove a field from a message—only the top-level data type is affected.

Best Practice: Message Schema

Use shallow data structures for message schema, and give each message its own unique top-level data type.

Reusability

If you follow the best practice regarding message schemas, it is clear that the top-level data types in message schemas will never be reused. What, then, does get reused? The answer is the data types used to define that top-level data type. Case in point: the Address data type from Figure 9-5. Addresses appear in many places, not just order status messages. Address data types are reusable, and reusability is what common data models are all about.

Common Data Models

The idea of common data models is to minimize the number of representations you have of any given concept. In other words, you want to share the representation across a number of schemas.

In designing common data models, you have to consider what, exactly, is being shared. Is it the representation of a single entity? Is it that entity plus its relationships to other entities? What about the other relationships of those other entities? Let's start with the representation of an entity.

Representing an Entity

Although the goal of common data models is to minimize the number of representations you have, for many concepts it is unrealistic to expect to have only one representation. Consider the four representations of customer shown in Figure 9-6. Case (a) is what you normally expect of a common data model representation: a `Customer` data type that includes all of the information about the customer (ignoring related concepts for the moment—these will be covered shortly).

But sometimes you don't want all of this information: You just want to indicate which customer you are talking about. This gives you case (b), a `CustomerRef` data type containing the minimal information required to identify the customer, here just the `customerID`. The Nouveau Health Care `Payment Manager` uses this type of representation to reference information being managed by other services (Figure 6-10). Case (b), however, has a significant limitation: It is not particularly human readable given that it is just a number. This gives you case (c), an enhanced `CustomerRef` data type that includes enough information to make the identity human readable.

Case (d) is a fourth commonly encountered representation that is not a complex data type at all: It is a simple data type for just the bare-bones identifier. This could be used as the type of an element belonging to some other complex data type that has a relationship with the customer.

To maintain consistency between these representations, the data types in cases (b) and (c) should be strict subsets of the data type defined in case (a). The field names and sequence of fields should remain the same, as should the data types for each of the fields. Similarly, for case (d), the simple data type should be the same type used for the `customerID` field in the other cases.

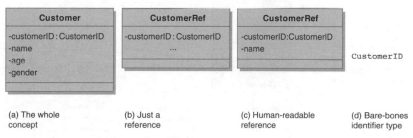

Figure 9-6: *Representations of an Entity*

You may wonder why the data types in cases (b) and (c) aren't just the data type of case (a) with the `name`, `age`, and `gender` fields made optional. The reason is that, with optional fields, you never know what data elements to expect. A data structure defined with this data type would be inherently ambiguous. The creator of the data structure would not know which fields ought to be populated, and the recipient of the data structure could never be sure when to expect the optional fields to be populated. Sure, this information could be added to the service specification, but then both the producer and consumer would have to study the specification to understand what is required and what is expected.

Representing an Association

A similar set of choices arises when you consider the representation of an association between two entities (Figure 9-7). Consider how you would represent, from the `Sales Order Line Item`'s perspective, its association with the `Product` entity. In case (a), the `Product` entity is explicitly represented. In the XML manifestation of this, the `Sales Order Line Item` contains an entity named `orderedProduct` whose type is a complex data type representing `Product`. There is then the

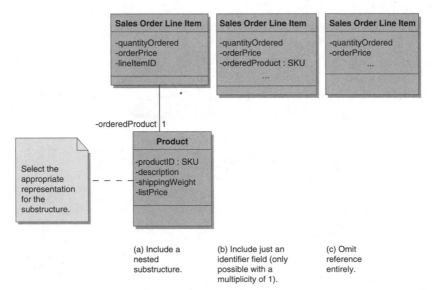

Figure 9-7: *Representing an Association between Entities*

additional choice as to which representation of `Product` you wish to use, as discussed in the previous section.

In case (b), the representation chosen for the product is just the `orderedProduct` field with the simple data type `SKU` that serves as an identifier for the product. Case (c) is even simpler—there is no representation of the product at all in the `Sales Order Line Item`.

Designing an XML Schema

Given the choices available for representing entities and associations, how do you go about designing data structures? The process is relatively straightforward and involves the following steps:

1. Using the domain model, identify the entities and associations that need to be communicated.
2. For each entity and association, determine the type of representation that will be used.
3. Identify (if using common data models) or create the information model for the data structure.
4. Consider common data model implications and review and refine as appropriate.
5. Create the XML schema for the data structure.

When you want to reuse data types in the data structure, you'll probably iterate this design as you consider how the data types would be used in other data structures.

Let's look at an example of this process. Chapter 5 discussed a `getOrder()` operation whose response included the `Sales Order`, `shipTo` and `billTo Address`, and `Sales Order Line Items` (Figure 9-8).

Let's suppose now that you want to implement another operation, `getOrderDetails()`, that returns a richer set of information—more like the data set back in Figure 9-3. Furthermore, in doing so, you'd like to reuse data structures where possible. A sketch of this operation is shown in Figure 9-9. Your challenge is to define the `Get Order Details Response`.

These steps are illustrated in the following sections.

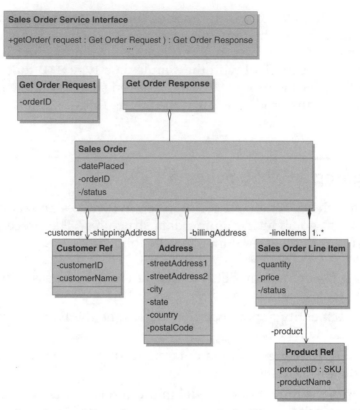

Figure 9-8: *Interface and Data Structures for getOrder()*

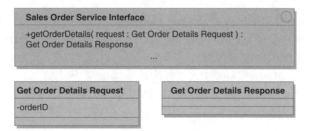

Figure 9-9: *Sketch of getOrderDetails() Interface and Data Structures*

Identify Required Entities and Associations

Figure 9-10 shows the domain model for the sales functional area with the elements to be included in the message highlighted. From this you can see that there are a significant number of elements (and their relationships) that need to be represented.

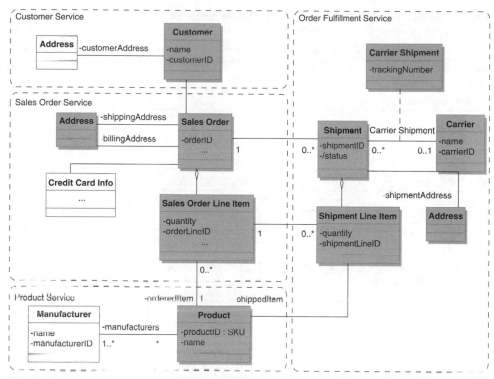

Figure 9-10: *Entities and Associations Required for Get Order Details Response*

Determine Entity Representations

If you just looked at the domain model and ignored the fact that you might want to re-use some of the data types in other data structures (or ignored existing data types that you might want to re-use), you might end up with the representation types shown in Table 9-1 for the entities in the Get Order Details Response.

Similarly, you might end up with the association representations shown in Table 9-2.

Create the Information Model

Putting all of these representations together and adding the attribute details, you get the information model shown in Figure 9-11.

One feature of this representation that is worth noting is the embedded reference to Sales Order Line Item that is included in the Shipment Line Item. Because XML is tree-structured, Shipment Line Item can

Table 9-1: *Entity Representations for Get Order Details Response*

Entity	Representation
Customer	Human-readable reference
Sales Order	Details
Sales Order Line Item	Details
Address	Details
Product	Human-readable reference
Shipment	Details
Shipment Line Item	Details
Carrier	Human-readable identifier
Carrier Shipment	Identifier

Table 9-2: *Association Representations for Get Order Details Response*

Association	Representation
Sales Order – Customer	Customer as nested substructure of Sales Order
Sales Order – billingAddress	Address as nested substructure of Sales Order
Sales Order – shippingAddress	Address as nested substructure of Sales Order
Sales Order – Sales Order Line Item	Line item as nested substructure of Sales Order
Sales Order Line Item – Product	Product as nested substructure of Sales Order Line Item
Sales Order – Shipment	Shipment as nested substructure of Sales Order
Shipment – Shipment Line Item	Shipment Line Item as nested substructure of Shipment
Shipment Line Item – Product	Product Ref as nested substructure of Shipment Line Item
Sales Order Line Item – Shipment Line Item	Sales Order Line Item ID embedded in Shipment Line Item
Shipment – Carrier Shipment	Carrier Shipment ID embedded in Shipment
Shipment – Carrier	Carrier as nested substructure of Sales Order

only be a child of one data type, in this case Shipment. The embedded reference is a means of indicating this other relationship.

Now compare this information model with the one shown in Figure 9-8. The model of Sales Order is almost identical—with one significant exception. The detailed response has Shipment as a child of Sales Order, while the basic get order does not. This means that either you

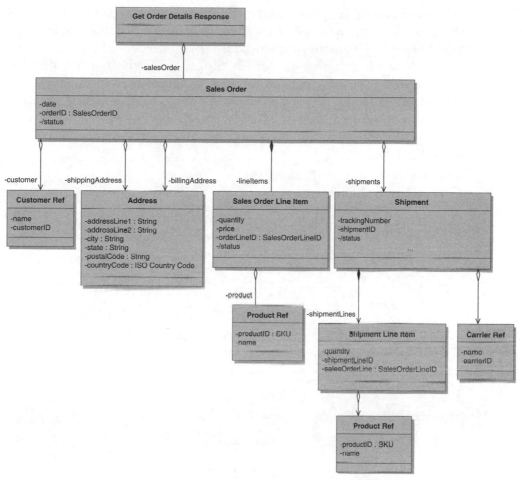

Figure 0 11: *Get Order Details Response Information Model—First Cut*

need two data types for Sales Order or you need to make the shipments association optional. Both have their drawbacks.

Creating other representations for Sales Order is working against the goal of minimizing the number of representations of each entity. Thus it would be preferable (if it turns out to be practical) to use the same representation. Making the shipments association optional has the drawback that neither the sender nor recipient of the data structure can be sure whether the association is supposed to be present. This not only forces both parties to refer to the specification for the particular operation to determine whether the association should be present, but it also creates the possibility of run-time errors.

There is a third option: Make the shipments association a child of the root Get Order Details Response (Figure 9-12). Here the association between Shipment and Sales Order is represented by an embedded reference to Sales Order in Shipment. Whether or not the shipments information is required is now determined by the top-level data structure—Get Order Details Response. This is appropriate since that data structure is specific to the operation. Now you have a reusable representation for Sales Order and (most likely) one for Shipment as well.

Create the Schema

Once you have settled on the information model, you can create the XSDs for its implementation. But before this is done, you need to consider how the shared XSDs will be organized.

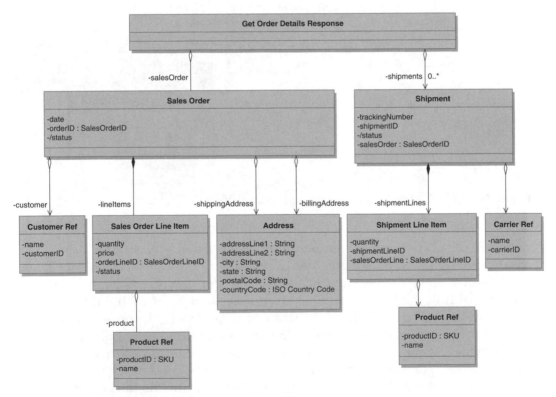

Figure 9-12: *Get Order Details Response—Final Cut*

Organizing Schema and Interfaces

When you design your common data models, other schema, and interfaces, you must consider how the XSDs and WSDLs containing the type and interface definitions should be organized. The namespace in which each definition is placed should indicate the scope over which the definition is to be considered a "standard." Common scopes include

- Interface
- Abstract service
- Functional area
- Line of business
- Enterprise
- Public domain

Figure 9-13 shows the scoping structure for the data types and interfaces mentioned in the Sales Order example. Note the use of schema folders to contain schema definitions and wsdl folders for interface definitions. This maintains clear separation between these two definition types in an otherwise similar scoping structure.

Operation-specific data structures such as Get Order Details Response are placed in the interface scope to which they belong (e.g., salesOrderServiceInterface). This avoids conflicts with other similarly named data structures belonging to other interfaces. Sales Order and Sales Order Line Item, along with their respective identifiers, are specific to the abstract salesOrder service, but are not specific to any given interface.

Similarly Shipment and Shipment Line Item and their respective identifiers are specific to the orderFulfillment service in the fulfillment functional area. Carrier, Carrier Ref, CarrierID, and TrackingNumber are specific to the carrier service, which is also a part of the fulfillment functional area. Manufacturer, Manufacturer Ref, and ManufacturerID are part of the manufacturer service in the procurement functional area. For brevity, the interfaces of these and other services are not shown in this figure.

More generic information is placed in higher-level services placed in the enterprise scope. Customer, Customer Ref, and CustomerID are in the enterprise-level customer service. Product,

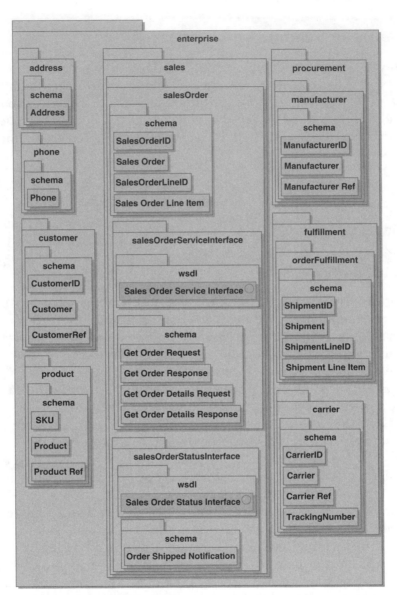

Figure 9-13: *Data Structure Packaging*

Product Ref, and SKU belong to the enterprise-level product service. Address and Phone are in their respective services, also at the enterprise level. Again, for brevity, the interfaces to these services are not shown in this figure.

Example Schema

The schema and interface definitions corresponding to Figure 9-13 are contained in Appendix A.

Summary

The data structures that appear in an enterprise's messages, databases, and files are often related to one another. Since components often need to map information from one to another, understanding these relationships is important. This same understanding can also be used to guide their design and simplify this mapping.

The requisite understanding begins with a domain model, a representation of the concepts and relationships that occur naturally in the real world. Concepts are sketched in this model, with only attributes like identifiers and values that drive major business process decisions being captured. Relationships focus on the multiplicity that can occur in real-world situations. Getting multiplicity right is important, for it gets cast in concrete when you create actual data structures. It is good practice to maintain a comprehensive domain model for an enterprise.

Information models are more detailed than domain models. They strive for completeness in the information they represent, and for this reason they are more difficult to maintain. In practice, information models typically only cover a small subset of the domain model, and they are used to capture the information to be represented in a component or its interfaces as that component is being designed. Such models are typically created in preparation for designing actual data structures. Note that if two different components or data structures are implementing the same concepts from the domain model, their respective information models may differ in details.

When designing data structures you have to decide how much structure to leave in the representation. Too much structure can make it difficult to assemble the data structure or find information in it. Too little structure requires additional rules to interpret the information in the data structure.

Common data models seek to minimize the number of representations for a given entity, but you will generally need more than one. Typically you want a full-blown representation with all the details, a human-readable reference, and a bare-bones identifier. There are a number of ways in which associations can be represented as well.

When you use common data models, it is a good practice to let the top-level entity in a communication be a data structure specific to the operation being invoked. The children of this top-level entity are the reusable data types of the common data model.

Designing data structures starts with understanding the relevant part of the domain model and ensuring that the multiplicities of its associations are clearly understood. From this, you prepare an information model that adds the details to be represented. Then at this point you consider which common data model data types to incorporate. Finally, you generate the actual schema for the message (or database).

Part III

Service Architecture Patterns

Chapter 10

Building-Block
Design Patterns

Objectives

To be of use, a service must become part of a solution, with some of the required solution functionality being provided by the service. This chapter explores a number of building-block design patterns related to the division of responsibility between the service providers and the solution components that consume those services.

After reading this chapter, you should be able to describe the design patterns related to

- Separating interface and business logic

- Using services to access back-end systems

- Using a rules service to define a business process

- Providing information to a rules service

- Returning variant responses

- Supporting multiple service consumers

Solution Architecture Decisions

In implementing a service-oriented architecture, the solution architect is faced with a number of decisions (Figure 10-1). When there are different types of service consumers, can they all share service operations, or are separate operations more appropriate? When back-end systems are to be accessed, should they be accessed directly or should each back-end system be wrapped with its own service? Should there be a single service containing all the intervening logic between the front-end systems and the back-end systems, or should the functionality be partitioned into a composite of services? And finally, what functionality belongs in the service as opposed to the front- and back-end systems?

The answers to these questions are explored in the following sections.

Separating Interface and Business Logic

The broadest of the solution architecture questions concerns the division of responsibilities between the service and the front- and back-end systems. In the pre-SOA generation of systems, front-end systems generally interacted directly with back-end systems or with a mediation layer whose interfaces directly reflected back-end system interfaces. In

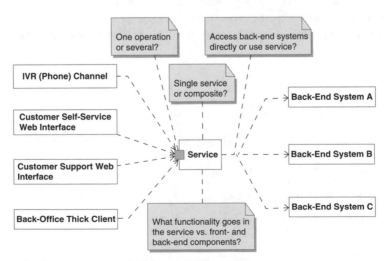

Figure 10-1: *Some Solution Architecture Questions*

these designs, the front-end systems contained two types of logic: interface logic and business logic. The interface logic dealt with the interactions of users or other systems that required access to the back-end systems. The business logic mapped these interactions to the back-end system interfaces, deciding when such interactions were appropriate and coordinating multiple interactions when required.

The disadvantage of this approach is that adding a new type of front-end interface (e.g., a new channel for providing business services) required not only implementing the new interface but also replicating the business logic. This not only drove up the cost of adding new channels for doing business, it significantly increased the cost of evolving the business logic.

Design Pattern: Separate Interface and Business Logic

Evolving to a service-oriented architecture affords the opportunity to refactor and separate the business logic from the interface logic (Figure 10-2). When done with an eye toward the different types of front-end systems, this would make it possible to have a single business logic implementation support more than one interface.

Consider the online banking example of Figure 10-3. Here the application server (the front-end system) guides the bank customer through the process of transferring funds between accounts. It also contains the business logic that coordinates the two interactions with back-end systems and provides the required transactional behavior.

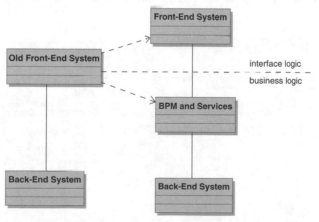

Figure 10-2: *Separating Interface and Business Logic*

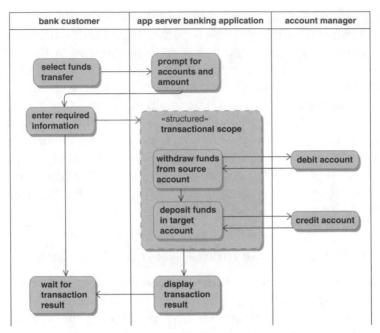

Figure 10-3: *Front-End System with Both Interface and Business Logic*

Now take a look at the refactored architecture of Figure 10-4. With this architecture, any front-end system could invoke the banking service's transferFunds operation. Furthermore, the banking service could be modified to provide access to other types of back-end systems

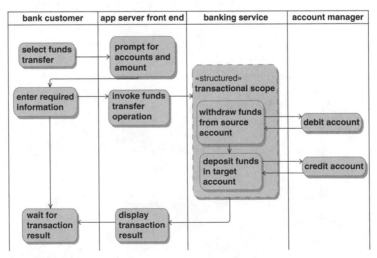

Figure 10-4: *Business Logic Factored into a Service*

(accounts belonging to other banks, for example) without requiring alterations to the front-end systems.

Such refactoring provides a more flexible architecture, but it does come at a price: You need to modify the front-end system to realize the benefits. An appropriate time to do this refactoring is when you have a business justification for modifying the front-end system anyway or, even better, you have a need for a new front-end system. The refactoring can then be incorporated into that project, which will lessen its cost. Once the refactoring is done, refactoring the other systems will cost less since the service already exists.

Best Practice: Separate Interface and Business Logic

As front-end systems need to be changed for business reasons, take the opportunity to factor interface and business logic, separating out the process coordination business logic. Depending upon the nature of the coordination, the associated logic may become a service or be incorporated into the overall orchestration logic for the complete business process

---

A common practice, but one to be assiduously avoided, is the introduction of a service that simply re-presents the existing back-end system interfaces recast in new technology (e.g., XML and WSDL/SOAP). Such efforts provide no immediate business value, and the only long-range value they provide is some measure of technology isolation between front- and back-end systems. The problem with this approach is that it doesn't make any inroads on improving the existing solution design. Instead, it tends to preserve the tight coupling between front- and back-end systems that necessitates frequent front-end system changes as back-end systems evolve. It is difficult to find a sound return-on-investment justification for such projects.

Using Services for Accessing Back-End Systems

Should business services that access back-end systems do so via other services? Not necessarily. The business service that needs to access the back-end system already presents an abstracted interface. The question then is whether there is justification for wrapping the back-end access with another service.

When considering a service that wraps back-end systems, bear in mind that a useful service requires a relatively stable interface. This means that the interface must expose an abstracted version of the back-end system capabilities. It also means that the interface must remain stable over time as the back-end system evolves. Conceptualizing such an interface requires an engineering investment, and therefore the decision to develop the service must be viewed as an investment decision.

There are a couple of situations that would justify the development of a service to wrap back-end system access:

- Two or more services need to access the same back-end system operations and could benefit from the stability of a service interface. The justification here is that only one service (the back-end wrapping service) needs to be updated when back-end systems are updated.
- These are back-end business operations that need to be accessed directly by other business processes. The justification here is similar: Only the wrapper service needs to be updated when the back-end systems are updated.

Deciding not to build a back-end wrapping service does not mean that the use of some assistive technology may not be appropriate for accessing the back-end system—far from it. The use of adapters that simplify access to the back-end system has its advantages. Recognize, however, that with adapters the resulting interface is not intended to remain stable as the end-point system evolves. They are not services.

Best Practice: Service Wrappers around Back-End Systems

Only build service wrappers around back-end system interfaces when you can make the case that two or more services or business processes require access to the same interfaces.

Rule Service Governing Process Flow

Rules, business rules in particular, are often used to make decisions in business processes. This section explores the relationship between a rule-driven service and a process manager in situations in which the business process is being orchestrated. Two architectural issues arise in these situations: the relationship between the process manager and the rule service, and the relationship between the rule service and the sources of data upon which the rules operate.

An example will help to motivate the discussion. In the health care arena, the question often arises as to whether a medical procedure for a given individual is covered by a health care plan. This question arises in a number of business processes including the handling of health care claims and pre-authorization of health care procedures.

This example is interesting for a couple of reasons. For one, the answer to this question determines the course of business processes— and in this case, more than one process. For another, answering the question requires access to a diverse set of information, such as the dates during which the person was a member of the health care plan, the date (actual or proposed) of the service, the coverage extensions mandated by regulations, and the existence of prior related services. Keep this example in mind as you read each of the following design pattern discussions.

Design Pattern: Rule Service Separated from Process Manager

There are two basic patterns for managing flow with rules. The patterns differ regarding where the rules are located with respect to the process flow logic. In one case the rules are strictly separated, and in the other they are fully integrated. Let's take a look at the design pattern for the separated case.

In most processes where rules are employed for decision making, there are well-defined decision points in the process, each of which has relatively few outcome branches (Figure 10-5). When rules are employed in these situations, it is because the decision as to which of the branches to take is complex, even though the number of possible outcomes is small. In these cases, it is relatively easy to separate the rule service (which interprets the rules) from the process manager, as shown in the figure. The process manager asks the rule service to determine the decision result, but the process manager determines what the process should be for each result.

This separation leads to process definitions that are easy to understand and validate. The process determines when questions should be asked of the rule service and defines what the process should look like for each possible result. The process manager retains full control over the process, which is consistent with the concept of an orchestrated process.

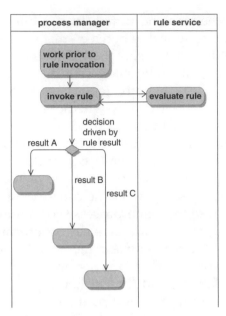

Figure 10-5: *Rule Service Separated from Process Manager*

This pattern is not a panacea. For its use to make sense, the latency involved in invoking the rules must be reasonable with respect to the execution time of the process. Furthermore, the overhead of supplying the data upon which the rules operate must be acceptable (more on this shortly). Nevertheless, because of its simplicity, this is the preferred design pattern as long as it is performance feasible.

The TIBCO ActiveMatrix® Decisions software is specifically designed to play the role of the rule service. TIBCO BusinessEvents™ is also well suited for this role.

Design Pattern: Rule Service as Process Manager

The opposite extreme to separating the rule service from the process manager is that the rule service becomes the process manager (Figure 10-6). The rules determine what the next process activity should be and the rules service then executes the activity (or at least manages its execution).

This pattern is efficient and provides the utmost in flexibility: Any activity can be invoked at any time if the rules call for it. But this flexibility is, in fact, a drawback as well: It is difficult for someone to under-

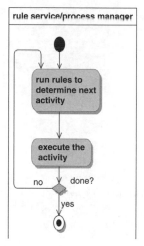

Figure 10-6: *Rule-Defined Process*

stand the process flows that can occur for various sets of circumstances, and therefore it is difficult to validate that the process flows are appropriate. For this reason, this pattern should be considered a last resort, to be used in situations in which it is not practical to statically define the process structure. Even then, it is likely that one of the hybrid approaches described in the next section will be more appropriate.

TIBCO BusinessEvents is well suited to implement the combined role of rule service and process manager.

Hybrid Rule-Process Approaches

There are business processes for which the entire process cannot be defined in advance. This commonly occurs when a business process contains an activity that designs (or defines) the ultimate deliverable of the process, then defines the process for creating that deliverable, and finally executes that newly defined process to create the deliverable (Figure 10-7).

To make this approach practical, the deliverable is usually an assembly of standard building blocks, each of which has a well-defined standard process for its implementation (Figure 10-8). The deliverable design characterizes how (and in what sequence) these building blocks are assembled. Based on this design, the process for creating the deliverable is defined by organizing the standard building-block processes into an overall process for creating the deliverable.

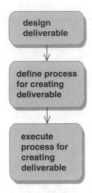

Figure 10-7: *Process with Design Activity*

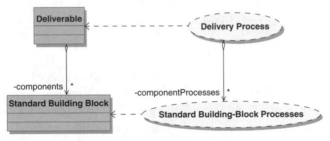

Figure 10-8: *Structured Deliverables and Delivery Processes*

This type of process can be implemented in a number of ways, some of which are managed (orchestrated) and others are unmanaged (choreographed). Focusing on the options for managing the process, and specifically employing a rules service, it turns out that the rules service can be employed in both the styles described earlier.

Design Pattern: Rule Service Assembles Process Definition

One option is to have the rules service assemble the process for creating the deliverable and then have the process manager oversee the execution of that process (Figure 10-9). This requires process definitions that the rule service can operate upon and that the process manager be capable of accepting a process definition and then executing it. The details of doing this vary widely depending upon the technology used for process management and are beyond the scope of this book.

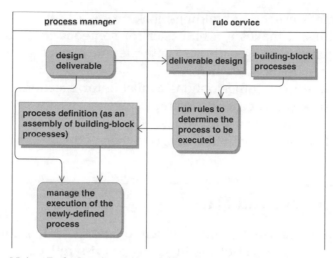

Figure 10-9: *Using Rule Service to Assemble a Process Definition*

Design Pattern: Rule Service Directs Process Manager

The other option is to have the rules engine actually invoke each of the building-block processes (Figure 10-10). This is a bit simpler both from the rule service and process manager perspectives since it does not involve the dynamic creation of new process definitions. Because the

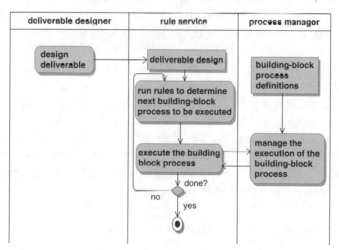

Figure 10-10: *Rules Engine Invoking Building-Block Processes*

rule engine is executing building-block processes rather than individual activities, it makes it a bit easier for someone to understand the overall process than was the case with the rule service as process manager pattern discussed earlier.

There are many other options available for executing this type of business process. The design patterns given here are just illustrative examples showing the use of a rules service in this context. They are not intended to provide comprehensive coverage of the design alternatives.

Rule Services and Data

Rules require information upon which to operate and, in turn, provide information to the rest of the business process reflecting the conclusions of the rules. The following sections describe two common design patterns for providing rules with access to information.

Design Pattern: Rule Client Provides Data

A common means of providing data to the rule service is that the client invoking the service provides all the data required by the rules and receives the results of evaluating the rules as a data structure returned by the service (Figure 10-11).

This is an architecturally simple design for the rules service, since it is fully self-contained and only requires one interface. The down side is that the client has to assemble all of the required data and pass it to the rules service. If the data set is large, and especially if the data is largely repetitive from invocation to invocation, this may not be an optimal design from a performance perspective. You are trading performance for simplicity.

The simplicity of this design pattern, however, provides simplified design-time opportunities for defining rules. Rule engines that provide spreadsheet-like interfaces for rule definitions (including TIBCO BusinessEvents) generally follow this model, with one axis of the spreadsheet representing the elements of the input data and the other axis representing the elements of the result.

Design Pattern: Rule Service Acquires Data

The other alternative is for the rule service to acquire some or all of the data required by the rules (Figure 10-12). In this design pattern the rule client typically provides some context information with each

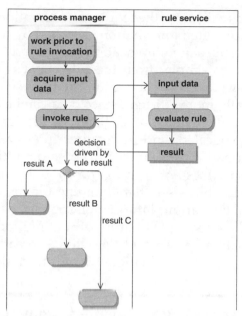

Figure 10-11: *Rule Client Provides Data*

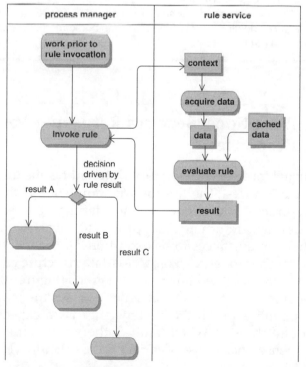

Figure 10-12: *Rule Service Acquires Data*

invocation. The remainder of the required information is then acquired by the rule service. Often information is cached by the rule service as well and used in subsequent invocations.

This approach is simpler from the rule client's perspective: It no longer has to be aware of the scope of information required by the rules. It is also potentially more efficient, since data can be cached from one invocation to the next. On the other hand, the design of the rules service is more complicated since it requires interfaces to the various sources of information and rules for obtaining that information. Although the client does not need to know the details of the information, it does need to be aware that obtaining the result depends upon the availability of the various information sources.

Because of the open-ended nature of the information used in the rules, it is generally not practical to provide a spreadsheet-style interface for business users to define the rules for this design pattern.

Information about TIBCO BusinessEvents Usage

This book only scratches the surface of rule-based designs and the use of TIBCO BusinessEvents. More information will be provided by the upcoming book, *Architecting Complex Event Processing Solutions with TIBCO*, and in the corresponding TIBCO Education course offerings. This book and course explore rule-based patterns in depth.

Business Exceptions: Services Returning Variant Business Responses

It is not unusual for a service to return different results under different business circumstances. The question is, how should these different results be returned? You might consider defining one set of circumstances as "normal," returning an appropriate data structure, and consider all other circumstances to be exceptions, throwing WSDL faults. Another approach is to return a response data structure capable of representing all of the expected business variations (Figure 10-13).

When should you choose one approach versus the other? The general rule of thumb is that if the circumstance is an expected business condition, don't throw a WSDL fault; rather, return it as part of the expected response, that is, use a variant data structure. The reason for

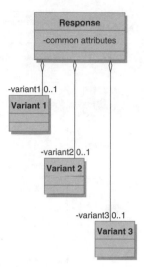

Figure 10-13: *Variant Response Structure*

this is because receiving a WSDL fault generally breaks the process flow in the receiving component. In Java and .NET, for example, you invoke a web service within a `try ... catch` construct. A WSDL fault results in control being passed to the `catch` block of the construct—it jumps you out of the process flow in the `try` block.

Consider the banking example of Figure 10-14. In this scenario, a bank customer is attempting to transfer funds from one account to another. In the event that the source account has insufficient funds to cover the transaction, the bank's policy is to determine whether the customer has a credit line sufficient to cover the transaction and use those funds instead. In this example, WSDL faults are only being raised for unexpected conditions, with business variations being communicated with a variant response. Thus the account manager service does not raise an exception if there are insufficient funds: It simply returns a variant response. The business logic is easy to understand in this example.

Now consider how this scenario would look if WSDL faults are raised by services for variant business conditions (Figure 10-15). The fact that a fault breaks out of the logic flow in the `try` portion of the construct makes it difficult to implement logic that gracefully handles variant responses. The example still has top-level `try ... catch construct 1`, as this is still needed to define the transaction scope,

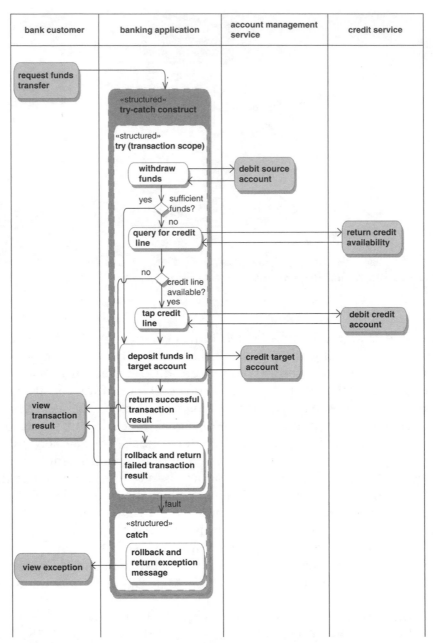

Figure 10-14: *Handling Business Variations with Variant Responses*

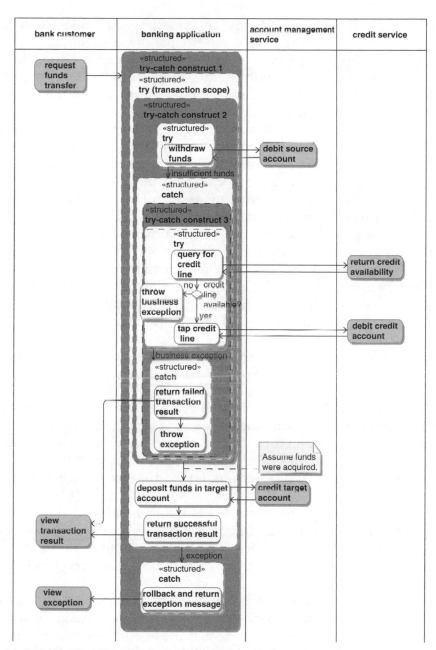

Figure 10-15: *Handling Business Variations by Raising Exceptions*

catch non-business exceptions, and rollback the transaction. However, each service interaction that needs to handle a business variant response needs its own `try ... catch` construct to identify and handle the variation. Thus the withdraw funds request to the account management service is in `try ... catch construct 2`, with the insufficient funds business variation being handled in the `catch` block. But it gets more complicated. Handling the insufficient funds variation requires obtaining credit, which has its own business variation (insufficient credit) and therefore requires `try ... catch construct 3`. This construct has a `catch` block for the business variation (no credit line), which displays a transaction result for the customer (which could even extend an offer of a credit line!). If you wanted to add more business logic to handle the offer, that would have to be placed in this `catch` block as well.

Understanding the process flow requires a thorough understanding of `try ... catch` block behavior. Completion of the execution in either the try or catch block of the construct will pass control onto the next statement after the construct unless an unhandled exception is raised, thus the need to throw an exception in the `catch` block of `construct 3` after the failed transaction result is returned. But that's not enough. You also need to understand that any fault occurring in a `catch` block will propagate to the next outer scope. Therefore, a fault occurring in the `catch` block of `construct 3`, which happens to be located in the `catch` block of `construct 2`, will propagate to `construct 2`'s `catch` block. By the same rule, the fault will propagate to the `try` block of `construct 1`, which means that its associated `catch` block can process this fault (if it has the correct catch clause . . .).

The way this example is constructed, it is assumed that a normal exit from `try ... catch construct 2` indicates that funds were successfully obtained. This requires that all other conditions raise exceptions that will propagate back up to `construct 1`'s `catch` block. Got it? No? That's the point.

Comparing these two diagrams, it is easy to see how the business logic becomes obscured if WSDL faults are used for variant business conditions. The conclusion then is that if the business process has a planned response for a business variation, don't use a WSDL fault to communicate the variation. Use a response data structure that can represent all of the variants instead.

Best Practice: Expected Business Variations

If a service returns different results for different business conditions and the business process logic needs to distinguish between these results, return the results as a single response data structure capable of representing all the variations. Do not use WSDL faults to return the variant results.

Asynchronous JMS Request-Reply Interactions

The Problem with Temporary Destinations

The default ActiveMatrix BusinessWorks behavior for JMS request-reply interactions, and a common pattern for all JMS request-reply service consumers, is that for each request, a temporary JMS destination is created for the corresponding reply (Figure 10-16). The replyTo property of the Request Message contains the destination to which the

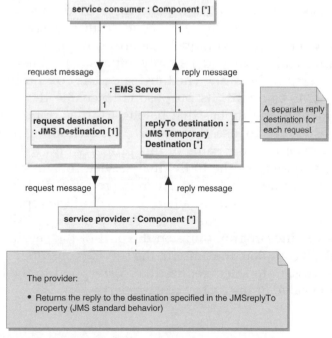

Figure 10-16: *Using Temporary Destinations for JMS Replies*

reply is to be sent. In this pattern there can be multiple components with service consumers and multiple components with service providers.

The default behavior provides a reasonable design pattern for synchronous interactions, but it is not suitable for asynchronous interactions. This is because the temporary destinations do not survive the loss of connectivity between the components and the EMS server. Thus a restart of either component or a breakdown in communications between them will cause the loss of the reply destination and its associated message. Typically when you do asynchronous interactions, the intent is to ensure that the exchange completes even if the participants are restarted or communication is temporarily lost.

Asynchronous Request-Reply: Single Reply Destination

One pattern that can be used for asynchronous request-reply interactions involves creating a single reply destination for all requests regardless of how many components[1] submit requests (Figure 10-17). The use of this pattern involves three JMS message properties, only two of which are standard. The first, `JMSReplyTo`, is a standard property used to indicate the destination to which the reply should be sent. The consumer sets the value, and the provider uses it to determine where to send the reply. The second, `JMSCorrelationID`, is a standard property used to uniquely identify a request. The consumer sets the value, and the provider simply returns the value in the same-named property of the reply. The third, a `Selector` property, is not part of the JMS standard. Its purpose is to enable the service consumer to identify the replies that belong to it, as opposed to other service consumers. To use this pattern, a convention needs to be established regarding the name of this property and the values that will be used to identify the individual service consumers. The consumer sets the value of this property in the request, and the provider returns the value in the same-named property of the reply. Note that returning this property value by the provider is not JMS-standard behavior—specific programming on the part of the service provider is required. To complete the pattern, the service consumer uses a JMS selector expression to select replies that correspond to the consumer based on the value of the `Selector` property.

---

1. Just to be clear here, we are talking about separate components (e.g., ActiveMatrix BusinessWorks engines), not threads within a component.

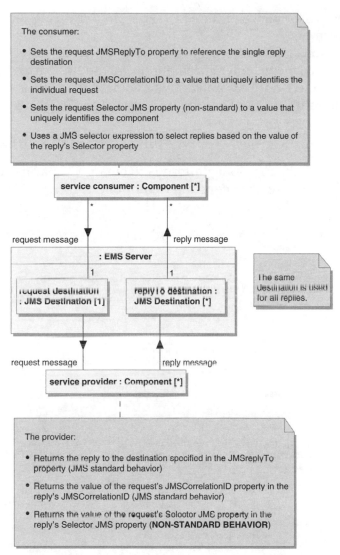

The consumer:

- Sets the request JMSReplyTo property to reference the single reply destination
- Sets the request JMSCorrelationID to a value that uniquely identifies the individual request
- Sets the request Selector JMS property (non-standard) to a value that uniquely identifies the component
- Uses a JMS selector expression to select replies based on the value of the reply's Selector property

service consumer : Component [*]

request message   reply message

: EMS Server

request destination : JMS Destination [1]   reply To destination : JMS Destination [*]

The same destination is used for all replies.

request message   reply message

service provider : Component [*]

The provider:

- Returns the reply to the destination specified in the JMSreplyTo property (JMS standard behavior)
- Returns the value of the request's JMSCorrelationID property in the reply's JMSCorrelationID (JMS standard behavior)
- Returns the value of the request's Selector JMS property in the reply's Selector JMS property (**NON-STANDARD BEHAVIOR**)

Figure 10-17: *Asynchronous Request-Reply with a Single Reply Destination*

One drawback to this pattern is that the use of the `Selector` property is not part of the JMS standard; it is part of the design pattern, and its appropriate use by both service consumers and service providers needs to be enforced in order for the pattern to work. Another drawback is that if the volume of requests is high and one of the service consumers is slow to retrieve its replies (or is off-line for some period of time), the accumulating replies for this slow consumer may adversely impact the performance of the EMS server in delivering replies to the other consumers.

A variation of this pattern that gets rid of the need for the `Selector` property is to use a consumer-specific prefix for the `JMSCorrelationID` values and select on that prefix. This avoids the need for the service provider to return the `Selector` property value.

Asynchronous Request-Reply: Multiple Reply Destinations

A variation on the previous pattern is to create a separate reply destination for each service consumer component[2] (Figure 10-18). The

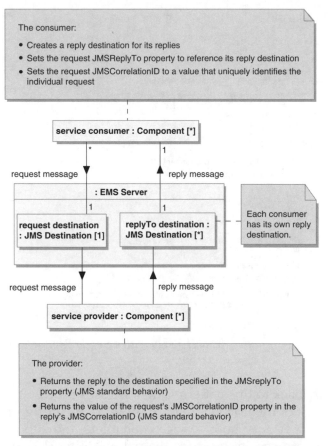

Figure 10-18: *Asynchronous Request-Reply with Multiple Reply Destinations*

---

2. Again, just to be clear, we are talking about separate components (e.g., ActiveMatrix BusinessWorks engines), not threads within a component.

service consumer component creates the reply destination (or it is created administratively at the time the consumer is deployed) and uses it as the `JMSReplyTo` destination for all requests. It uses `JMSCorrelationID` to uniquely identify each request. Note that all service provider behavior is in conformance with the JMS standard: No special programming is involved.

The only real disadvantage to this pattern is the need to create a reply destination for each service consumer and communicate the name of that destination to the consumer in such a way that it can supply it as the value of the `JMSReplyTo` property and subscribe to replies from that destination.

Supporting Dual Coordination Patterns

Although it is desirable for a service to support different kinds of service consumers with a single interface, differences in consumer coordination patterns can make this difficult. Generally, consumers that expect quick responses deliver small work requests using a synchronous request-reply pattern. Consumers that deliver large work requests, on the other hand, usually expect to wait longer for the responses and tend to use an asynchronous request-reply pattern. While different coordination patterns often require different interfaces, it is possible to present an interface that can be used with both synchronous and asynchronous coordination patterns.

In order to support both synchronous and asynchronous coordination patterns, the request submitted to the interface must indicate which type of coordination is desired. Figure 10-19 shows such a request, with a Boolean field indicating whether an immediate response (i.e., synchronous interaction) is required.

Figure 10-20 shows the processing of this request. Based on the value of the immediate response flag, the service provider either performs the work immediately and returns the result or returns a promise to do the work later. The data structure returned in Figure 10-20 is an example of a service returning a variant business response, which was discussed earlier in this chapter.

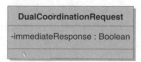

Figure 10-19: *Dual Coordination Request*

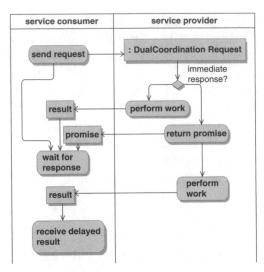

Figure 10-20: *Dual Coordination-Pattern Processing*

In the case of an asynchronous interaction, the service eventually performs the work and returns the result using a second asynchronous interface. To make life simple, it is a good idea to use exactly the same data structure definition for both the synchronous and asynchronous response. Thus only one data structure definition is needed and the same service consumer logic can be used to process both synchronous and asynchronous responses. The `payClaim()` operation of the `Claim Payment Interface` in the Nouveau Health Care example uses this design pattern.

Summary

When approaching an SOA-based solution architecture, there are a number of questions facing the project architect. When there are multiple front-end systems to be supported, can they be supported by a single operation or are separate operations required? When back-end systems need to be accessed, should they be accessed directly, or should those interfaces themselves be wrapped in a service? Should the service contain all of the logic, or should it be factored into several services and combined in a composite service? Finally, what logic properly belongs in front- and back-end systems as opposed to the service(s) in between? This chapter has examined these questions and some design patterns that they motivate.

Many existing front-end systems (e.g., applications in application servers) interact directly with back-end systems. These systems contain a mixture of interface and business logic. The problem with this approach is that adding a new interface (new channel for doing business) requires not only defining the new interface logic but also replicating the pieces of business logic. This drives up the cost of implementing new business channels and of evolving the business logic.

The introduction of services as intermediaries between front- and back-end systems affords the opportunity to re-factor the interface and business logic, placing the business logic in the common shared services and leaving the front-end systems with pure interface logic.

Rules are often used to guide the flow of managed (orchestrated) business processes. There are a number of design patterns that can be used for this purpose. One good pattern separates the rules from the business process and uses the rules to answer business process questions. The process manager then takes these answers and decides what branch of the process to pursue. This makes the overall process flow very clear. The extreme opposite embeds the rules in the process manager and uses the rules after the completion of each activity to determine what activity to perform next. Although this has the ultimate in flexibility, it makes it very difficult to understand what the process looks like under different circumstances and validate the process.

Some processes cannot be defined in advance. Typical of these are processes that design something and then implement what has just been defined. Generally these designs are assemblies of predefined building blocks, each of which has a standard process for its implementation. Defining the business process to implement the design then consists of assembling these building-block processes. Depending upon the capabilities of the rules engine and process manager, the rules engine can either assemble the implementation process, handing it off to the process manager for execution, or manage the overall process by directing the process manager to execute each individual building block process as required.

Rules operate on data, and the manner in which the data is provided is an important architectural decision. In one design pattern, the party that invokes the rules provides all the required information and receives information (the rule conclusions) in return. This makes for a simple interface but may require the repetitive movement of the same information in different invocations. Another design pattern has the rules service obtaining and caching the information it needs. Even though this increases execution efficiency, it introduces additional interfaces and dependencies into the architecture.

Often a service needs to return different information under different business conditions. Using WSDL faults for the different conditions makes it difficult to structure the service consumer's business logic. A best practice is to design the normal return data structure to accommodate the variant information sets required under the different circumstances.

When asynchronous interactions occur using EMS as a transport, the design pattern used to return the replies needs to be selected. The default JMS behavior, using temporary destinations, is inappropriate for asynchronous interactions. One design pattern is to use a single reply destination for all responses. However, if there are multiple service consumers, each consumer must use JMS selectors to identify their responses. If some consumers are slow in receiving their responses, this may have adverse performance consequences. Another design pattern is for each service consumer to have its own reply destination.

When a service needs to support both synchronous and asynchronous coordination patterns for the same logical operation, this does not necessarily require separate operations. There is a design pattern in which the request indicates whether an immediate response is required, and the response indicates either the actual response or (in the asynchronous case) a promise to perform the work later. A second interface is used to return the asynchronous responses returning the same data structure that was used in the synchronous response.

Chapter 11

Load Distribution and Sequencing Patterns

Objectives

There are times when there is more work to be done than a single instance of a component can handle. When this occurs, you need to distribute the load between two or more instances of the component. This chapter explores a number of design patterns that can be used for this purpose.

Some types of work, such as bank account deposits and withdrawals, are sensitive to the sequence in which the activities are executed. Load distribution presents a challenge in this regard. This chapter explores design patterns that distribute load while preserving sequencing.

After reading this chapter you will be able to

- Identify and select appropriate load distribution patterns for Enterprise Message Service and ActiveMatrix Service Grid.

- Identify and select appropriate load distribution patterns that preserve sequencing.

Using IP Redirectors to Distribute Load

A common way to distribute load that has requests being sent using a network-based protocol (e.g., TCP/IP) is to use an IP redirector (Figure 11-1). This is commonly done for HTTP and SOAP over HTTP requests. The IP redirector has a list of candidate service providers to which incoming requests can be directed. Some IP redirectors have mechanisms for determining the workload and status of the service providers, and they use this information when forwarding requests.

Using JMS Queues to Distribute Load

Another common approach to distributing load is to send requests via a Java Message Service (JMS) queue (Figure 11-2). JMS queues deliver each message to exactly one subscriber—in this case one of the service providers. If you are using Enterprise Message Service as your JMS server, you need to make sure that the `exclusive` property for the queue is not set.

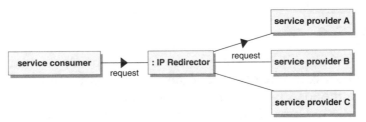

Figure 11-1: *Using an IP Redirector to Distribute Load*

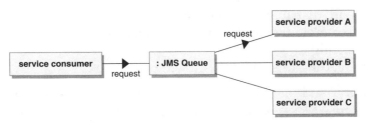

Figure 11-2: *Using JMS Queues to Distribute Load*

Partitioning JMS Message Load between Servers

When the volume of message traffic exceeds the capacity of a single JMS server, the traffic must be split between servers. The easiest way to do this is to move some destinations to another JMS server (Figure 11-3). This distributes the message traffic to the different servers.

Planning for Future Partitioning

To facilitate the movement of destinations from one server to another, it is good practice to group related destinations and use a different JMS connection factory for each group (Figure 11-4). The structured names discussed in Chapter 8 provide a good basis for this organization.

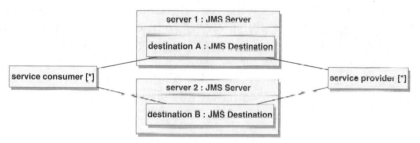

Figure 11-3: *Partitioning JMS Message Load between Servers*

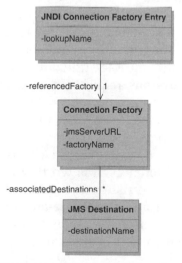

Figure 11-4: *Grouping JMS Destinations with Connection Factories*

Partitioning by line of business or functional area is generally sufficient, although functional areas with high aggregate message volume (rule of thumb: 10,000 messages/second peak for a Enterprise Message Service server) may want to consider further partitioning by service name or even interface name for the high-volume services. JMS clients then use JNDI lookups to locate these connection factories.

Once this type of grouping is done, moving destinations to another server is relatively straightforward as long as message sequencing is not a requirement:

1. Create the required destinations on the new JMS server.
2. Update the JNDI entry for the connection factory.
3. Stop the old JMS server.

Stopping the old server will break the JMS client connections. JMS clients, when they use the JNDI lookup to find the connection factory, will be directed to the new JMS server. Messages still on the old server can be moved to the new server using a temporary client that subscribes to the destinations on the old server and republishes the destinations to the new server. Note that this temporary client should not use JNDI lookups!

Partitioning by Nature of Traffic

All network communications for a given Enterprise Message Service server are handled by a single thread. As a consequence, large messages sent to one destination may adversely impact the delivery of small messages sent to another destination on the same server.

If you examine typical message utilization patterns, it is common to find that most synchronous request-reply interactions involve relatively small messages, require a timely response, and do not require message persistence. On the other hand, one-way fire-and-forget messages tend to be larger, have a longer service-level agreement (SLA) for delivery, and do require fail-safe message persistence.

Because of these differences, it is worthwhile to consider whether the segregation of non-persistent synchronous request-reply traffic from persistent asynchronous and fire-and-forget traffic would be appropriate. For similar reasons, you may want to consider segregating application traffic from administrative traffic.

A Word of Caution Regarding Over-Partitioning

Partitioning involves a certain amount of administrative inconvenience and manual policy enforcement. The conventions for grouping destinations and associating the groups with connection factories need to be documented and shared. JMS administrators need to follow the conventions, and JMS clients need to use the correct connection factories to access the destinations. Before you define partitioning policies, you need to weigh the benefits against the administrative overhead. Convince yourself that message partitioning is (or will be) necessary before setting up the policies, and keep it as simple as you can.

Enterprise Message Service Client Connection Load Distribution

There is a practical limit to the number of client connections that one Enterprise Message Service server can service. Although the limit depends to some extent on message size and peak delivery rate, a rough rule of thumb is that a single EMS server can service between 200 and 500 clients. When you see a design with numbers of clients in this range or above, you should do some performance prototyping with your expected message size and rate to determine the number of clients that are practical in your environment.

The following sections describe patterns for distributing client load across multiple EMS servers under the assumption that the total message volume does not exceed capacity of a single server. If message volume exceeds this limit, you will need to combine these patterns with the partitioning patterns of the previous section.

Client Load Distribution: Topic Pattern

The pattern for distributing client load for topics (Figure 11-5) takes advantage of two EMS features: routing and load balancing. Routing of topics allows messages to be published to one EMS server and delivered to a client connected to another EMS server. Load balancing is a client configuration feature that allows the client to have a list of EMS servers to which it could connect. The client determines which server has the lowest load (either in terms of the number of client connections or volume of message traffic) and connects to that server. For

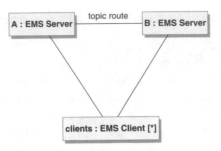

Figure 11-5: *Client Load Distribution: Topic Pattern*

this pattern to work, topics must be defined as `global` (a destination property) and routed among the EMS servers. In addition, the `max_connections` server configuration parameter should be set to limit the number of connections that a server will accept. For configuration details, consult the *TIBCO® Enterprise Message Service™ User's Guide*.[1]

Client Load Distribution: Queue Pattern

Distributing client load with queues is a bit more complex than with topics (Figure 11-6). This is because a queue can only be "owned" by

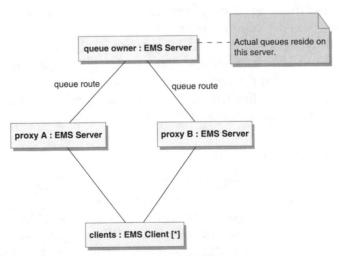

Figure 11-6: *Client Load Distribution: Queue Pattern*

1. Product documentation can be found at http://docs.tibco.com.

one EMS server. Access via other "proxy" EMS servers is possible, but all of the proxies must be routed directly to the server that owns the queue. Scaling client connections then requires creating a number of proxy EMS servers and configuring the client's load balancing parameters to choose among them. In this pattern the queues must be defined as `global` and be routed between the servers. As with the topic pattern, the `max_connections` parameter should be set to limit the number of connections that a given proxy server will accept.

Client Load Distribution: Combined Patterns

The topic and queue patterns for client load distribution can be readily combined, with the proxy servers of the queue pattern serving as the topic EMS servers (Figure 11-7). Note that the routing configuration is different for topics and queues.

Load Distribution in ActiveMatrix Service Bus

There are a number of design patterns that can be used to achieve load distribution with ActiveMatrix Service Bus. The following sections explore these patterns.

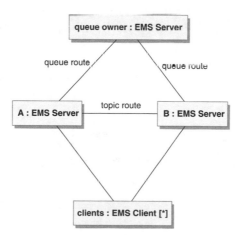

Figure 11-7: *Client Load Distribution: Combined Topic and Queue Patterns*

ActiveMatrix Service Bus Load Distribution Using Virtual Bindings

If you recall, communications between ActiveMatrix Service Bus nodes occurs via an EMS server that has a configuration managed by the ActiveMatrix Administrator. This communications takes place via JMS queues. If you use ActiveMatrix Service Bus Virtualization bindings and deploy a service consumer on one node and a number of service providers on other nodes, the workload will be distributed among the service providers by the queue (Figure 11-8).

ActiveMatrix Service Bus Load Distribution of Promoted Services

Communications between SCA promoted services and the components that implement them occurs via JMS queues if the promoted service and implementing components are deployed on different ActiveMatrix Service Grid nodes. For example, Figure 11-9 shows a `LoadDistribution` composite comprising a `promotedService` and a `serviceProvider`. If the `promotedService` is deployed on one ActiveMatrix Service Grid node and the `serviceProvider` is deployed on another, then the communications between them will occur via a JMS queue whose configuration is managed by the ActiveMatrix Administrator.

The fact that this communications occurs via a JMS queue makes it possible to do load distribution by deploying more than one instance of the service provider on different nodes (Figure 11-10). This approach works regardless of the transport binding used for the promoted

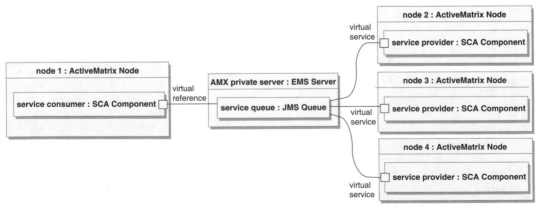

Figure 11-8: *ActiveMatrix Service Bus Load Distribution Using Virtualization Bindings*

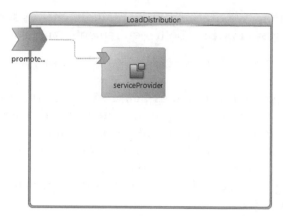

Figure 11-9: *SCA Representation of a Service*

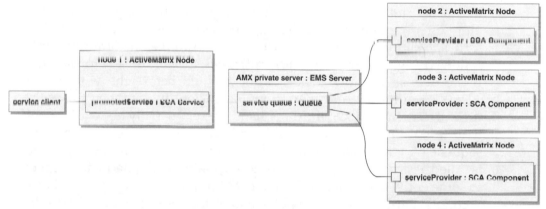

Figure 11-10: *ActiveMatrix Service Bus Load Distribution Using Promoted Services*

service. This means that you can get load distribution for your SOAP over HTTP services without using an IP redirector!

The Sequencing Problem

Load distribution and sequencing (the need to process messages in a particular order) appear to be fundamentally incompatible concepts. Load distribution allows activities to happen in parallel with a non-deterministic relationship between activity completion times, while sequencing requires that the results of processing one message become available before the results of processing the next message. In the following sections we examine these requirements in some detail and then examine ways in which both requirements can be accommodated.

Sequencing

The requirement that certain messages be processed in a specific order is not uncommon, with the required sequence defined by the order in which the messages were originally sent from a single source. Figure 11-11 illustrates this type of requirement. The source sends `input 1` and `input 2` to the service in a particular sequence and expects the corresponding outputs to be delivered to the ultimate destination in the same order.

Limited Sequencing: Partial Ordering

In practice, total sequencing of all messages is rarely required. What is more often required is that the sequencing of messages *pertaining to a particular entity or entities* be preserved. For example, the order of transactions being performed *on a particular bank account* must be preserved: If the deposit that was made is not credited before the withdrawal occurs, then the account may show insufficient funds when the withdrawal is attempted. On the other hand, there is usually no requirement that the transactions associated with one bank account maintain sequencing with respect to any other account. This form of sequencing is called a *partial ordering*. Partial ordering is always defined with respect to some entity or defined collection of entities (in this example, the bank account). Partial ordering enables one of the most powerful and efficient solutions to the sequencing versus load distribution dilemma.

Although partial orderings are commonly found, it should be noted that a partial ordering is often a simplifying assumption with respect to the real-world situation being modeled. For example, in the discussion earlier regarding the bank accounts, the assumption was made that the activity associated with one account was totally independent of the activity associated with other accounts. But what about the transfer of funds from one account to another within the same bank? If one account

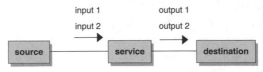

Figure 11-11: *The Sequencing Problem*

is credited before the other is debited, where did the money come from? Such situations require additional logic, often treating the two account operations as a single transaction. In such cases, the work involving the individual account operations cannot be treated independently, which is the underlying assumption for partial ordering. When choosing to do load distribution using partial ordering, the architect must test the validity of the partial ordering assumptions against the actual business requirements before assuming that partial ordering provides a sequencing that satisfies the business requirements.

Patterns That Preserve Total Sequencing

The simplest architecture that preserves sequencing is, of course, an architecture in which there is exactly one component performing each operation and each component performs its operations in first-in-first-out (FIFO) order. This is referred to as a single-threaded design pattern, since each component must be single threaded to get this behavior. Another approach involves the addition of a component that has the role of managing the work of other components to ensure sequencing. This is referred to as a sequence-manager design pattern. These two design patterns are described in the following sections.

Single-Threaded Pattern

All TIBCO messaging services by default preserve message sequencing between a given sender and a given recipient.[2] Given this, what is needed to achieve a single-threaded solution is to ensure that each component in the architecture receives and processes only one message at a time. This solution can only be scaled by increasing the processing speed of each component.

Single-Threaded Solutions with ActiveMatrix BusinessWorks

For ActiveMatrix BusinessWorks, implementing a single-threaded solution requires making the sequencing rule for the process starter a constant expression. Since every message will evaluate to the same

---

2. Exceptions can arise if an EMS message selector is used by the client that returns a message *other* than the first in the topic or queue or if an expiration time for the message was set, and the message was not delivered within the specified time period.

value, and the engine will only process one message at a time for messages with the same value, then all messages will be processed in the order received.

Single-Threaded Solutions with ActiveMatrix Adapter for Database

For a single-threaded operation, the number of publication, subscription, and request-response threads (whichever is appropriate) must be set to exactly 1 for the desired service.

Single-Threaded Solutions with the ActiveMatrix Adapter for Files

As a subscriber, the file adapter is always operating in the asynchronous mode: It will accept files whenever it is asked to. It is not inherently single threaded. To obtain single-threaded behavior for a file adapter subscriber, there can only be one publisher to the file adapter, and that publisher must itself be single threaded. In other words, the sequencing must be preserved at the publishing end.

For a single-threaded publication, the publication service must be set to synchronous mode, and only one instance of the adapter may be running listening to the file source.

Single-Threaded Solutions with Other Adapters

For other adapters, please consult the individual adapter documentation to determine the configuration requirements needed to preserve sequential processing.

Sequence Manager Pattern

If all the messages need to be sequenced and multiple components are required to handle the load, then load distribution requires the introduction of a sequence manager (Figure 11-12). The sequence manager's role is to ensure that inputs are processed in the proper order. The implementation specifics of this design pattern are not given here, as they tend to vary widely from application to application. However, there are some common characteristics of the pattern that warrant a general discussion.

The basic style of the sequence manager pattern is that each time a component is ready to process an input, it asks the sequence manager whether or not the message can be processed. There are several possi-

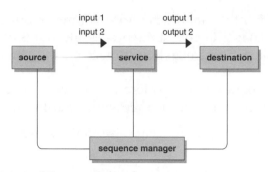

Figure 11-12: *Sequence Manager Pattern*

ble variations, one being where the asking component blocks, waiting for the answer, and then when the manager determines that the message can be processed, it sends the reply. And in another, the requesting component does not block but listens for asynchronous messages from the manager indicating the message can now be processed. In any case, the sequence manager pattern requires a relatively complex protocol between the processing components and the manager, and all processing components must be capable of participating in this protocol. The implication is that all of the participating components must be explicitly designed to use the protocol.

The sequence manager approach requires a significant volume of communications between the processing components and the manager. At a minimum, each processing component must check with the manager before processing a message in order to determine whether processing is permissible at this time, and it must communicate again to report the fact that processing has been completed. The number of coordinating communications can easily exceed (by a factor of 2 or 3) the number of application communications whose processing is being coordinated. The communications latency and the raw performance of the sequence manager itself can become the limiting factor in the overall system throughput.

The design of the sequence managing protocol itself can be complex, particularly when failure and recovery scenarios for individual components and the sequence manager are taken into consideration. It is usually a requirement that the sequence manager itself be fault tolerant, which adds further complexity, and the sequence manager often doubles as an agent for ensuring that the processing of the messages themselves is fault tolerant. Such fault-tolerance requirements require the sequence manager to persist the processing status of each message, which has an additional negative impact on the sequence manager performance.

Taking these issues into consideration, sequence manager solutions are generally practical under the following conditions:

- The total ordering of *all* messages is required and load distribution is required.

- The volume of throughput is low enough that the sequence manager performance and additional coordination traffic volume do not present significant design problems.

- All components requiring sequencing can be customized to use the coordination protocol.

Load Distribution Patterns That Preserve Partial Ordering

As discussed earlier, there are situations in which sequencing is only required with respect to some entity such as a customer, an account, or an order. In these situations, maintaining the processing order with respect to that entity—that is, a partial ordering—is sufficient to satisfy the business requirements. If this is the case, and sufficient information to uniquely identify the entity is carried along with each message, then additional load distribution patterns become available. For each of the following patterns it is assumed that the message carries with it values that uniquely identify the entity in question.

The underlying concept of these patterns is that partial ordering will be preserved with any load distribution mechanism that consistently assigns work associated with a given entity to the same worker component and that has worker components that either process messages in a FIFO manner or distribute the load further using the same distribution rule.

Preserving Partial Order Sequencing in ActiveMatrix BusinessWorks

ActiveMatrix BusinessWorks has an explicit mechanism for maintaining partial order sequencing. In the process starter, there is an optional `sequencing key` whose value is an xpath expression that yields a value. Within an engine, messages for which this value is the same are guaranteed to be processed in the sequence received. In the bank account example, if the xpath expression references the account number, then all messages with a given account number will be processed in the order received. [3]

Two-Tier Load Distribution Preserving Partial Ordering

When you need to preserve partial-order sequencing and distribute load, you can use a two-tier load distribution pattern (Figure 11-13). This pattern requires workers to individually preserve partial ordering of their work. The work is then distributed among the workers by a dispatcher that preserves partial ordering; that is, it always distributes work associated with a specific entity to the same worker.

Implementing Two-Tier Load Distribution Preserving Partial Ordering

The two-tier load distribution pattern that preserves partial ordering can be implemented in ActiveMatrix Service Bus using ActiveMatrix BusinessWorks for the workers (Figure 11-14) and the Mediation implementation type for the dispatcher. The dispatcher uses a Custom Mediation Task that accepts the value identifying the entity (i.e., the result of the xpath expression) and uses a hash function to determine which worker should get this particular request. Each worker has its own JMS queue to which the dispatcher sends the requests. The processes implemented in BusinessWorks similarly use the same xpath expression for their sequencing key.

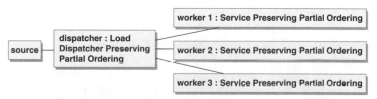

Figure 11-13: *Two-Tier Load Distribution Preserving Partial Ordering*

---

3. At the time of this writing, a sequencing key was not yet available for processes initiated by the Service activity from the Service palette.

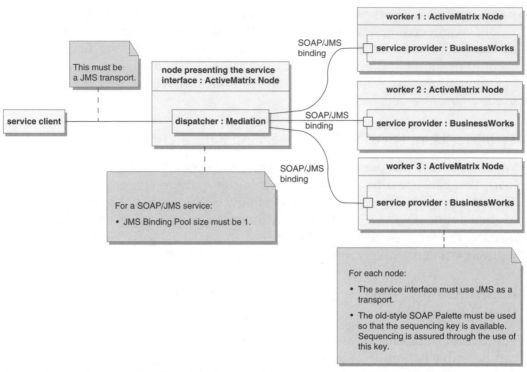

Figure 11-14: *Implementing Two-Tier Load Distribution Preserving Partial Ordering*

For this pattern to work, there are a number of additional constraints that need to be followed. The service client must use a JMS transport, either XML over JMS or SOAP over JMS, to submit requests. The dispatcher must be in its own ActiveMatrix node and the `JMS Binding Pool` size on that node must be set to 1. The ActiveMatrix BusinessWorks processes must use the SOAP Event Source activity from the SOAP palette as the process starter and use the `sequencing key` of this activity.[4]

Summary

When the volume of work exceeds the capacity of a single component, that work must be distributed among multiple workers. One common

---

4. If a sequencing key becomes available on the Service activity of the Service palette, it could be used in this pattern as well.

way is to use a dispatcher to distribute the work among a number of workers. When requests come in via HTTP, it is common to use an IP redirector for this purpose. Another common approach is to use a JMS queue to which multiple workers subscribe.

For performance reasons, the dispatcher approach does not work for JMS messaging servers. When the aggregate volume of traffic exceeds the capacity of a single messaging server, the traffic must be partitioned between two or more servers by assigning different JMS destinations to different servers. The use of JNDI lookups when clients connect to servers makes it easier to migrate destinations from one server to another. It is often a good idea to partition based on the nature of the traffic as well, separating request-reply traffic that does not require persistence from one-way traffic that does.

JMS servers are limited in the number of client connections they can handle. The Enterprise Message Service routing capabilities provide a convenient way to spread client load across multiple servers and still ensure that messages can be delivered to their intended destinations. Different patterns are required for topic and queue routing.

ActiveMatrix Service Bus uses JMS queues for internal communications. This provides additional design patterns for distributing workload. When both service consumers and service providers are deployed within the ActiveMatrix Service Bus, the use of Virtualization bindings allows any number of service providers (workers) to be deployed on different nodes and the load will automatically be distributed among them. Similarly, if a promoted service and the service providers are deployed on different nodes, requests sent to the promoted service will be distributed among the service providers. This even allows SOAP over HTTP requests to be distributed without requiring the use of an IP redirector.

Since load distribution allows work to be processed in parallel, it does not preserve sequencing. In fact, to preserve sequencing you either need to use single-threaded components and sequence-preserving communications or you need to introduce a sequence manager into the design.

In many cases, the actual business requirement is to preserve sequencing with respect to some entity, such as a bank account. In these cases, load can be distributed as long as the dispatcher sends all work associated with a given entity to the same worker. Individual workers may perform work in parallel as long as they do not violate the sequencing requirement.

Chapter 12

Data Management Patterns

Objectives

Data plays a key role in business processes. As such, you need to carefully consider how that data is managed. At the most concrete level, you need to consider where individual pieces of data reside and whether or not they are replicated in different components. Broadly speaking, there are five patterns that can be used for data management:

1. System of Record

2. System of Record with Cached Read-Only Copies

3. Replicated Data with Transactional Update

4. Edit Anywhere Reconcile Later

5. Master Data Management

The following sections explore these patterns. After reading this chapter you will be able to describe these five data management patterns and the pros and cons of each.

System-of-Record Pattern

The simplest data management pattern is to have a single system of record (Figure 12-1). All data resides in a single system, and any component that uses or modifies the data uses that system's data access interface to read or update the information. From a data management perspective, this is the simplest approach. All of the logic needed to maintain the consistency of the data resides in the system of record.

This pattern is rarely found in the enterprise, for a variety of reasons, both conceptual and practical. At the conceptual level, a single system of record may have difficulty scaling: There may be too much data and too much access activity for one system to practically manage all of it. The use of this pattern may also introduce a reliability problem: If the system of record is down, or network problems prevent access to it, no work can be accomplished.

Having said this, there are emerging technologies that are beginning to make this pattern viable. TIBCO ActiveSpaces®, for example, can manage large datasets (in excess of a terabyte) in memory and distributed across many machines with built-in redundancy management (i.e., fault tolerance). These same capabilities are available in TIBCO BusinessEvents.

At the practical level, enterprises tend to acquire commercial off-the-shelf (COTS) software packages to support different parts of their operations. An order management package might be acquired to handles sale orders and a fulfillment package to handle shipments. Each of these packages manages its own set of data, but there is usually some overlap. To the extent that each piece of data resides in only one of these packages, you still have the System-of-Record pattern. However, if there is replicated data, the System-of-Record pattern does not apply. A fulfillment package, for example, typically contains some information about the

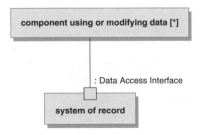

Figure 12-1: *Single System-of-Record Pattern*

orders that are being filled: The order information is replicated. Among enterprise IT systems, there is typically a lot of overlap among the information being maintained by different packages in the enterprise.

For all these reasons, the System-of-Record pattern represents an ideal, the pursuit of which is desirable but may not always be achievable. Nevertheless, the more data that is managed in this manner, the easier it is to manage that data. If you have a choice, and the reliability and performance constraints permit, this is the preferred pattern.

System of Record with Cached Read-Only Copies Pattern

One of the problems with the System-of-Record pattern is that of performance: Frequent access to system-of-record data can potentially overwhelm the capabilities of the system. If a significant portion of the data access is read only, then copies of the data can be cached and read-only access can occur via the cache (Figure 12-2). This pattern retains the notion of the system of record and requires that all updates to the data be applied directly to that system. In this pattern, the system of record notifies the caching components of changes to the data. If this notification occurs as the changes occur and the cache updates as soon as the notification occurs, the cached data will be kept up to date in nearly real time.

A common variation on this pattern is to update the caches with periodic batch updates. This increases the likelihood that the cached data will be out of date and requires more peak-load resources to update the cache than if the changes were communicated in real time as they occur.

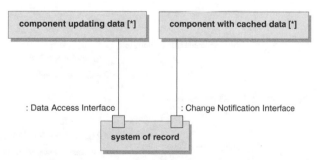

Figure 12-2: *Single System of Record with Cached Read-Only Copies Pattern*

A limiting factor in the use of this pattern is the requirement that components updating the data do so via the system of record. Many applications have interfaces for editing data, and if it is not the designated system of record for that data, you have a problem. These applications typically have their own copy of the data, which they update first. Only then can other systems be notified of the change. They are not designed to participate in the System-of-Record pattern. For these systems, you are forced to use the Edit-Anywhere-Reconcile-Later pattern.

Replicated Data with Transactional Update Pattern

If you cannot identify (and enforce) a single system of record for data, then you end up in a situation in which multiple systems have copies of the data and no one system contains the definitively correct data. In such cases, you need to identify the pattern that you will use to maintain consistency between the various copies of the data.

One pattern for maintaining consistency is to use a distributed transaction to update the replicated copies of the data (Figure 12-3). Here a component wishing to change the data utilizes interfaces provided by the multiple systems to perform a distributed transactional update of all copies. Note that it is possible for the updating component to also be one of the systems that is storing the data.

Even though this may seem like a nice approach, the reality is that most systems are not designed to participate in distributed transactions. This is particularly true for large, COTS software packages.

Even if the individual systems are designed to participate in a distributed transaction, such transactions can introduce a reliability problem: If any of the participants is unavailable or unreachable (due to a

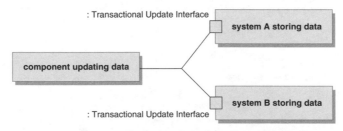

Figure 12-3: *Replicated Data with Transactional Update Pattern*

communications problem), the data update cannot be performed. This likely means that the larger business process, of which the data update is a part, cannot proceed further. For these reasons, the Replicated-Data-with-Transactional-Update pattern is rarely found in practice. More commonly, you will encounter the Edit-Anywhere-Reconcile-Later pattern.

Edit-Anywhere-Reconcile-Later Pattern

A commonly found pattern in enterprise systems is the Edit-Anywhere-Reconcile-Later pattern shown in Figure 12-4. In this pattern, the data can be edited in any system that happens to contain it. At some point the changes that have been made to that system are conveyed to other systems containing the same data so that they can be correspondingly updated.

The problem with this pattern is that if updates are applied to multiple systems at the same time, their corresponding change notifications may cross paths and cause each system to update using the other system's data. This leaves the two systems with inconsistent data. *The longer the delay between the original change and the other system's update, the more likely it is that there will be data inconsistencies.* This is a major argument for real-time notification and update. However, you can never guarantee consistency with this pattern.

This pattern is very common in the enterprise IT environment. The typical COTS software package edits and manages its own data. Other COTS packages do the same. If there is overlap in the data between the two systems, then change notification and update are

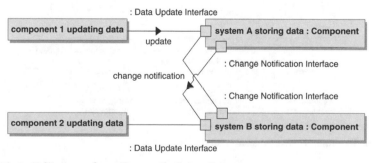

Figure 12-4: *Edit-Anywhere-Reconcile-Later Pattern*

required to maintain consistency. It is common to "instrument" these systems to detect data changes and update other systems.

This most common occurrence of this pattern involves reference data (customer, partner, product, etc.) that typically appears in many systems. This is also information for which inconsistencies may cause significant business problems. To minimize the inconsistencies and resolve them when they occur, the preferred approach to maintaining distributed reference data is to use the Master-Data-Management pattern.

Master-Data-Management Pattern

The problem of minimizing, identifying, and reconciling inconsistencies among multiple sources is particularly important for reference data (e.g., information about customers, products, and partners). As the previous discussion of the Edit-Anywhere-Reconcile-Later pattern made clear, simply publishing the changes and having other systems subscribe to those changes and update their data cannot ever guarantee consistency and does nothing to resolve inconsistencies should they arise.

The Master-Data-Management pattern (Figure 12-5) is commonly employed to address this problem. The master data manager defines

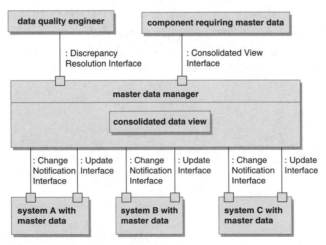

Figure 12-5: *Master-Data-Management Pattern*

a consolidated data model encompassing the reference data distributed across all of the systems. It also defines mappings of each system's subset of master data into that model. This model is used for several purposes.

One of the purposes is to aid in maintaining the data in the individual systems containing master data. Each of these systems has two interfaces: a notification interface that is used to inform the master data manager that changes have occurred, and an update interface that is used to update information when changes occur elsewhere. When a change occurs in one system, the master data manager maps the change into the consolidated data model and then uses the mappings to the other systems to update their data as required. Note that these two interfaces may be add-ons to the underlying systems in the form of service wrappers or adapters.

Another purpose of the consolidated model is to present a comprehensive logical view to components requiring access to master data. This not only provides a uniform view of the data but also isolates the components from the details of the underlying systems. In some variations of the pattern this view is strictly for queries. In other variations it may be used to update the master data as well. It is worth noting that some master data management products can only support a low volume of activity on this interface. As such, the view they present is not well suited to providing this information for use in high-volume transactional business processes.

Despite the presence of the master data manager, discrepancies can still arise, if for no other reason than the data was inconsistent initially. Thus an important aspect of a master data manager is an interface through which discrepancies can be identified and resolved. This is typically a human interface, since in most cases someone will have to investigate in order to determine which of the conflicting values is correct.

The TIBCO Collaborative Information Manager is designed to play the master data manager role in this pattern. It supports the definition of the consolidated data model and its mapping to the subsets found in individual systems. It enables the definition of processes for handling data change and discrepancy resolution. It also provides a query interface that can support a high-volume of activity and thus support transactional business processes that require access to reference data.

Summary

Data is an essential element in all business solutions. A significant architectural concern is determining the design patterns that will be used to ensure that the data being used is correct. If each data element resides in exactly one place (its system of record) then this is easily managed with the System-of-Record pattern. However, this design pattern has difficulty scaling and may have adverse reliability characteristics.

If most of the data access is read only, then the scalability pressure can be relieved by adding cached read-only copies of the data and accessing the data copies. This is the System-of-Record-with-Cached-Read-Only-Copies pattern. This pattern requires mechanisms for recognizing that the system-of-record data has changed and updating the cached copies. Latency in the update may render the cached data obsolete, and for each business process you must consider the consequences of working with obsolete data and select the actual source of data appropriately.

Another approach is to allow data to be replicated in multiple locations and to use distributed transactions to simultaneously update all copies. This is the Replicated-Data-with-Transactional-Update pattern. Although this pattern keeps the data consistent, it may have adverse reliability consequences since an unavailable participant will keep the update from occurring and hence keep the business process requiring the update from proceeding further. Furthermore, few COTS packages (the likely owners of the data) are designed to participate in such transactions.

A commonly found approach is the Edit-Anywhere-Reconcile-Later pattern. Here data can be edited anywhere it is found, and data changes are communicated to other systems that use these notifications to update their local copies of the data. This pattern typically arises when multiple COTS packages are used and there is overlap in the data that they maintain. Unfortunately, this pattern can never guarantee consistency of the data.

An approach to dealing with the data inconsistency arising from the Edit-Anywhere-Reconcile-Later pattern is to introduce a master data manager. This is the Master-Data-Management pattern. The manager defines a unified data model encompassing the data from the various systems. It receives notifications when the data in the underlying systems changes and updates the other systems accordingly. It also presents interfaces that expose the unified view of the data and allow components to read and possibly update the data using that view. Finally, it provides interfaces through which the inevitable data discrepancies can be viewed and resolved.

Chapter 13

Composites

Objectives

Many solution components—whether services or entire solutions—are compositions of components, *composites* for short. This chapter examines a number of architectural choices that you will encounter when building composites. After reading this chapter you will be able to:

- Describe the concept of a composite and the difference between a composite service and a composite application.
- Identify and select appropriate composite implementation technologies.
- Identify and select appropriate composite service design pattern.
- Identify and select appropriate composition and management styles.
- Describe the process for architecting a composition.

What Is a Composite?

A composite is an assembly of components that provides a specified behavior. There are several aspects of a composite that the architect needs to consider:

- Behavior: What is the purpose of the composite and what behavior does it need to exhibit in order to achieve that purpose?

- Wiring: What are the components and how are they logically wired together to form the composite?

- Behavior management: How are the behaviors of the individual components combined to create the required behavior of the composite?

- Implementation: How is the logical structure of the composite implemented, particularly the wiring between the components?

Specifying a Composite

A composite is expected to play a specific role in a larger design. This is pretty obvious for a composite that happens to be a service (i.e., a composite service), but it is also true of a composite application or solution. As a result, each composite must be specified in the manner described in Chapter 6. Note that even though the chapter describes the specification in terms of services, it applies to composite applications as well. The only real difference is that for composite applications, the high-level descriptions (the one-line description and abstract) will likely be used during the budgetary process for the project rather than as a means of identifying a service suitable for some particular use. [1]

The specification defines the "black box" view of the composite, including its interfaces, its observable behavior and state, and its intended utilization scenarios. In architecting the composite, the design challenge is to ensure that the constituent parts, when wired together, actually conform to the specification.

In the following sections, the Payment Manager specification from Chapter 6 will be used as the composite example.

Architecting a Composite

A composite architecture involves the same three elements as any architecture: an architecture pattern, one or more process descriptions, and a mapping of the processes onto the architecture pattern.

---

1. For a discussion of solution and application requirements and specification, see Chapter 8: "The Artifice of Requirements" in Paul C. Brown, *Implementing SOA: Total Architecture in Practice*, Boston: Addison-Wesley (2008).

Composite Architecture Pattern

The architecture pattern for the composite defines the components of the composite and the manner in which the interfaces of those components are wired together. The composite wiring defines the architecture pattern of the composite. It identifies the components, their interfaces, and the communications channels between the interfaces.

Figure 13-1 shows the architecture pattern for the Payment Manager. This pattern has two primary components: a Payment Manager Composite and an Operational Data Store (ODS). In this design, the ODS is not shown as part of the Payment Manager Composite. This is typical when the physical instance of the database to be used is not

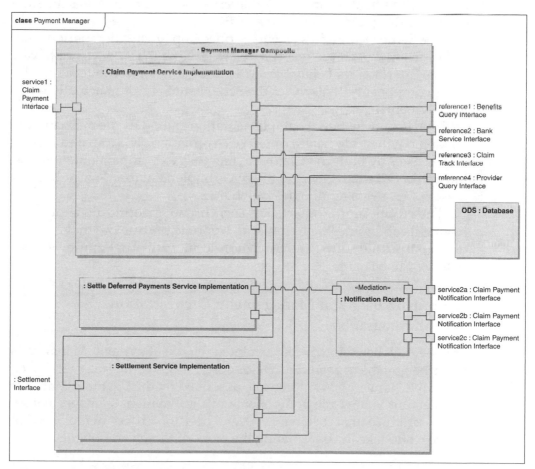

Figure 13-1: *Payment Manager Architecture Pattern*

dedicated to the component. The fact that the database is not part of the composite actually reflects a change to the specification for the Payment Manager, as it introduces an external component upon which the Payment Manager depends. The logical and physical design of the ODS is part of the Payment Manager, but its implementation depends upon a database that is operated independent of the Payment Manager.

The Payment Manager Composite comprises four components: the Claim Payment Service Implementation, the Settle Deferred Payments Implementation, the Settlement Service Implementation, and the Notification Router.

The Claim Payment Service Implementation is the component that handles invocations of the Claim Payment Interface. For immediate payments it manages the entire process, utilizing the Settlement Service to make the actual payments. For deferred payments, it leaves the state of the pending settlements in the ODS.

The Settle Deferred Payments Service Implementation periodically settles payments that have been deferred. Note that it does not have a service interface: Its behavior is driven by timers, not invocations by other components. It also uses the Settlement Service to actually make the payments.

The Settlement Service Implementation embodies the mechanics of making payments to health care service providers. It is a shared service that is used by both the Claim Payment Service Implementation and the Settle Deferred Payments Service Implementation, since both of these components require this capability.

The Notification Router takes asynchronous notifications of claim payments and routes them to the appropriate party. Note that as additional parties are added at the business level, additional routing entries will need to be made.

Composite Behavior Management: Orchestration and Choreography

The overall behavior to be exhibited by the Payment Manager is described by the triggered behavior descriptions contained in its specification (Chapter 6). What must be described by the Payment Manager architecture is how the components of the Payment Manager collectively produce that behavior. A key decision to be made is what approach to take in coordinating the work of these components.

Broadly speaking, you have a choice between two approaches for coordination: orchestration or choreography.[2] With orchestration, one of the components managers the delivery of the overall behavior: It directs the other components, telling them specifically what actions to take and when to take them. Figure 13-2 illustrates the concept, with the service playing the role of the process manager. The service directs each of the participants to perform their tasks, ensures that they complete successfully, and returns the response to the original request. The service is in charge of the overall composite behavior.

Although the orchestration example shows participants A and B to be part of the composite, the same pattern applies when they are not. The only difference is in the specification of the composite. If the participants are external to the composite, then they will be shown in the composite specification, as will the service's interactions with them. If they are part of the composite, then they will not be indicated in the specification, only in the service architecture document.

With choreography, there is no overall process manager. Instead, the wiring of the components, combined with the behavioral specification of

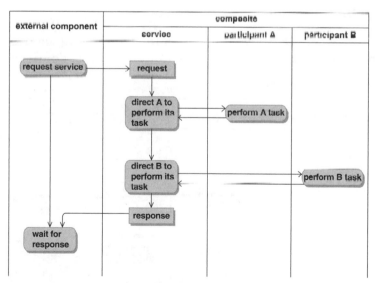

Figure 13-2: *Example of the Orchestration Design Pattern*

2. Stephen A. White and Derek Miers, *BPMN Modeling and Reference Guide: Understanding and Using BPMN*, Lighthouse Point, FL: Future Strategies Inc. (2008), pp. 29–31.

each component, delivers the desired behavior. Figure 13-3 illustrates this behavior. Here the service accepts the request, directs participant A to perform task A, and then has no further involvement. Participant A performs its task, directs participant B to perform task B, and then has no further involvement. Participant B performs its task and returns the result to the original requestor. No one component is in charge of the composite behavior.

Choreography gets more complex when asynchronous events are involved (Figure 13-4). Here the execution of the overall process relies on the occurrence of some asynchronous event, such as the expiration of a timer or the occurrence of another interaction.

As with orchestration, the participants in the choreography pattern may or may not be part of the composite. The only difference is whether these participants appear in the service specification or only in the service architecture.

For the Payment Manager Composite, immediate payments are orchestrated, but the deferred payments use choreography with asynchronous events.

Composite Processes

For a composite, the processes it executes are the triggered behavior mappings documented in the composite specification. For the Payment

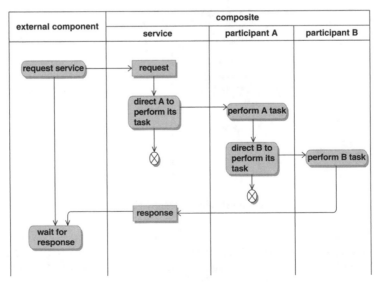

Figure 13-3: *Example of the Choreography Design Pattern*

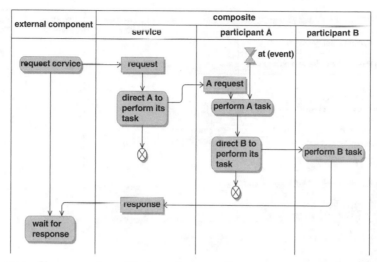

Figure 13-4: *Choreography with Asynchronous Events*

Manager, these are the Deferred Payment Behavior (Figure 6-11), the Settle Deferred Payments Behavior (Figure 6-12), and the Immediate Payment Behavior (Figure 6-13). Be sure to include the exception handling scenarios in your design!

Composite Mappings

To complete the architecture of the composite, each of the triggered behaviors defined in the composite specification needs to be mapped onto the components of the composite. Figure 13-5 shows the mapping of the Deferred Payment Process onto the composite. Note that while all of the activity here is orchestrated, this is not the end of the payment process: Settle Deferred Payments must also execute before the health care service provider is actually paid.

The mapping of the Settle Deferred Payments Process (the completion of the health care service provider payment) onto the composite is shown in Figure 13-6. Note that the beginning of the process is triggered by the expiration of a timer, not some interaction with another component. The mechanics of the actual payment have been factored out into a Settlement Service so that they can be reused in the immediate payment scenario.

The mapping of the Immediate Payment Process onto the composite is shown in Figure 13-7. Note that the Settlement Service is again used for the actual mechanics of making the payment.

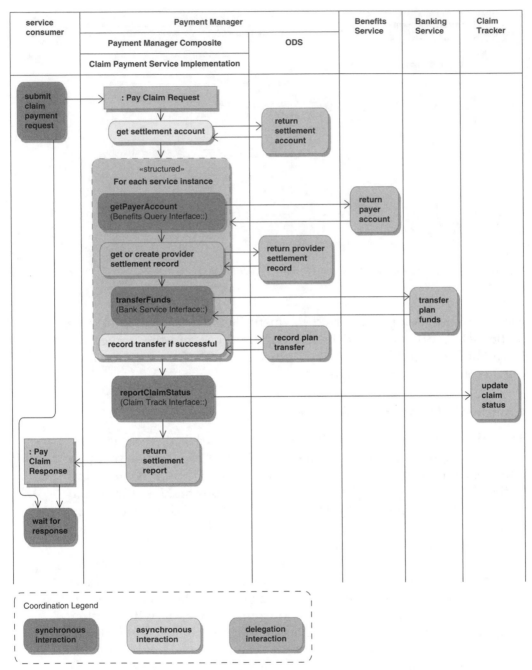

Figure 13-5: *Deferred Payment Composite Mapping*

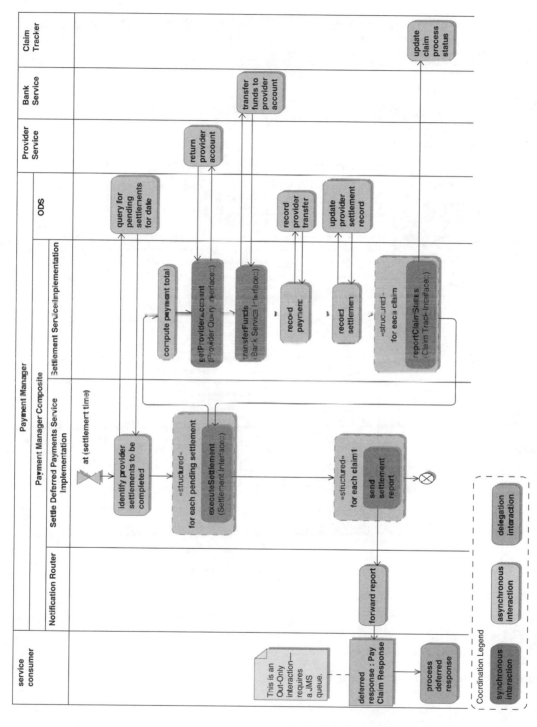

Figure 13-6: *Settle Deferred Payments Process Mapping*

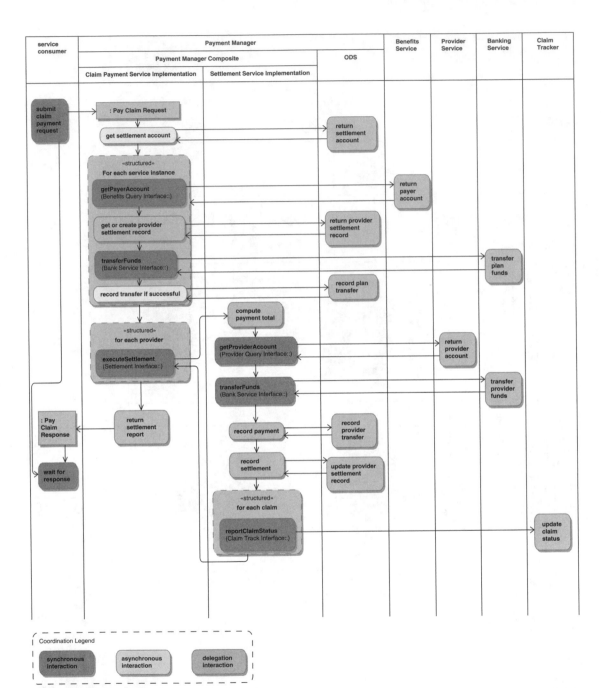

Figure 13-7: *Immediate Payment Composite Mapping*

Completing the Component Specifications

Once the architecture of the composite has been defined, the specifications for the individual components need to be defined. If any of the components are intended to be reusable services, then a separate specification document must be created for each of these. For non-reusable components, their specification information can simply be included in the architecture document for the composite. Note that the same set of information is required in either case.

The Process of Architecting a Composite

The process of architecting a composite tends to be somewhat iterative in nature. It begins by defining a trial set of components, defining the composite architecture pattern, and selecting a behavioral management style. Then, one by one, the triggered behavior (from the composite specification) is mapped onto the components. The process of doing the mapping will lead to refinements in the components and the architecture pattern.

Once all of the processes have been mapped (be sure to map the exception scenarios), the individual component specifications can be completed.

Composite Services and Applications

The term *composite service* has two similar but distinct meanings, both of which are valid. In one, the service itself is a composite of components as discussed earlier in the chapter. In the other, the service utilizes other services that are not components of the "composite service." The distinction becomes apparent when you look at the specification for the service. When the underlying services are, themselves, part of the composite service, they do not appear in the service specification: They are part of the service architecture. When the underlying services are independent, then they appear in the service specification as part of the service context: Their interfaces appear as referenced interfaces, and the triggered behavior mappings show their participation in the behavior of the composite service.

A composite application is an application comprising multiple components. In other words, it is a distributed application. The performance of application work requires the coordinated participation of its constituent components.

The distinction between a composite application and a composite service is primarily one of intended use. A composite service provides functionality that is intended to be invoked by other system components in order to become part of an application or business process. Composite applications, on the other hand, provide usable functionality for users. This functionality might be in the form of a tool (e.g., an analytics engine such as TIBCO Spotfire®) or it might be an entire business process.

Information Retrieval Design Patterns

Some composite services gather information from multiple sources and return it to the service consumer. There are two design patterns that can be used for this purpose: Cascading Control and Cached Information.

Cascading Control Pattern

In the Cascading Control Pattern, when the composite service is invoked it turns around and makes calls on the underlying services to retrieve the required information (Figure 13-8). This is probably the first pattern that comes to mind when you are conceptualizing a composite service. But be aware of the performance implications. Every invocation of the composite service requires invocations of the underlying services, and the composite's response time depends on the performance of the underlying services.

Cached Information Pattern

An alternative to the Cascading Control Pattern is the Cached Information Pattern (Figure 13-9). In this pattern, rather than having the composite service retrieve information from its underlying services, the underlying services instead notify the composite when information

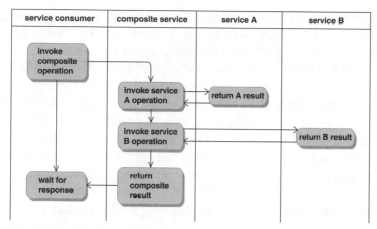

Figure 13-8: *Cascading Control Pattern*

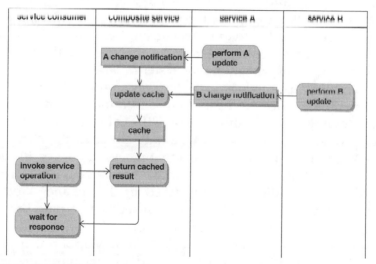

Figure 13-9: *Cached Information Pattern*

changes. The composite then caches this information so that it is available locally when a service client asks for it.

Note that in the Cached Information Pattern, the nature of the underlying service interfaces is different than in the Cascading Control Pattern. For cascading control, the underlying services present request-reply interfaces (typically synchronous), while for cached information they present notification interfaces. The choice of pattern impacts the interface design of the underlying services.

The Cached Information Pattern is used by fedex.com for package status reporting. Underlying systems, which are responsible for managing the progression of packages from origin to destination, publish notifications of package status changes. A composite service at fedex.com, using the Cached Information Pattern, subscribes to those notifications and caches the package status information. When a customer goes to fedex.com and wants to know the status of a package, the composite service uses a local lookup from its cache rather than an interaction with a back-end system to provide the package status.

Lookup and Cross Reference

A common type of information retrieval is a lookup: A piece of data is used as a key for looking up a corresponding piece of information. You might use a currency to look up the current exchange rate, or use the identifier of an entity in one system to locate the corresponding identifier for the same entity in a different system.

Frequent lookups can lead to performance problems, particularly if the information resides on disk. The use of a memory-resident cache can considerably speed up this process. TIBCO BusinessWorks™ Smart-Mapper provides the ability to cache data either in the ActiveMatrix BusinessWorks instance or in a separate process that is readily accessible by multiple BusinessWorks instances. Lookups are performed by BusinessWorks activities that are placed in the BusinessWorks processes that require the data. The cache is kept up to date by actively monitoring the underlying reference information and updating the cache when it changes. BusinessWorks™ SmartMapper also provides BusinessWorks activities that can create and manage the cross-reference information.

ActiveSpaces™ is also well suited for this task. The TIBCO Active-Matrix BusinessWorks™ Plug-in for ActiveSpaces Software makes it easy to use the ActiveSpaces capabilities in a BusinessWorks process.

TIBCO ActiveMatrix Composite Implementation

Defining the Composite

Figure 13-10 shows the Payment Manager composite represented in SCA notation. Creating this representation in TIBCO Business Studio is the first step toward implementing the composite in the TIBCO ActiveMatrix platform.

Selecting Implementation Types

The next step is to choose the implementation type for each component (Figure 13-11). In this case, ActiveMatrix BusinessWorks is selected for each of the three service implementations and a Mediation implementation type for the Notification Router.

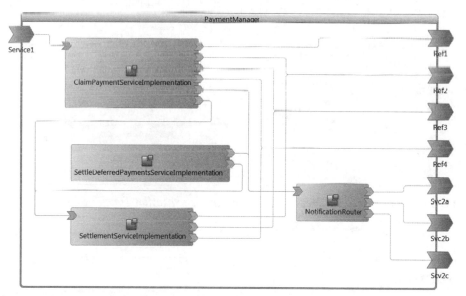

Figure 13-10: *SCA Representation of the Payment Manager Composite*

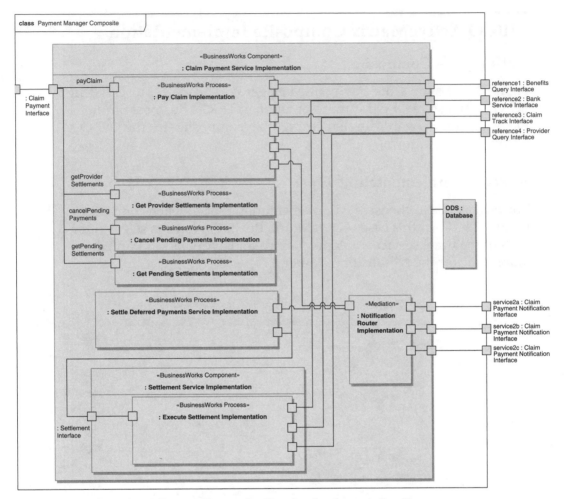

Figure 13-11: *Payment Manager Composite Showing Implementation Types*

Summary

A composite is a collection of components wired together for some purpose. The specification for the composite indicates the externally observable structure and behavior of the composite, while its architecture defines how that structure and behavior are actually provided.

Architecting a composite is very much like architecting any other component. You determine the components you want as part of their interfaces and define the architecture pattern describing how they are

composed and wired together. You map the observable process definitions from the composite's specification onto the architecture pattern for the composite. This defines the required behavior for each of
the individual components. You then complete the specifications for
the individual components in preparation for their design and
implementation.

Composite services are composites that present functionality for
use in larger composites—they are services. Composite applications
are distributed applications that present functionality to support users
either in the form of tools (e.g., an analytics tool) or in the form of business processes.

Some composite services are used to gather data from multiple
sources. There are two design patterns that can be used for this purpose: the Cascading Control Pattern and the Cached Information
Pattern. Cascading control uses request-reply interfaces on the underlying services to retrieve the information when it is required. The
cached information pattern relies on notification interfaces on the
underlying systems that publish changes to the required information,
which is then cached in the composite service.

The BusinessWorks SmartMapper uses the Cached Information
Pattern to efficiently provide lookup and cross-reference information
to ActiveMatrix BusinessWorks processes. It also provides the ability
for BusinessWorks processes to actively manage the underlying reference data.

Part IV

Advanced Topics

Chapter 14

Benchmarking

Objectives

A benchmark is a standard against which things can be compared. The term is also used to refer to a standardized test or experiment with results, that when the test is applied to different systems, can be used to compare those systems.

In the development environment, these two meanings are practically inseparable. The benchmark results (i.e., the standard) can only be understood by understanding both the test that produced the results and the configuration of the system under test. Two sets of results from two different systems cannot be fairly compared unless the same test was used and the configurations of both systems are clearly understood. In fact, if there isn't enough information for you to reproduce the test results, there isn't enough information for you to understand and apply those results to your situation!

This chapter discusses the conduct of benchmark tests and documentation that is required for the test results to be meaningful to other people. After reading this chapter, you will be able to

- Describe how a benchmark test should be conducted.
- Describe how benchmark tests results should be documented.
- Describe how to benchmark complex components.
- Identify the resource with a limitation that determines a component's capacity.

Misleading Results

The Bathtub Test

Imagine wanting to benchmark the rate at which you can consume water. In designing the test, you want to ensure that your measurement is not adversely impacted by a limitation in the available supply of water. Consequently, you design the test to drink from a high-pressure fire hose.

There's no question here that the hose can supply water at a faster rate than you can drink, but is this a fair test of capacity? When you run the test, you find yourself gasping for air and trying to keep from drowning, activities that certainly detract from your optimal consumption of water. The test is, somehow, flawed, at least with respect to measuring your drinking capacity.

Although this example is a bit absurd, it serves to illustrate a common flaw in what are purported to be capacity measurement tests. In message-based systems, these often take the form of loading up a message queue with millions of messages, turning on the message consumer, and looking at the rate at which the consumer actually processes the messages. This is often referred to as the bathtub test and, in reality, it is not a capacity measurement at all but rather an overload test. Let's see why.

Figure 14-1 shows a typical performance curve for a component. The horizontal axis shows the steady-state rate at which inputs are presented to the component, and the vertical axis shows the steady-state rate at which the component completes the work, here characterized as

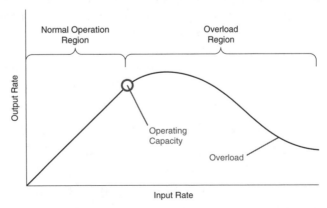

Figure 14-1: *Typical Performance Curve*

the production of an output. Over some range of input rates, the output rate exactly tracks the input rate: The component is performing work at the same rate at which it is being presented with work.

As the input rate increases you eventually reach a point beyond which the component can no longer keep up with the increasing demand. This is the point that defines the operating capacity of the component.

Beyond the operating capacity, you are in the overload region and the behavior of the component is different. Inputs are arriving faster than they are being processed, and either they are being lost altogether or they are piling up in a buffer. If they are piling up in a buffer, that buffer has a finite capacity, and when you reach that capacity something bad is going to happen. Therefore, extended operation in this region is inherently unstable.

But there are consequences for operating in the overload region even before it becomes unstable. Resources that would otherwise be applied to doing useful work in the component are now being dedicated to managing the buffer. Initially, this may just manifest itself as a falling-off of output rate, but as the input rate increases further, the output rate levels off and then begins to decline. It typically declines to some level substantially below the nominal operating capacity of the component.

The bathtub test (or fire hose test) immediately pushes the component well into the overload region. Even though it may be useful in determining whether a component is well behaved (at least for some period of time) when overloaded, it does not give you any true indication of the component's operating capacity.

Disabling Features

Another common source of misleading results is running the benchmark test on a component that is not configured as it would be in production. Some common examples are

- Using asynchronous disk writes for benchmarking when synchronous interactions will be used in production
- Running without security policies in place when security policies will be used in production
- Running without transaction management when transactions will be used in production
- Running without logging when logging will be used in production

Test Harness Design

Inappropriate design of test harnesses can also lead to misleading results. For example, it is common to use a Java sleep() operation to introduce a delay in a loop that sends inputs to the component under test. However, this operation generally takes a millisecond or longer to execute, even if the specified time delay is zero. Thus the maximum rate at which this loop can generate inputs is less than 1,000 per second.

Gathering the data can also have an impact on the measured test results. The techniques used for data capture and recording require careful consideration. If these activities are being performed on the machine upon which the component under test is running, they will consume machine resources and thus reduce the apparent capacity of the component.

Determining Operating Capacity

In order to effectively determine the operating capacity of a component, you need a test setup similar to that shown in Figure 14-2. In addition to the system under test, this test setup has three essential ingredients:

1. A mechanism for supplying inputs at a controlled rate
2. A mechanism for measuring the actual input rate
3. A mechanism for measuring the work completion rate (typically a result or output)

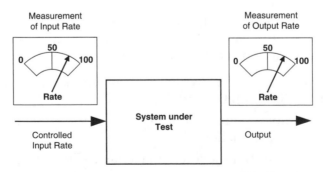

Figure 14-2: *Test Setup for Determining Operating Capacity*

Given such a test setup, the operating capacity is determined as follows:

1. Set the input rate.
2. Wait for the output rate to stabilize. Note that under some overload conditions, stabilization may never occur.
3. Record the input and output rates.

This sequence is repeated for various input rates until you are able to construct a performance curve similar to that of Figure 14-1. It will probably require some experimentation to determine the operating capacity for the set of conditions being tested. You may want to do further experimentation with tuning and operating parameters of the system under test to determine their impact on operating capacity.

Documenting the Test Design

In order for the test results to be interpreted appropriately, the reader needs to understand how the test was set up and executed. A good litmus test here is that there needs to be enough information for the reader to reproduce the test result. Only with this degree of information will the reader be able to understand the results and their implications.

The basics of documenting the test design are the same as for a solution: You need to document the overall architecture and then supply additional details as required.

Test Harness Architecture Pattern

Documenting the architecture begins with the architecture pattern (Figure 14-3). In all cases, the component under test is deployed on a machine (or virtual environment) whose resources are fully dedicated to that component. Typically there is only one instance of the component on one machine, and its capabilities are the focus of the test. If the focus of the benchmark is on distributing load across multiple instances of the component under test, the architecture pattern should clearly indicate both the component deployment and the load distribution mechanism being employed.

Test harnesses require careful consideration: You want to make sure that the limitations you ultimately measure are those of the component

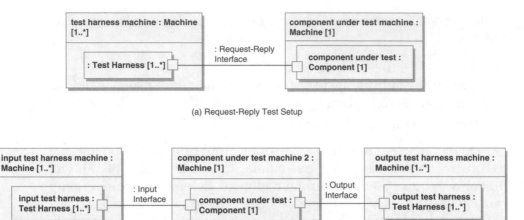

(a) Request-Reply Test Setup

(b) Straight-through Processing Test Setup

Figure 14-3: *Test Design Architecture Pattern Examples*

under test and not the test harness. Test harnesses should be run in their own dedicated machines. To fully load the component under test or to handle the volume of output, multiple instances of the test harnesses may be required, possibly running on multiple machines.

Communications infrastructure needs to be considered as well, particularly if the component you are testing is a messaging server. The Enterprise Message Service, when run on an appropriate platform, can saturate 100 Mbit and 1 Gbit networks—and possibly even 10 Gbit networks.

The details of the test environment must also be documented. Here you must use some discretion as to the necessary level of detail, but the governing criteria should be whether the detailed item might impact the test results. Table 14-1 shows a typical set of details for the machine on which the component under test is being run. Table 14-2 shows the setup for the machine running the test harness, and Table 14-3 shows the network details.

Test Harness Process Mapping

For most tests, the process design is trivial: Send a request, get a reply. There is little benefit in documenting the process by itself, and so attention immediately turns to the mapping of the process onto the architecture pattern. Figure 14-4 shows such a mapping for a simple request-reply test scenario.

Table 14-1: *Component under Test (Repeat for Each Machine)*

Processor	
CPU Type	X86
Number of CPUs	1
Cores/CPU	2
Clock Speed	2.66 GHZ
Memory	3 GB
Network Interface Card	
Bandwidth (Mbit/second)	1,000
Half/Full Duplex	Full
Disk	
Number of Spindles	1
RPM	10,000
Average Seek Time (ms)	4.7
RAID Configuration	N/A
Access Bandwidth	50 MB/second
FT RAM Buffer	No

Table 14-2: *Test Harness (Repeat for Each Machine)*

Processor	
CPU Type	X86
Number of CPUs	1
Cores/CPU	?
Clock Speed	2.66 GHZ
Memory	3 GB
Network Interface Card	
Bandwidth (Mbit/second)	1,000
Half/Full Duplex	Full
Disk	
Number of Spindles	1
RPM	10,000
Average Seek Time (ms)	4.7
RAID Configuration	N/A
Access Bandwidth	50 MB/second
FT RAM Buffer	No

Table 14-3: *Network Configuration*

Network	
Backbone Bandwidth	1 Gbit

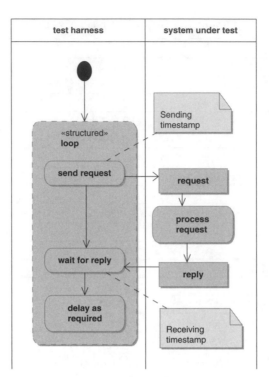

Figure 14-4: *Simple Test Process Mapping*

Documenting the mapping is important, as it provides a means for identifying limitations in the test setup. In this case, there are at least several potential issues with this test setup. One issue is that there is communications latency after sending the request and before receiving the reply, and this latency will be part of the measurement. Another issue is that after the reply has been received it may take some time before another request is sent. For example, using a `sleep()` call in Java for the delay (which is required to control the request rate) will introduce a measurable delay even if the argument to the call is zero. This limits the rate at which the test harness is capable of sending requests, and it may limit it to a rate that is less than the operating capacity of the component under test. Yet another issue might be the time it takes for the test harness to record the measurements, which may further limit the rate at which the harness sends requests.

For all these reasons, you may want to alter the design of the test harness to ensure that it can fully load the system under test. One

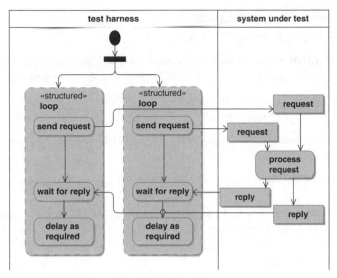

Figure 14-5: *Two-threaded Test Harness Mapping*

approach might be to use a multi-threaded design for the test harness (Figure 14-5). Alternatively, you may want to deploy multiple instances of the test harness, potentially on multiple machines. However, regardless of the approach taken, it is incumbent on the test designer to document the design and configuration of the test harness so that the reader of the test results is in a position to evaluate the harness design and its likely impact on the test results.

Experimental Parameters

Often there are parameters that can be varied in the experiment. The variables that are important depend on the nature of the components and the nature of the tests being performed. In conducting your benchmarks, you will have to determine which parameters are important for your benchmarks. Some common examples include

- Test harness parameters
  - Degree of parallelism required to fully load the component (e.g., number of test harnesses or number of threads in each test harness)
  - Size of data set

- Component under test parameters
  - Number of threads in the component
  - The number of concurrent sessions allowed (e.g., the value of the ActiveMatrix BusinessWorks MaxJobs parameter)
  - Constraints on the number of activities that can occur in parallel (e.g., the sequencing key in ActiveMatrix BusinessWorks)
  - Sizes of buffers (e.g., prefetch settings on Enterprise Message Service clients)
  - The number of connections allowed

Some of these parameters will remain the same for all test runs, while others you will intentionally vary to determine their impact on the component's performance. For each test run, the values of all parameters must be documented.

Test Results

The final aspect of the test that must be documented is the data that was collected (Figure 14-6). This data includes the test parameter settings and all of the measurements that were made. Once again, decisions have to be made about what to measure, and the criteria should be things that might impact the test results. Typical measurements include (in addition to input and output rates) calculated data rates, latency, CPU utilization, memory utilization, disk access rate, disk bandwidth utilization, and network bandwidth utilization. Note that the disk and network numbers are generally calculations based on other measurements and settings (input rate, message size) and an understanding of component behavior.

To make the data more useful, it is a good idea to provide the data in graphical form as well. Figure 14-7 shows the basic input versus output rate graph. Note the falloff of the output rate as the input rate rises. This is a clear indication that the operating capacity has been identified, assuming that the appropriate tuning adjustments have already been done.

Experimental Paramters

Message Size (KB)	5
Worker Threads	10

Test Data

Input Message Rate (messages/sec)	Input Data Rate (KB/sec)	Output Message Rate (messages/sec)	Output Data Rate (KB/sec)	Latency (ms)	CPU Utilization (% of available CPU)	RAM Utilization (MB)	Disk Access Rate (accesses/sec)	Disk Bandwidth Utilization (MB/sec)	Network Bandwidth Utilization (KB/sec)
1	5	1	5	2	0%	150	3	0	10
2	10	2	10	2	0%	150	6	0	20
5	25	5	25	3	0%	150	15	0	50
10	50	10	50	3	1%	151	30	0	100
20	100	20	100	4	1%	151	60	0	200
50	250	50	250	4	3%	153	150	1	500
100	500	100	500	5	5%	155	300	2	1,000
200	1,000	200	1,000	5	10%	160	600	3	2,000
500	2,500	500	2,500	6	25%	175	1,500	8	5,000
1,000	5,000	1,000	5,000	6	50%	200	3,000	15	10,000
2,000	10,000	1,250	6,250	10	100%	250	3,750	19	16,250
5,000	25,000	800	4,000	38	100%	400	2,400	12	29,000
10,000	50,000	500	2,500	120	100%	650	1,500	8	52,500
20,000	100,000	350	1,750	343	100%	1,150	1,050	5	101,750
25,000	125,000	1	5	150 000	100%	1,400	3	0	125,005

Figure 14-6: *Test Data Example*

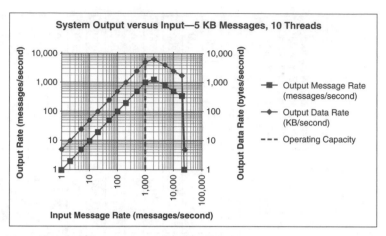

Figure 14-7: *Graph of Input versus Output Rates*

Benchmarking Complex Components

Benchmarking complex components is, well, complex! Such components typically perform multiple activities, and these activities can be of different types. Complicating things further, different types of activities may consume different levels of resources. Components that manage processes fall into this category, with ActiveMatrix BusinessWorks and TIBCO ActiveMatrix® BPM being common examples.

What makes the benchmarking of these components complex is that there are virtually an infinite number of ways in which the activities can be combined into processes that are then executed by the components. The likelihood that your process will be similar enough to a given benchmark process for those benchmark results to be useful is very small. So how do you go about establishing useful benchmarks for components like these?

The answer is to obtain data about individual aspects of component behavior that you can then combine analytically to get some reasonable estimate of your design's performance. So what data do you need? In general, you need three kinds:

1. Overhead benchmarks
2. Individual activity benchmarks
3. Common scenario benchmarks

Overhead Benchmarks

Simply interacting with a component has some overhead associated with it. The idea of overhead benchmarks is simply to understand what this overhead is. To make such measurements, you want to identify the simplest (lightest weight) activities that the component is capable of doing. For ActiveMatrix BusinessWorks, this might simply be returning an inbound message. For ActiveMatrix® BPM, this might be starting a trivial business process (one with one activity and no data) or performing an activity that does no work.

The measurements you get from overhead tests will give you an upper bound on what is possible. If you find the maximum rate at which ActiveMatrix BusinessWorks can start a trivial process that just returns a result, adding work to that process can only lower the rate. However, understanding that maximum rate in itself gives you important information. If your solution requires a particular piece of work to be done at a particular rate and that rate exceeds (or even comes close to) the maximum for a BusinessWorks instance, you know immediately that it will take multiple instances of BusinessWorks to do the job.

When setting up overhead benchmarks, the first thing you need to do is identify the basic scenarios to be tested. For ActiveMatrix BusinessWorks, this might be the running of a trivial process. For ActiveMatrix BPM, this might be the starting of a trivial process and the execution of a trivial activity. To aid you in identifying the scenarios, think about the way in which the component will interact with the other solution components, and then ask yourself what patterns are involved and what constitutes a "minimal" version of each scenario. When identifying the scenarios, take the interaction mechanism into account: A SOAP over HTTP interaction will have different overhead than a SOAP over JMS interaction.

Once you have identified the relevant scenarios, you then run a baseline performance test for each scenario as described in the previous section. Keep data structures minimal in size.

After the baseline has been established, identify the parameters that might affect the result. These may be test harness parameters (e.g., message size) or component parameters (e.g., the number of worker threads in ActiveMatrix BusinessWorks). For each of the parameters, define a range of values to be tested. Then, for each parameter value, repeat the entire baseline performance test.

Individual Activity Benchmarks

Once the baseline overhead has been established, you can begin to benchmark individual activities. For each activity of interest, add the activity to one of the test scenarios for which you have a baseline overhead benchmark. Repeat the baseline test with the activity added, with an initial focus on minimizing the amount of work done in the activity. The difference between the baseline results and this set of results gives you the overhead of executing the activity you are testing.

Once the overhead for the activity has been established, you can identify the parameters that might impact its execution. In addition to those mentioned before (test harness and component parameters), you probably want to look at the possible configurations of the activity itself. For example, if you are looking at the data transformation activity in ActiveMatrix BusinessWorks, you might want to consider varying the size of the data structure, the complexity of the data structure, and the complexity of the transformation. To keep this from becoming an open-ended experiment, you need to have some idea of how this activity will be used in your solution and make sure that your experiments reflect the nature of that use.

As with the overhead measurements, once you have identified the relevant parameters, you want to repeat the baseline test for each new parameter setting. This set of results will help you understand the resource requirements for the activity.

Be cautious in your evaluation of activities that rely on other components. Interactions with the file system, databases, and messaging services will depend as much on the performance of those components as they will on the component you are trying to benchmark. Make sure you understand and account for those external components.

Benchmark Common Scenarios in which Activities Interact

Over time you will come to recognize certain component usage patterns that arise repeatedly in your design. For example, you might have many cases in which a front-end system makes a SOAP over JMS call to a service implemented in ActiveMatrix BusinessWorks, and this service does a database lookup and returns the results. When you look at the BusinessWorks design, you have a Service that invokes a process containing a JDBC activity with data transformations before and after the JDBC activity. Since this is a common pattern appearing in many solutions, it makes sense to invest in benchmarking its performance.

This will provide the data you need to do capacity planning when this pattern is employed.

Interpreting Benchmark Results

So you are running a benchmark test and, looking at the input and output rates, you identify what appears to be the operating capacity. You'd like to know, first of all, that the component is truly running at its maximum capacity and what resource limitation ultimately determined that capacity. This section provides you with some information you can use to help answer these questions.

When you graph resource utilization data against input rate, the resulting curves give you the information you need to determine which resource is the limiting factor in performance. The following sections show how you can use these curves to identify the resource limitations listed here:

- CPU
- Network bandwidth
- Disk performance
- Memory
- Test harness limitations

Identifying the Capacity Limit

The first step in identifying the resource limitation is to establish the nominal operating capacity as determined by your present benchmark test results. This is done by graphing the input versus output rate, as was done in Figure 14-7, and identifying the point at which the input/output curve begins to deviate from a 45-degree slope. Graphing latency as well (Figure 14-8) can help identify the operating capacity: You'll usually see a sharp change in the slope of the latency curve when you reach the operating capacity.

There is an additional feature of this graph that is worth noting: As the message rate is increased beyond the operating capacity, a second break in both the output and latency curves occurs. The output rate drops near zero, and the latency jumps way up. At this point, the

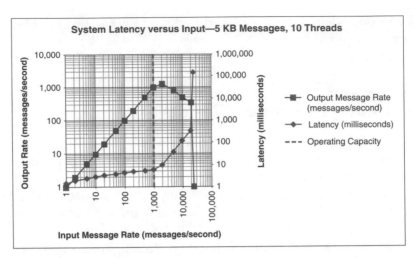

Figure 14-8: *Latency versus Input Rate*

component is effectively doing no work at all! From an architecture perspective, you then want to ensure that your design will never push the component into this operating region.

In this graph and all of the others that will be presented, the output rate curve is always shown for comparison. The key things you will be looking for are the slope of the resource utilization curve and the relative location (in terms of input rate) of the break in this curve versus the break in the output curve. In general, a flattening in the resource curve that coincides with the break in the output curve is an indication that this is the resource that is limiting the output rate. Let's look at some examples.

Identifying CPU Utilization Limits

Figure 14-9 shows CPU utilization and output rate for a situation in which the CPU utilization is not the limiting factor in component performance. Note that even after the operating capacity has been reached, the CPU utilization curve continues in a straight line beyond the operating capacity limit. This indicates that there was more CPU capacity available when the operating capacity was reached.

Figure 14-10 shows what the curve looks like when CPU utilization is the limiting factor in output rate. Note that the break in the CPU utilization curve occurs precisely at the point where the output rate curve begins to deviate from a 45-degree slope. Beyond this point, there is no

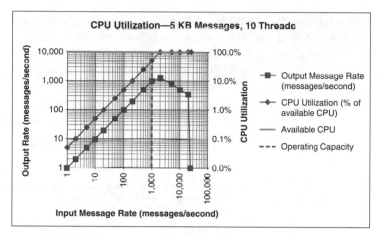

Figure 14-9: *CPU Utilization Not Limiting Output Rate*

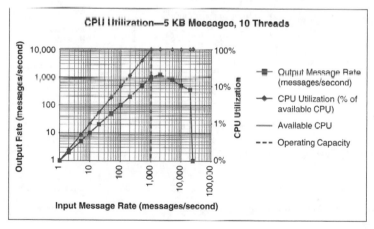

Figure 14-10: *CPU Utilization Limiting Output Rate*

increase in CPU utilization because there isn't any more to consume! This is the indication that a lack of CPU availability is limiting the output rate.

Identifying Network Bandwidth Limits

Graphing network bandwidth utilization and output rate, you get a curve similar to Figure 14-11 when network bandwidth is not the limiting factor. Note that this bandwidth utilization is generally a computed rather than a measured number. In this case, the component under test is receiving a 5 KB data structure and returning the same structure. Therefore the data rate is 10 K times the input rate. Note that the data rate continues to increase steadily well beyond the operating capacity. It is not the limiting factor.

Figure 14-12 shows the curve when the network bandwidth is the limiting factor. This is the same component under test, but to make the network bandwidth the limiting factor, the size of the input and output

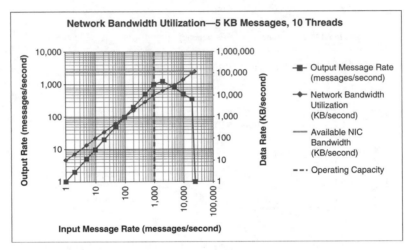

Figure 14-11: *Network Bandwidth Not Limiting Output Rate*

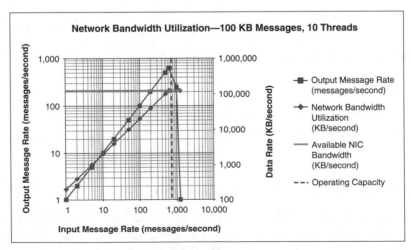

Figure 14-12: *Network Bandwidth Limiting Output Rate*

data structures had to be increased to 100 KB. Showing the actual network interface card (NIC) bandwidth on the graph makes it even clearer that the bandwidth limit has been reached. Note that in this case the operating capacity is now lower than before.

There is an important lesson in this example regarding test harness and component parameters: The settings of these parameters can alter the apparent capacity of the component under test, often erroneously. In this case, the test never reached the operating capacity of the component under test. Instead, it ran into what might be best described as a test harness limitation: It ran out of network bandwidth.

On numerous occasions TIBCO customers have reported supposedly poor benchmark results with Enterprise Message Service only to discover upon investigation that they had run into a network bandwidth limitation such as a 10 Mbit or 100 Mbit NIC card or switch. This is why it is so important to graph resource utilization in these benchmark tests so that you really understand the nature of the limit you have encountered.

Identifying Disk Performance Limits

Identifying disk performance limits is complex, for a variety of reasons. Nevertheless, it is an important consideration. As with network bandwidth, it is not practical in most environments to measure disk access. You have to work with computations—estimates.

Disk performance shows up in a variety of guises. The obvious cases are file operations being performed by the component. A bit less obvious are the database accesses. If you have appropriate benchmarks for the database that reflect your component's usage patterns, you can use those. However, if you are designing your own database you may have to do your own benchmark or, failing that, your own estimates.

There are two different types of measurements that are relevant to disk access. One is the rate at which requests for disk access occur, which is commonly measured in terms of I/O operations per second (IOPS). The other is the rate at which data is being transferred to and from the disk, commonly referred to as the disk data transfer rate and is measured in bytes/second.

It also makes a difference whether the component is reading or writing to the disk: Read requests can be answered from a cached buffer, so you need some estimate as to the likelihood that the result you are looking for is already in the cache. Write performance depends upon the writing strategy: synchronous or asynchronous. Synchronous writes need to wait for the physical disk. Asynchronous writes update an in-memory buffer before returning control to the component: The physical disk update occurs asynchronously. Note that, while efficient, asynchronous writes run the risk of data loss in the event of a power failure: Critical data should always be written synchronously.

Disk architecture comes into play as well. There are a number of options, each with its own set of performance characteristics:

- Single disk spindle (physical)
- Solid-state drive
- RAID array of physical disk spindles
- Storage subsystem with redundant battery-backed buffers

When a single physical disk is being used, calculations regarding disk performance are fairly straightforward. First, you need to calculate the average rotational latency of the disk. This is the average time it takes for the disk to rotate so that the sector you want is under the read/write head of the disk. The disk speed, in revolutions per minute (RPM), is part of the disk specification, which can be looked up online and is typically printed on the physical disk as well.

$$avgRotationalLatency_{sec} = \frac{1}{(diskSpeed_{rpm}/60) \times 2} = \frac{30}{diskSpeed_{rpm}}$$

For a 10,000 RPM disk, the average rotational latency is 3 milliseconds.

Next, you need to calculate the time it will take to transfer the data to or from the disk. The transfer rate, in bytes/second, is also part of the disk specification. Note that if there are several rates given, you probably want the lowest of the rates.

$$dataTransferTime_{sec} = \frac{messageSize_{bytes}}{transferRate_{bytes/sec}}$$

For a disk with a transfer rate of 100 MBs and a 1 KB message to be saved, the data transfer time is 1 microsecond.

Finally, you combine these numbers to obtain the average access rate. The average seek time is another parameter from the disk specification and reflects the time it takes for the disk head to move to the proper track.

$$avgAccessRate_{accesses/sec} = \frac{1}{avgSeekTime_{sec} + avgRotationalLatency_{sec} + dataTransferTime_{sec}}$$

The seek time for the disk being used as an example is 2 milliseconds. The sum of the seek time and average rotational latency is 5 milliseconds. The data transfer time is so small in relation to this value that it can be ignored. This yields an average access rate of 200 accesses per second (IOPS) for this single disk.

The specifications for solid-state drives generally give the access time or rate and the read and write rates. Typical numbers for a solid-state drive at the time of this writing are random reads at 40,000 IOPS, random writes at 50,000 IOPS, sequential read data rates at 415 MB/second and write data rates at 260 MB/second.

Calculating access rates for RAID arrays is significantly complicated, as it depends upon the type of disk, the number of spindles in the array, the RAID configuration, the mixture of read and write operations, and the size of the dataset being transferred. There are a number of online calculators that you can use to determine the actual rates, such as Marek Wolynko's IOPS calculator at http://www.wmarow. com/. For a comprehensive discussion of RAID array performance, see Chapter 3 of Somasundaram and Shrivastava's *Information Storage and Management: Storing, Managing, and Protecting Digital Information*.[1]

Calculations for storage subsystems, particularly those with battery-backed memory, are so dependent upon the design of the storage subsystem and the mechanisms used to access them that you will have to search online or consult the vendor to determine the characteristics of the system you are using.

Contention for the disk is another issue you need to take into consideration. Disks tend to be shared resources, and it is often difficult to determine the actual level of disk utilization. For this reason, your computations regarding disk performance should be taken as upper

---

1. G. Somasundaram and Alok Shrivastava, *Information Storage and Management: Storing, Managing, and Protecting Digital Information*, Indianapolis: John Wiley & Sons (2009).

bounds: It is unlikely that you will ever reach this level in practice. Because of the likelihood of disk contention, if your calculations indicate that you need a significant portion of disk I/O capability for your component, you probably need to do an actual benchmark of your component utilizing the disk. You also need to have a discussion with the organization responsible for storage regarding disk performance in production versus the test environment in which you do your benchmark.

Because of contention and differences between storage subsystems in development, test, and production environments, it is often difficult to perform benchmark tests with the storage subsystem you intend to use. As an alternative, if you can disable (bypass) the disk access in the component under test, you can run a benchmark test against this modified component. Also determine the relevant disk access rate (IOPS) limit for your intended storage subsystem. If you then overlay the IOPS limit on your benchmark curve (Figure 14-13), you can then determine what the operating capacity would be if it were constrained by the disk performance.

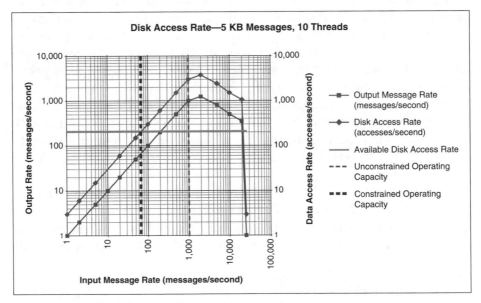

Figure 14-13: *Estimating Disk Access Rate Limitations*

Identifying Memory Limits

When it comes to determining resource requirements, memory is a bit different from other resources. Although it is possible to run performance benchmarks with different amounts of memory available to the component, it is typically not very convenient to do so. Furthermore, the real question is, usually, how much memory does this component require? To answer this question, it is best to run the benchmark test on a system that has more memory than you believe the component will require. As part of the benchmark experiment, record the amount of memory that the component is using for each data point and graph the results. You'll likely get a graph that looks something like Figure 14-14.

There are a couple of features of this graph worth pointing out. One is that as the operating limit is approached, memory utilization begins to climb. This is likely an artifact of garbage collection on the heap: As the input rate climbs, increasing numbers of data structures are being allocated and freed on the heap and the garbage collector is lagging behind. Beyond the operating capacity, the rate memory utilization continues to climb. In this region inputs are arriving faster than they

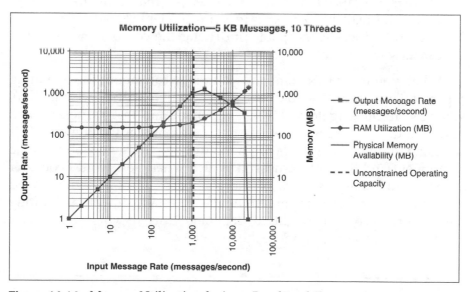

Figure 14-14: *Memory Utilization during a Benchmark Test*

are being processed, and the increased memory utilization may reflect the outstanding requests being buffered in memory.

When you collect this data, be sure that you have allowed the component to run for a long enough period of time for the memory utilization to stabilize. If it does not stabilize (i.e., continues to climb), you may have what is known as a memory leak—memory being allocated for each request that is never recovered. This is an indication of a long-term reliability problem for the component. So-called burn-in tests that run components for days or weeks are intended to identify this type of problem.

Identifying Test Harness Limits

When you are running a benchmark and have identified what appears to be the operating capacity, it is important that you understand what the limiting factor was in the test. In particular, it is important to determine whether it was the component itself of the test harness that ultimately constrained the result. If you have reached an apparent capacity limit and you can't identify system resources that have reached their limits, then there are two possibilities:

1. There is a component design characteristic that limits its ability to utilize the available resources (e.g., insufficient threads), or
2. The test harness is incapable of driving the component to its full capacity.

When you reach this point and you really care about the operating capacity (i.e., your intended utilization warrants further investigation), you need to investigate both the component and test harness design until you understand why you are not seeing higher throughput. This is when you would begin playing with tuning parameters on both the component and the test harness. It is also when you would consider adding additional instances of the test harness (both sending and receiving). In any case, if you are unable to establish what is limiting the performance, you ought to document this in your benchmark results—it may be important to the reader.

Using Benchmark Results

When you are reading the results of a benchmark test, you need to ask yourself whether you understand the test that was actually run. The best way to answer this is to find out whether there is enough information for you to set up the test yourself and re-create the results. If the answer is no, then it is questionable whether you can determine how to use these benchmark results to predict the performance of the design upon which you are working. Sadly, a great many published benchmarks lack this level of detail.

The next question is, of course, how does the benchmark test scenario relate to the design you are evaluating? Ideally, they are identical, in which case you can apply the results directly. But in many cases the benchmark will only reflect part of your design—you'll have to do some interpolation and interpretation to draw conclusions about your design.

One critical question relates to the comparability of the resources available in the benchmark environment and in your component's environment. Are the CPU, network bandwidth, disk performance, and memory all comparable? More importantly, are they fully available for your component's use?

Ensuring that resources are actually available is often harder than it appears. I recall once in preparation for running a benchmark asking repeatedly whether there was anybody else using either the network or the database upon which the component under test depended. The answer was repeatedly "No!" Nevertheless, within seconds of starting the test, a voice from the other side of the cubicle wall exclaimed, "What happened to my database?" The difficulties in knowing what resources are actually available and obtaining commitments for their use (i.e., reserving their capacity) should not be underestimated. However, it is particularly important to do so when your estimates indicate that you may be using 10 percent or more of a resource.

Often you will not have access to the resources needed to perform the benchmark test you would like to perform, particularly when it requires high-end machines with multiple CPUs. In such cases, you may need to do scaled-down experiments and extrapolate those results. If you do so, be sure that your experimental results will scale to accurately predict the performance of the production system.

Finally, when in doubt, do your own benchmark! Only then will you know for certain that you understand the resources required to obtain the throughput your component requires. This should actually be part of the test plan for any component that has performance critical to the overall solution's performance.

Summary

The purpose of benchmarking is to provide reference information that you can use to predict the expected performance of individual components in your solution designs. Benchmarking requires more than a single data point. So-called benchmark results that provide a single data point hopefully represent a component running at its nominal operating capacity, but even there you have to understand the conditions under which the test was performed in order to make use of the result.

For a benchmark to be useful, you need to understand the actual test that was performed in sufficient detail that you could repeat the test and obtain the same results yourself. This requires understanding the architecture pattern of the test setup; the mapping of the test scenarios onto this pattern; and the details of the component, machine, and network configurations.

Some types of tests can lead to misleading results. Loading a queue with millions of messages and then turning on a component that is supposed to process those messages may well push the component into overload, giving results that are not necessarily indicative of the component's actual capabilities.

A well-conducted benchmark test requires that the rate of input be controlled and that a series of tests be run making measurements at different input rates. The input rate is ramped up, at a minimum, until the output rate of the component begins to fall behind the input rate. The maximum input rate for which the output rate matches defines the operating capacity of the component. You may have to play with tuning parameters to find the true maximum.

Benchmarking complex components such as ActiveMatrix Business-Works and ActiveMatrix BPM requires several series of tests. One series measures the basic overhead of the component and establishes an upper bound on the rate at which the component could perform work. Additional series explore the performance impact of individual activities. Taken together, these results can be used to anticipate the performance of a more complex design.

When an apparent limit has been reached in a benchmark test, it is important to identify the limiting factor: CPU availability, network bandwidth limitations, disk performance limitations, memory limitations, or other causes such as the settings of tuning parameters. Only when you understand the nature of the limitation can you be sure that you have identified the true operating capacity of the component.

Using benchmark results requires understanding the relationship between the benchmark test design and your component design. Unless you understand the benchmark test design in sufficient detail to be able to reproduce the test results, it may be difficult to determine the extent to which the test results can be interpreted in terms of your design. When in doubt, run your own benchmark test, particularly for components having performance that is critical for the overall solution performance.

Chapter 15

Tuning

Objectives

Maximizing the performance of components deployed in ActiveMatrix Service Bus and ActiveMatrix BusinessWorks requires an understanding of the threading architecture of these products and the related tuning parameters. This chapter provides an overview of the threading models for these products and the major tuning parameters. Additional details may be found in the respective product documentation.

After reading this chapter you will be able to

- Describe the threading architecture and related tuning parameters used in ActiveMatrix Service Bus nodes.

- Describe the threading architecture and related tuning parameters used in ActiveMatrix BusinessWorks engines when deployed alone and as a component in an ActiveMatrix Service Bus node.

ActiveMatrix Service Bus Node Architecture

Back in Chapter 2 we reviewed the ActiveMatrix Service Bus deployment options for service interfaces, components, and references, but did not discuss the mechanics of how those elements interact with each other. This section explores the details of those interactions. There are two aspects that need to be understood: the use of threads within a node and the use of JMS queues as a communications media between nodes.

The manner in which deployable elements (service interfaces, components, and references) interact is configurable. There is a default behavior, which will be explored first, and there are two types of policy sets that can alter that default behavior. One is the Threading policy set that changes the thread pool assigned to a service interface or reference. The other is the Virtualize policy set that forces communications that would otherwise remain entirely within the node to occur through the messaging bus instead.

Before we look at the behavior, there are some basics that need to be covered.

Thread Pools

Threads in ActiveMatrix nodes are organized into thread pools. Each node has

- A JCA[1] thread pool
- A JMS Binding thread pool (a subset of the JCA thread pool)
- A virtualization thread pool
- Zero or more named thread pools
- Zero or more HTTP Connector thread pools

JCA Thread Pool

The JCA thread pool is configured by three node parameters:

1. **Core Pool Size**: The target minimum size of the JCA thread pool. These threads are not created when the node starts. Instead, if the current thread pool contains fewer than this many threads, each request for a thread will result in the creation of a new thread, even if an existing thread is idle. This will continue until the pool reaches the Core Pool Size. The default value is 5 at the time of this writing.

2. **Max Pool Size**: The upper bound on the number of threads in the JCA thread pool. The default value is 250 at the time of this writing.

---

1. J2EE Component Architecture

3. `Keep Alive Time`: The amount of time an idle thread will remain in the JCA thread pool before being reclaimed. Only threads in excess of the core pool size are reclaimed. The default value is `60` seconds at the time of this writing.

JMS Binding Thread Pool

The JMS Binding thread pool is a subset of the JCA thread pool. At the time of this writing, this thread pool is configurable only by setting its parameters in the node's `.tra` file. The parameters are:

- `java.property.com.tibco.amf.binding.jms.sharedresource.pool.minsize`: The minimum size of the JMS Binding pool. The default value is 5 at the time of this writing.

- `java.property.com.tibco.amf.binding.jms.sharedresource.pool.maxsize`: the maximum size of the JMS Binding pool. The default value is 25 at the time of this writing.

Virtualization Thread Pool

This is the default pool of threads used for virtualization communications. There are no configuration parameters for this thread pool, and its size is unbounded. Through the use of threading policies, named thread pools can be used for virtualization communications.

Named Thread Pools

Additional thread pools can be created either at design time or deployment time. The process involves two steps. The first is to create what is termed a Thread Pool but is, in reality, a Thread Pool Template. This can be done either in TIBCO Business Studio or in the ActiveMatrix Administrator. The template is given a name and has the following significant parameters:

- `Core Pool Size`: The target minimum size of the thread pool. These threads are not created when the node starts. Instead, if the current thread pool contains fewer than this many threads, each request for a thread will result in the creation of a new thread, even if an existing thread is idle. This will continue until the pool reaches the Core Pool Size. The default value is 2 at the time of this writing.

- `Max Pool Size`: The upper bound on the number of threads in the thread pool. The default value is 10 at the time of this writing.
- `Keep Alive Time`: The amount of time an idle thread will remain in the thread pool before being reclaimed. Only threads in excess of the core pool size are reclaimed. The default value is 30 seconds at the time of this writing.
- `Autostart Core Threads`: Indicates whether the core threads should be pre-created at the time the node starts. The default value is No at the time of this writing.
- Priority: the default priority of the threads in the pool. The default value is 5 at the time of this writing.
- Rejection Policy: The policy applied when there is no thread available for the task. Possible values are
  - `Abort`: The task is aborted and an exception is thrown.
  - `Blocking`: The task is blocked until a thread from the thread pool becomes available and picks up the task.
  - `Caller Runs`: The task is run in the calling thread.

  The default value is `Blocking` at the time of this writing.

Once the pool template has been created, you can use the template to create instances of this thread pool on selected nodes. The default name of the pool on the node will be the same as the name of the template. This name is important, for it is the way that the pool is referenced in policies, which is where the pools will be used.

HTTP Connector Thread Pools

By default, each HTTP Connector creates its own worker thread pool. By exception, a named thread pool may be assigned from which threads will be assigned. The connector-specific thread pool can be configured through the node's `.tra` file using the following parameters:

- `amf.node.connector.<connectorName>.threadpool.maxPoolSize`—the maximum pool size. As of this writing defaults to 250.
- `amf.node.connector.<connectorName>.threadpool.corePoolSize`—the target minimum pool size. As of this writing defaults to 10.
- `amf.node.connector.<connectorName>.threadpool.keepAliveTimeInSeconds`—the keep-alive time of threads in seconds, excluding the core pool. As of this writing defaults to 60.

In addition to the worker threads, the HTTP Connector defines another pool of threads called acceptor threads. These threads accept the operating system socket connection calls. They are taken from the thread pool being used by the connector, but they are not counted when computing the pool's maximum pool size.

The number of acceptor threads is configured on the HTTP Connection resource's `Acceptor Threads` parameter. If non-blocking sockets are used (the default), the recommended number of acceptor threads is 1. This is because the Java socket API synchronizes the accept call so only one thread can actually wait on accept. Hence there is no benefit to increasing the number of acceptor threads. If blocking sockets are used, the recommended number of acceptor threads is 20. By default, the size of the acceptor pool is 20 threads as of this writing.

Another important parameter on the HTTP Connector's configuration is `Accept Queue Size`. The size indicates how many connections waiting to be accepted will be queued by the operating system. When the queue is full, the operating system will start refusing connections. The default is 0. For non-blocking sockets, this means that if there is more than one connection that needs to be accepted at a time, one will be accepted and the others will be rejected. For blocking sockets, a 0 value will use the JVM's default accept queue size, which for Java versions 1.6 and 1.7 is 50.

Worker Thread Assignments

Worker threads are assigned to tasks at the physical interfaces of nodes, the bindings associated with a composite's promoted services and references, and the node's interface to the messaging bus.

HTTP bindings take their worker threads from the thread pool defined by the associated HTTP Connector. This is either the default pool created by the connector or an explicitly named pool.

Threads assigned in JMS Bindings, by default, are taken from the JMS Binding thread pool, which is a subset of the JCA thread pool.

Default SOAP/HTTP Thread Usage

Figure 15-1 shows a service (interface) and its implementing component deployed on the same node. Each inbound service request is picked up by one of the HTTP Connector acceptor threads ❶. These threads are taken from the thread pool designated by the HTTP

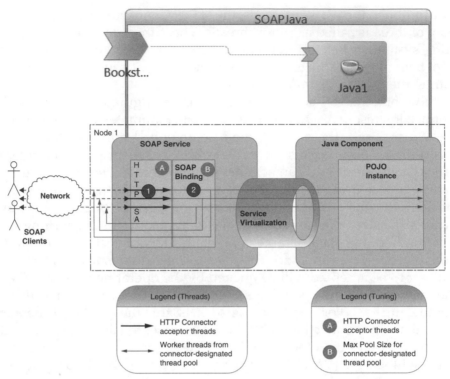

Figure 15-1: *Default SOAP/HTTP Thread Usage*

Connector's `Worker Thread Pool` property. If this property is absent (the default), the connector's thread pool is used.

The acceptor thread ❶ accepts the system call and hands it off to an HTTP Connector worker thread ❷ for execution. The worker thread is taken from the thread pool designated by the HTTP Connector. This thread handles all remaining work including the execution of the SOAP binding logic, the service virtualization work required to interact with the component, the execution of the service implementation, and the return of the HTTP response. In Figure 15-1 the implementation is a plain old Java object (POJO) instance, but the thread usage is the same for Mediation implementation types as well. Thread assignment for other implementation types is described later.

There are two tuning parameters associated with these thread assignments. The HTTP Connector's `Acceptor Threads` parameter determines the number of threads accepting socket connections. If non-blocking sockets are used, the recommended number of acceptor threads is 1. This is because the Java socket API synchronizes the accept call so only one thread can actually wait on accept. Hence there is no benefit to increasing the number of acceptor threads. If blocking sockets are used, the recommended number of acceptor threads is 20. For the thread pool associated with the HTTP Connector, its `Max Pool Size` parameter determines the total number of worker threads available.

Figure 15-2 adds an outbound SOAP over HTTP call to the picture. The thread doing the component work ❷ also performs the HTTP interaction and then resumes the execution of the component work. Upon completion of the component work, thread ❷ returns the HTTP response to the initial requestor.

Default JMS Thread Usage

The default thread usage for JMS or SOAP over JMS interactions is shown in Figure 15 3. The service consumer places the inbound request on the JMS queue. A JMS client/session thread (not from one of the thread pools) ❶ picks up the request and passes it to a worker thread ❷ from the JMS or SOAP/JMS binding. The worker thread is taken

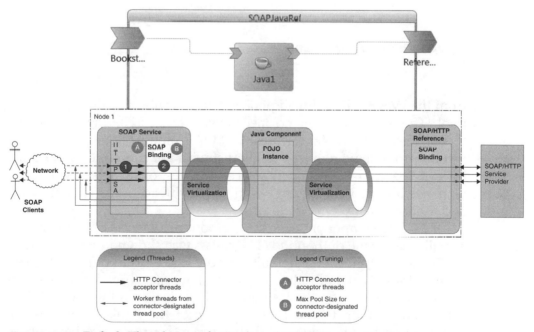

Figure 15-2: *Default Thread Usage for Outbound HTTP Communications*

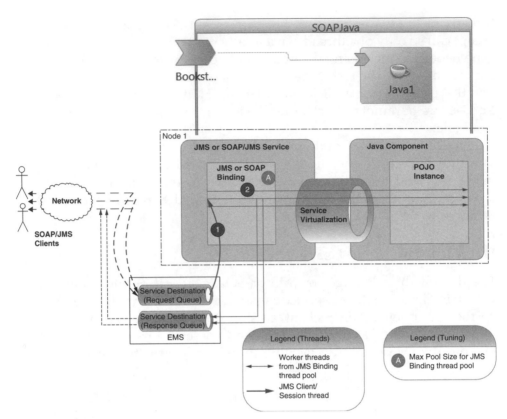

Figure 15-3: *Default JMS Thread Usage*

from the JMS Binding thread pool, which is a subset of the JCA thread pool. There is at present no mechanism for designating a different thread pool. Thread ❷ executes the SOAP binding logic, the service virtualization logic required to interact with the component, the component logic, and ultimately places the response message on the response queue. This pattern describes the thread usage for both Java and Mediation implementation types.

If the Java component makes an outbound SOAP/HTTP call, thread ❷ will execute the outbound HTTP call as was shown in Figure 15-2.

Figure 15-4 shows the default thread usage for outbound JMS communications. By default, the component's worker thread ❷ places the outbound message on the JMS queue. This thread is then released. A JMS client/session thread (not from one of the pools) ❸ listens for responses on the reply queue. When a response arrives, another worker

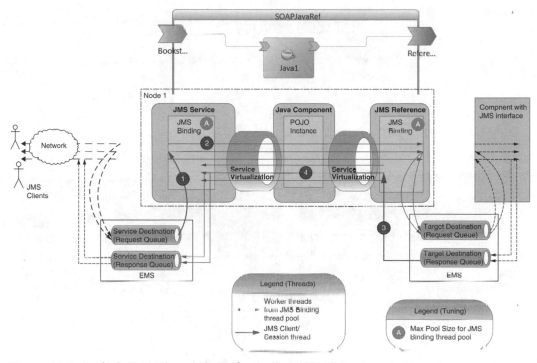

Figure 15-4: *Default JMS Thread Usage for Outbound JMS Communications*

thread ❹ is obtained from the JMS Binding's thread pool. Thread ❹ then resumes execution, ultimately placing the response to the original client on the reply queue.

Default Node-to-Node Communications Thread Usage

When a service and its implementing component are deployed on different nodes, the messaging bus is used for communications between the nodes. Figure 15-5 shows the thread utilization for an inbound HTTP call. On Node 1 the worker thread ❷ publishes the request to the JMS queue and blocks, waiting for the reply. On Node 2, the JMS client/session thread ❸ picks up the message and gives it to a virtualization worker thread ❹ from Node 2's virtualization thread pool. That thread executes the Java or Mediation logic and places the reply message on the response queue. Back on Node 1, the JMS client/session thread ❺ picks up the message and gives it to a worker thread ❻ from

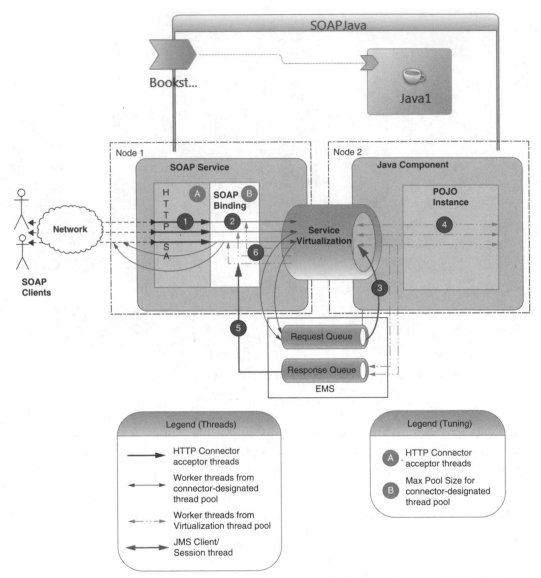

Figure 15-5: *Default Thread Utilization in Node-to-Node Communications with HTTP Input*

the virtualization pool. This thread hands the response to the blocked worker thread ❷, which then returns the reply to the original requestor.

Interactions that originate in JMS requests are a bit different (Figure 15-6). Here the worker thread ❷ that places the service virtualization request on the queue is immediately released. When the

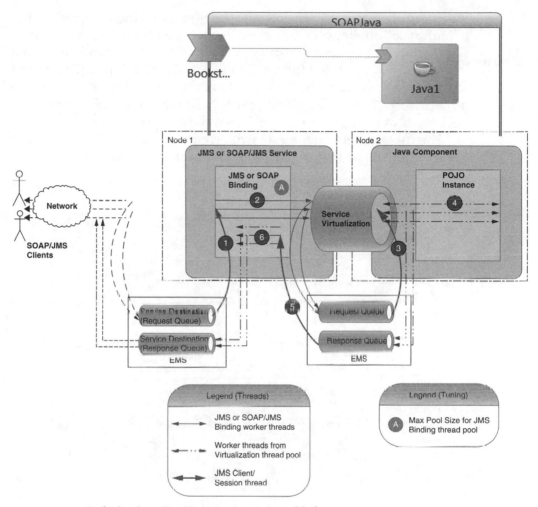

Figure 15-6: *Default Thread Utilization in Node-to-Node Communications with JMS Input*

response comes back, the JMS client/session thread ❺ obtains a new worker thread ❻ from the virtualization thread pool. This worker thread then completes the process of placing the client's response on the response queue.

Thread Usage with the Virtualize Policy Set

The virtualize policy set makes wired elements communicate as if they were on different nodes. When a Virtualize Policy Set is applied to any of the wired services or references (or to the composite as a whole, which applies it to all services and references in the composite), the communications between the wired elements will occur using the messaging bus. The resulting thread usage for an HTTP initiation is shown in Figure 15-7. Note that the thread usage is identical to that shown in Figure 15-5, except that here all the elements are deployed on the same node. This is, in fact, the intent of this policy: to make the interactions occur as if the components were deployed on separate nodes.

The thread utilization for a virtualize policy set and JMS initiation is shown in Figure 15-8. Again, note the similarity with Figure 15-6.

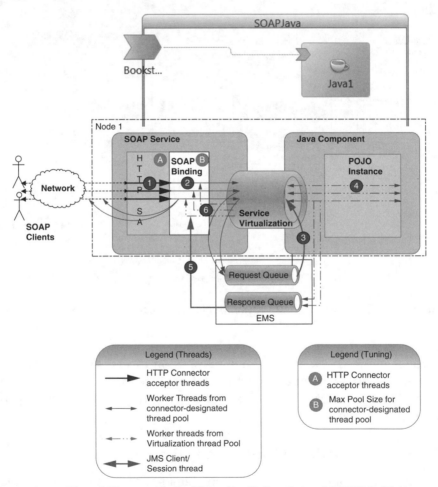

Figure 15-7: *Thread Usage with the Virtualize Policy Set and HTTP Initiation*

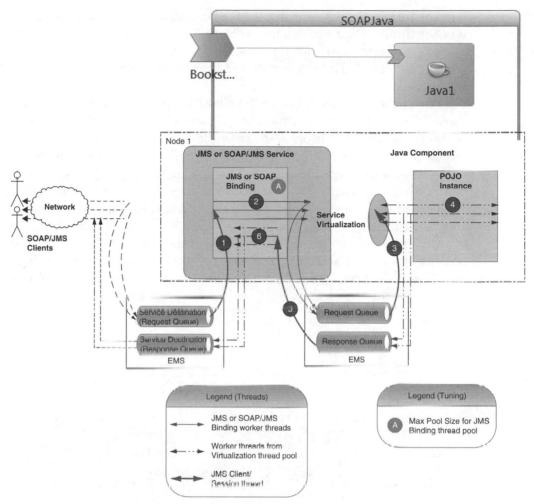

Figure 15-8: *Thread Usage with the Virtualization Policy Set and JMS Initiation*

Thread Usage with the Threading Policy Set

Any service or reference can have a threading policy set associated with it. Figure 15-9 shows the thread utilization when the threading policy set is associated with either a promoted service with an HTTP binding or with the component service to which it is wired. The HTTP Connector worker thread ❷ hands off control to a worker thread ❸ from the pool specified by the threading policy. The HTTP Connector worker thread blocks, waiting for the response. The threading policy worker thread ❸ completes the work of the Java (or Mediation) component and hands off the response to the blocked HTTP Connector worker thread ❷. The worker thread then returns the response to the SOAP client.

When the work is being performed by a JMS worker thread, the thread usage is slightly different (Figure 15-10). The JMS Binding worker thread ❷ hands off to the threading policy worker thread ❸, at which point the JMS Binding worker thread is freed. The threading policy worker thread completes the work of the Java (or Mediation) component and returns the JMS response message to the JMS client.

Threading Policy Sets can also be applied to references. Figure 15-11 shows the threading policy pool usage when the original worker thread is an HTTP worker thread. The HTTP worker thread ❷ executing the component code hands off to a worker thread ❸ from the policy-specified thread pool. That thread executes the outbound HTTP call and

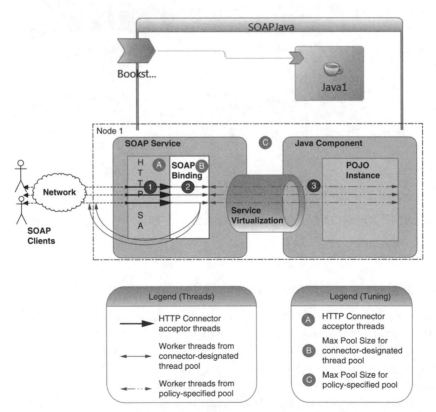

Figure 15-9: *Use of Policy-Specified Pool Threads with HTTP Worker Threads*

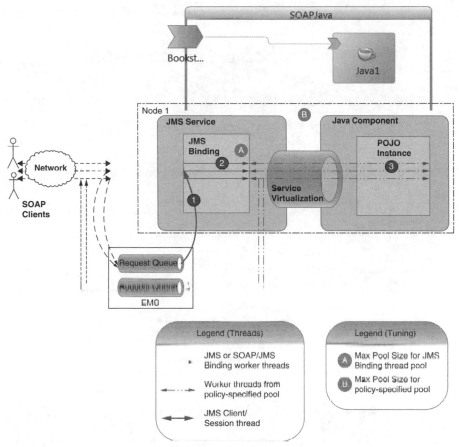

Figure 15-10: *Use of Policy-Specified Pool Threads with JMS Worker Threads*

blocks, waiting for the response. When the response is received, it is handed back to the HTTP worker thread ❷, which completes the component work and hands the ultimate response back to the SOAP client.

Figure 15-12 shows the use of policy-specified threads in a reference when the initial thread is a JMS worker thread. The JMS worker thread ❷ hands off to a thread ❸ from the policy-specified pool and is then released. Thread ❸ places the request on the outbound JMS queue and then it, too, releases. When the response comes back, a JMS client/session thread ❹ obtains a thread ❺ from the policy-specified thread pool and passes the message to it. This thread then completes the processing, ultimately placing the client's response message on the JMS queue.

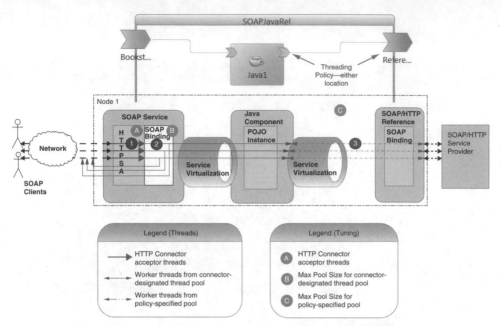

Figure 15-11: *Use of Policy-Specified Pool Threads in References with HTTP Worker Threads*

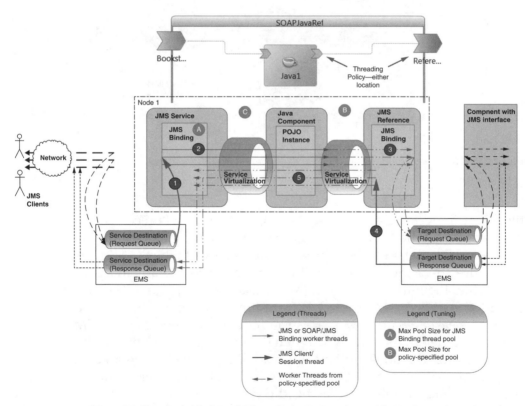

Figure 15-12: *Use of Policy-Specified Pool Threads in References with JMS Worker Threads*

ActiveMatrix BusinessWorks™ Service Engine Architecture

Thread Pools

ActiveMatrix BusinessWorks has three thread pools of interest:

1. Engine thread pool
2. Zero or one Tomcat thread pool
3. Zero or one HTTP Component thread pool

The ActiveMatrix BusinessWorks Service Engine has an additional thread pool:

- Invoke Partner thread pool

Engine Thread Pool

The engine thread pool threads actually execute the ActiveMatrix BusinessWorks process definitions. The number of worker threads is established by the `Engine.ThreadCount` property on the Active-Matrix BusinessWorks Service Engine instance.

Setting the ActiveMatrix BusinessWorks Service Engine HTTP Server Type

Although ActiveMatrix BusinessWorks can use the Service palette to provide services that are accessible in SCA composites, it can also directly provide service interfaces. HTTP service interfaces provided in this manner require an HTTP server configuration. BusinessWorks provides two HTTP server options: `Tomcat` and `HTTPComponent`. These are the allowed values of the `bw.plugin.http.server.serverType` property on the ActiveMatrix BusinessWorks Service Engine instance.

Tomcat Thread Pool

If Tomcat is selected as the HTTP server, two parameters are used for its configuration:

1. `bw.plugin.http.server.minProcessors`: This establishes the minimum number of HTTP server threads.
2. `bw.plugin.http.server.maxProcessors`: This establishes the maximum number of HTTP server threads.

HTTPComponent Thread Pool

If HTTPComponent is selected as the HTTP server, one parameter is used for its configuration:

- `bw.plugin.http.server.httpcomponents.workerThread`: This establishes the number of HTTP server worker threads.

Invoke Partner Thread Pool

The Partner definitions in ActiveMatrix BusinessWorks processes correspond to the references on the ActiveMatrix BusinessWorks Service Engine components in ActiveMatrix composites. Partner invocations use threads from the Invoke Partner thread pool. The number of threads in this pool is configured by the `InvokePartnerServiceActivityThreadPool.ThreadCount` property on the ActiveMatrix BusinessWorks Service Engine instance.

ActiveMatrix BusinessWorks Internal Architecture

The internal engine architecture of ActiveMatrix BusinessWorks is shown in Figure 15-13. Processes in BusinessWorks, called Jobs, are represented by data structures. These data structures represent the entire state of the job, including all data associated with the job.

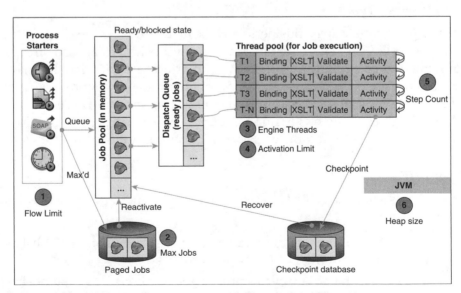

Figure 15-13: *ActiveMatrix BusinessWorks Internal Architecture*

Process Starters

Process starters create the job data structures and place them in the Job Pool in memory or page them to disk (see the section on Max Jobs). There are various types of process starters, differing in the sources of the events that start the jobs. Process starters include

- Adapter Subscribers (events from TIBCO Adapters)
- File Poller (recognizes file system changes)
- On Event Timeout (exception handling when a WaitFor activity times out)
- On Notification Timeout (exception handling for a Notify activity)
- On Shutdown (process to execute when the engine shuts down)
- On Startup (process to execute when the engine starts)
- Timer (starts process at a specific time or periodically)
- HTTP Receiver (receipt of an HTTP input)
- JMS Queue Receiver (receipt of a message from a JMS queue)
- JMS Topic Receiver (receipt of a message from a JMS topic)
- Receive Mail (receipt of an e-mail message)
- Rendezvous Subscriber (receipt of a Rendezvous message)
- RMI Server (receipt of an RMI request)
- Service shared configuration (associated with a WSDL portType, acts as a process starter for a collection of processes, each associated with a different WSDL operation of the portType)
- SOAP Event Source (receipt of a SOAP request)
- TCP Receiver (client requests a TCP connection—he process manages the subsequent dialog)

For most of the process starters, a thread is dedicated to each defined process starter in the deployed project. This thread listens for the event and creates the job data structure. The exceptions are the process starters involving HTTP and JMS.

Process starters using HTTP Connections have multiple threads. These threads are taken from either the Tomcat or HTTPComponent thread pools discussed earlier. Each process starter references an HTTP Connection that specifies the configuration to be used. Note that while the job is actually executed in an engine thread, the HTTP threads block until the job returns the required HTTP response.

JMS interactions are described in the following section.

JMS Process Starters

Depending on the job starter configuration, there are several possible configurations. The `Acknowledge Mode` parameter is the primary determinant in the configuration. When it is set to `Auto` (the default) or `Dups OK`, there is a single JMS process starter thread (Figure 15-14). This thread receives a JMS message, creates the job, and immediately acknowledges the message.

Another option is to set the `Acknowledge Mode` to `Client`, `Transactional`, or `Local Transactional` (Figure 15-15). With these options, the message is not acknowledged until a job activity explicitly indicates that it is time to do so. However, this also ties up the JMS process starter thread. For this reason, when the `Acknowledge Mode` is set to one of these values, another parameter comes into play: `Max Sessions`. This parameter specifies the number of JMS sessions (i.e., process starter threads) to allow for this process starter. The value of `Max Sessions` determines the number of JMS messages that can be processed concurrently.

There is a third option for `Acknowledge Mode` that is only available when the JMS server is a Enterprise Message Service server. This is the `TIBCO EMS Explicit Client Acknowledge` mode (Figure 15-16). Here the process starter does not block when the job is created and therefore the single starter thread can create multiple jobs.

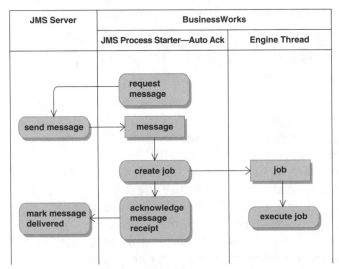

Figure 15-14: *JMS Process Starter with Auto or Dups OK Acknowledgement Mode*

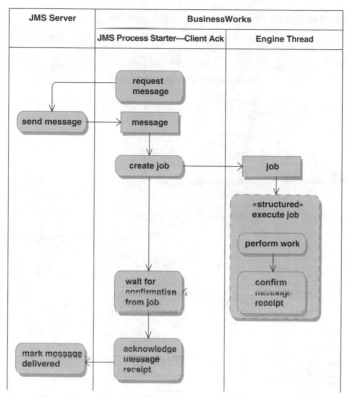

Figure 15-15: *JMS Process Starter with Client, Transactional, or Local Transactional Acknowledgement Mode*

Starting Jobs from the ActiveMatrix Service Bus

When ActiveMatrix BusinessWorks jobs are started through service invocation from the ActiveMatrix Service Bus, the node on which the ActiveMatrix BusinessWorks Service Engine is running plays the role of the process starter. Figure 15-17 shows the thread usage when the BusinessWorks process is invoked by an HTTP worker thread. The HTTP worker thread ❷ creates the BusinessWorks job and blocks, waiting for the result. The BusinessWorks job is then executed by a BusinessWorks engine worker thread ❸. The engine thread completes the work and hands the result back to the HTTP worker thread, which then returns the result to the original SOAP client.

Figure 15-18 shows the engine being invoked from a JMS worker thread. The JMS worker thread ❷ creates the ActiveMatrix BusinessWorks job and is released. A BusinessWorks engine worker thread ❸ executes the job and returns the response message to the SOAP client.

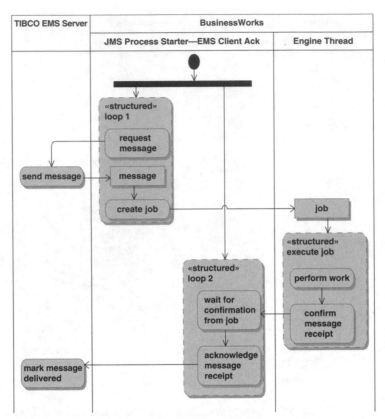

Figure 15-16: *JMS Process Starter with TIBCO EMS Explicit Client Acknowledge Acknowledgement Mode*

ActiveMatrix BusinessWorks Job Processing

By default, jobs are created and placed in the in-memory Job Pool. Jobs that are ready to run (as new jobs would be) are placed in the Dispatch Queue. When an engine thread becomes available (these are the same engine threads discussed earlier), the thread takes the job and begins executing the job activities. By default, the thread will continue to execute activities until either the process completes or an activity is reached that executes in a non-engine thread.

The following is a partial list of I/O activities that are executed by the engine thread:

- JMS Sender
- JDBC Query

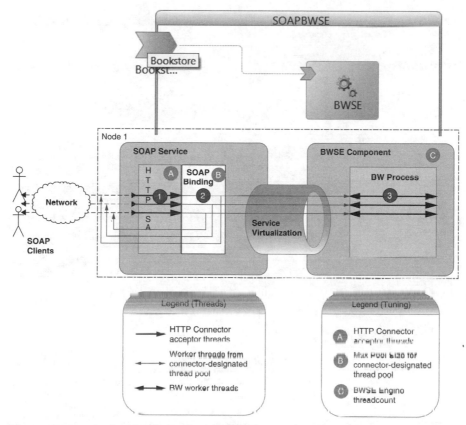

Figure 15-17: *ActiveMatrix BusinessWorks Service Engine Thread Usage with HTTP Worker Thread*

For these activities, the engine thread is blocked waiting for the I/O completion. Note that even if the process flow allows two or more of these activities to execute in parallel, in reality they never will: As soon as the thread begins executing one activity, it will remain blocked until that I/O completes.

The following is a partial list of I/O and other activities that execute in non-engine threads:

- Adapter Request-Response Invocation
- JMS Topic/Queue Requestor
- Send HTTP Request
- Send Rendezvous Request

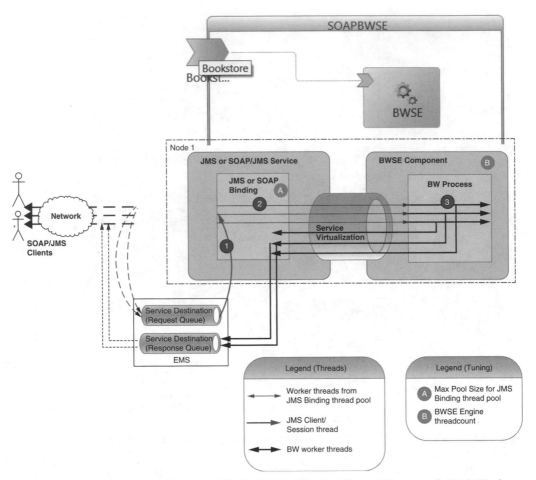

Figure 15-18: *ActiveMatrix BusinessWorks Service Engine Thread Usage with JMS Worker Thread*

- SOAP Request/Reply
- Wait, WaitFor, and Sleep activities
- Invoke Partner activities

Not only do these activities execute in non-engine threads, two or more of these activities can execute in parallel. If a process flow places two of the activities in parallel, the worker thread will initiate first one and then the other. If the first one takes long enough to complete, the two activities will be executing concurrently.

For a current listing of which activities execute in non-engine threads, please consult the product documentation.

When an activity executes in a non-engine thread and there are no other activities eligible for execution, the job is taken out of the dispatch queue and the engine thread is released to execute other jobs. When the activity completes, the result of that activity is added to the job and the job is again ready to run. If the job happens to be in the memory-resident Job Pool, it is placed in the Dispatch Queue. If it has been paged out, it will not be placed into the Dispatch Queue until it is paged back in.

When a job running in an ActiveMatrix BusinessWorks Service Engine engine thread ❸ uses an Invoke Partner activity to make an outbound call (Figure 15-19), it transfers control to an Invoke Partner worker thread ❹. The engine thread is then released to perform other work in the ActiveMatrix BusinessWorks engine. The Invoke Partner worker thread then performs whatever work is necessary. Note that this thread behaves like an HTTP worker thread: It blocks whenever it is waiting for a reply. When thread ❹ receives its response, it gives the response back to the BusinessWorks engine, which adds the response to the corresponding job. A BusinessWorks engine thread ❸ then resumes execution of the job.

This would be a good place to use a threading policy, associating it with the ActiveMatrix BusinessWorks Service Engine reference. If this is done, the Invoke Partner thread will obtain a worker thread from the policy-specified thread pool and hand off the request for processing. The Invoke Partner worker thread is immediately released (see Figures 15-11 and 15-12).

ActiveMatrix BusinessWorks Tuning Parameters

Max Jobs

One of the key tuning parameters in ActiveMatrix BusinessWorks is Max Jobs. This parameter limits the total number of jobs that can be held in the memory of a BusinessWorks engine.

The default value for Max Jobs is 0, which places no limit on the number of jobs that can be held in memory. Although this setting is convenient in a development environment, ActiveMatrix BusinessWorks should never be deployed in production with a 0 value. This is because this setting creates a situation in which BusinessWorks could potentially create an unbounded demand for memory. This would arise when, for a sustained period of time, the rate at which jobs are created exceeds the rate at which they are being completed.

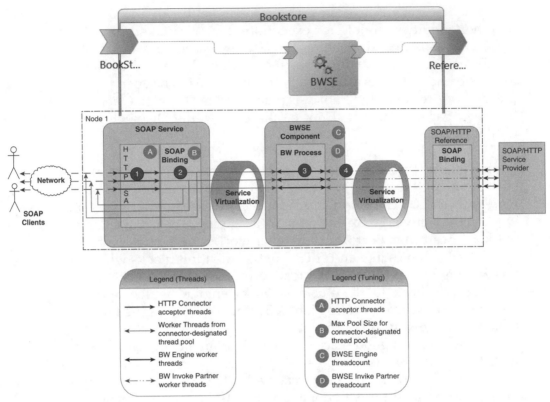

Figure 15-19: *ActiveMatrix BusinessWorks Service Engine Using Invoke Partner*

To determine the appropriate setting for `Max Jobs`, first determine the operating capacity of the ActiveMatrix BusinessWorks instance using the procedure described in Chapter 14. You will probably do some experimentation with the number of engine threads as part of that exercise. Then, while operating an engine steady-state at the operating capacity, observe the number of concurrent jobs. Note that if the engine is configured to run more than one type of job, you may want to run a mix of jobs at this point. Now observe the number of jobs running: This is your value for `Max Jobs`. Also observe the memory usage: This will tell you the amount of memory required to support running at the operating capacity.

Setting `Max Jobs` does more than limit memory demand: It also improves engine performance when the input rate exceeds the output rate. It does so by limiting the amount of work required for handling new jobs to just that required to create the job data structure and write it to disk.

Activation Limit

The ActiveMatrix BusinessWorks engine's `Activation Limit` parameter determines whether jobs are held in memory once they have begun executing. When `Activation Limit` is set, after a job is in memory and has started, it will remain in memory until it has completed. Note that this is true even if the job is waiting for an I/O to complete.

The primary use of `Activation Limit` is to govern execution in scenarios in which three conditions hold:

1. There are significant peak load demands that exceed the operating capacity of the ActiveMatrix BusinessWorks engine.
2. The jobs have I/O activities that execute in non-engine threads.
3. `Max Jobs` is being used to limit memory demand

If you set `Max Jobs` without setting `Activation Limit`, here's what can happen:

1. When a peak occurs in excess of `Max Jobs`, new jobs get paged to disk.
2. Jobs that are currently executing, when they hit the I/O activity that executes in a non-engine thread, also get paged to disk—behind the ones that are already there (it's a queue). In the meantime, new jobs are being paged to disk.
3. Because a job just got paged to disk, the first ready-to-run job is taken from the disk queue and loaded into memory. If it is a new job, when it hits the non-engine-thread I/O, it will get paged back to disk—behind any new jobs that were created while it was executing.
4. When an I/O completes, the result of the I/O is added to the job (on disk), but that job can't be loaded into memory yet.

What ends up happening is that the jobs for which I/O has completed are on the queue behind the new jobs that have yet to run. They don't get to run until the new jobs have run and have gotten to the point where they are waiting for their I/O to complete. In other words, the output rate of the engine deteriorates as was described back in Chapter 14.

Setting `Activation Limit` changes this picture. The jobs that are already started stay in memory, while new jobs get paged to disk.

When the I/O completes, they finish running. Only as they complete are new jobs given a chance to run. This gets jobs completed faster. Note that the setting of `Max Jobs` needs to account for the number of jobs waiting for I/O completion as well as the number of jobs that are actively running.

Flow Limit

The `Flow Limit` parameter is found on most job starters, but conspicuously not for a Service shared configuration (we'll talk about this case in a minute). `Flow Limit` determines the number of concurrent jobs that can be created by the job starter.

What happens to incoming requests once the `Flow Limit` has been reached depends upon the nature of the protocol being used. For protocols that have an upstream buffer (e.g., JMS, e-mail), the requests simply sit in that upstream buffer until the number of active jobs drops below the `Flow Limit`. For protocols without a buffer (e.g., HTTP), the excess requests are simply lost. For HTTP connections, Flow Limit is a shorthand way of setting the number of threads available for handling incoming HTTP connections. Please consult the product manual for more details.

Step Count

By default, once a job starts running it will execute all activities unless it runs into an activity that executes in a non-engine thread. The `Engine.StepCount` parameter can be used to alter this behavior. It determines the maximum number of activities that will be executed by a worker thread. If this limit is reached before the job completes, the worker thread will place the job at the end of the dispatch queue and obtain another job from the head of the queue.

This parameter is intended to be used when the engine is running a mixture of large, complex jobs and smaller, simple jobs. When set to an appropriate value, it keeps the large jobs from hogging all the engine threads by forcing them to pause and allowing other (hopefully smaller) jobs to get a chance to run.

This parameter should be used with caution, as its use can lead to unexpected behaviors. Setting it to too small a value will result in performance degradation due to more frequent worker thread switches. Using it in conjunction with `Max Jobs > 0` and with `Activation Limit` enabled can result in large jobs being paged to disk and waiting a long time before they get to execute again.

An alternative to the use of the Step Count parameter that should be strongly considered is the deployment of the different processes on different engines.

Summary

Threads in ActiveMatrix Service Bus nodes are organized into pools. Each node has

- A JCA thread pool
- A JMS Binding thread pool (a subset of the JCA thread pool)
- A virtualization thread pool
- Zero or more named thread pools
- Zero or more HTTP Connector thread pools

Worker threads are initially assigned to tasks at the physical interfaces of nodes. For promoted services and references, by default, the threads are taken from the pools associated with their bindings. For virtualization communications between nodes, by default, the threads are taken from the virtualization thread pool. In all cases, named thread pools can be associated with services and references using threading policies. These threads are then used in lieu of the default threads for performing work.

There is a difference in behavior between HTTP worker threads (threads from an HTTP Connector thread pool) and other worker threads. HTTP worker threads manage the initial socket connection created in response to the service client's call. When an HTTP worker thread hands off responsibility to another thread, it blocks until the other thread returns the expected response. All other worker threads are released when they hand off responsibility to another thread or send a JMS message. They block only when they are making an outbound HTTP call.

Communication within a node, by default, remains within the node and is handled by the worker threads of that node. Communication between nodes utilizes the ActiveMatrix messaging bus (a dedicated Enterprise Message Bus server instance). By exception, a Virtualize Policy Set can be used to force in-node communications to use the messaging bus. This enables a service consumer to distribute load between a service provider residing on the same node and other service providers residing on other nodes.

ActiveMatrix BusinessWorks and its companion ActiveMatrix BusinessWorks Service Engine have four thread pools of interest:

1. Engine thread pool
2. Zero or one Tomcat thread pool
3. Zero or one HTTP Component thread pool
4. Invoke Partner thread pool

The engine thread pool is the one that executes jobs in an ActiveMatrix BusinessWorks engine. The Tomcat or HTTPComponent thread pools are used for HTTP connections directly to the BusinessWorks engine (i.e., not through the ActiveMatrix Service Bus). The Invoke Partner thread pool is used for outbound calls from BusinessWorks to the ActiveMatrix Service Bus.

There are a number of engine-level parameters that can be used to tune ActiveMatrix BusinessWorks. These include

- Max Jobs
- Activation Limit
- Flow Limit
- Step Count

For JMS process starters, there are additional tuning parameters:

- Acknowledge Mode
- Max Sessions

Chapter 16

Fault Tolerance and High Availability

Objectives

Fault tolerance (FT) and high availability (HA) are techniques for improving the availability of a solution in the face of component failure. It is important to recognize that achieving fault tolerance or high availability for a solution does not necessarily require that every component of the solution be fault tolerant or highly available. Selecting appropriate coordination patterns for the solution may allow it to be fault tolerant or highly available even though some of the components involved are not. The Deferred JMS Acknowledgement Pattern is an example discussed later in this chapter.

Nevertheless, the starting point for most fault-tolerance and high-availability solutions begins with making at least some of the participating components fault tolerant or highly available. This chapter first explores patterns that do not depend on TIBCO product features, and then explores patterns that leverage product-specific features.

After reading this chapter you will be able to

- Describe the generic design patterns for fault tolerance and high availability
- Describe TIBCO-specific patterns for fault tolerance and high availability
- Identify and select appropriate generic and TIBCO-specific fault-tolerance and high-availability design patterns

Common Terms

Strictly speaking, fault tolerance is the ability of a solution to provide an uninterrupted capability despite the failure of one (or possibly more) of its components. In practical terms, this means that, given a service-level agreement (SLA) limiting the length of time it takes for a solution to complete a function, that SLA will still be met if there is a component failure.

Given that many of our solutions are expected to provide subsecond response, achieving fault tolerance (by this definition) is difficult and expensive to achieve. In practice, true fault tolerance is generally found only in widely used infrastructure: networks, storage subsystems, and some high-end databases. Most components instead provide high availability rather than fault tolerance.

High availability is the ability to restore a capability faster than it would normally take to simply restart, replace, or repair a component. Many times there is an additional requirement that data not be lost during this restoration process.

There are three terms that are collectively used to characterize high-availability solutions: availability, recovery time objective (RTO), and recovery point objective (RPO). Availability is the percentage of time that a component is available taken as a long-term average. For example, over the course of a year, a 99.999% available component is expected to be operational for all but five minutes of the year. But availability does not constrain the length of time for a single outage.

The RTO specifies the maximum outage time for a single incident—in other words, the amount of time you have to restore the functionality. Typically the RTO is a fraction of the permissible annual downtime given by the availability. A 99.99% availability component is allowed to be down 50 minutes during the year, but it might have an RTO limiting each individual outage to no more than 10 minutes. This component could then be down five times over the course of the year (assuming the RTO is met) without violating its availability constraint.

Data loss during a failover is also a concern. The RPO specifies the amount of data that is allowed to be lost in the event of a failure. The allowed loss is specified in terms of time—how many seconds (or minutes or hours) of data are allowed to be lost when a failure occurs. An RPO of one minute means that the loss of one minute's worth of data is permitted for each outage. An RPO of zero indicates that no data loss is permissible.

When discussing high availability, it is common for there to be two sets of performance targets, one for failure recovery within a data center and another for failover between data centers. The targets for data center failover tend to be less confining. An intra-site failover may have an RPO of zero (no data loss), while an inter-site failover may relax this to 10 minutes or so.

Deferred JMS Acknowledgement Pattern

As mentioned earlier, highly available solutions do not necessarily require that all components be highly available if the right coordination patterns are used. The most common coordination pattern is a request-reply interaction coupled with a retry of the request, at least under certain failure conditions. JMS has this pattern built in.

According to the JMS standard, given that a message has been delivered to a client and the client has not yet acknowledged receipt of the message, if the connection to the JMS client is lost, the message immediately becomes eligible for redelivery.

Components that have work triggered by the receipt of JMS messages can take advantage of this feature to avoid loss of work (Figure 16-1). Since the component acknowledges receipt of the JMS message only after its work has been completed, if anything happens to the component, the JMS server will redeliver the message.

This strategy works independent of the recovery strategy for the component. If there are multiple instances of the component subscribing to a JMS queue, the message will immediately be delivered to one of the other components. On the other hand, if there is only one

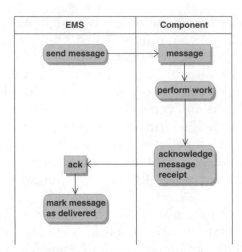

Figure 16-1: *Deferring JMS Message Acknowledgement to Avoid Loss of Work*

component, the message will be redelivered to that component when it is restored to service.

When you use this pattern, you must ensure that the JMS message itself is not lost. By default, messages sent to queues are persistent. For topics, the JMS client must send the message with the message delivery mode set to `PERSISTENT`. This will cause the JMS server to make a persistent copy of the message so that it will not be lost should the JMS server restart.

If your RPO is zero for a failover (i.e., no messages lost on failover) and you are using the Enterprise Message Service, be sure to set `[mode=sync]` in the `stores.conf` file to ensure that messages are synchronously written to disk as they are received by the server. By default, storage is asynchronous, meaning that messages are held in a memory-resident buffer and only periodically flushed to disk. Messages that are in this buffer at the time of an EMS failover will be lost.

Intra-Site Cluster Failover Pattern

The Intra-Site Cluster Failover Pattern (Figure 16-2) is a high-availability pattern for use within a data center. It is perhaps the most common high-availability pattern in use today. In this pattern, a component is installed on a machine that has a virtual host identity: a virtual host-

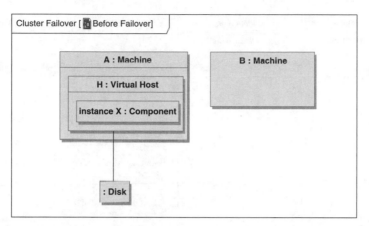

Figure 16-2: *Intra-Site Cluster Failover Pattern—Before Failover*

name and virtual IP address. Any disks that are being used are logically mounted on this virtual host. The disk is assumed to be fault tolerant, that is, part of a RAID array. Any state information that needs to be retained upon failover must reside on the disk.

When a failure occurs, the component is resurrected on a different machine (Figure 16-3) with the same virtual identity and with the same disks mounted. From the component's perspective, nothing has changed. Neither has anything changed from the perspective of the consumers of services provided by the component. This simplicity is the reason that this pattern is so common.

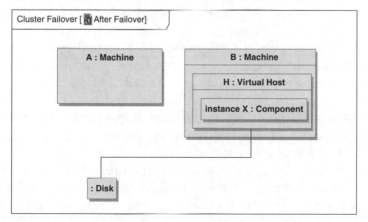

Figure 16-3: *Intra-Site Cluster Failover Pattern—After Failover*

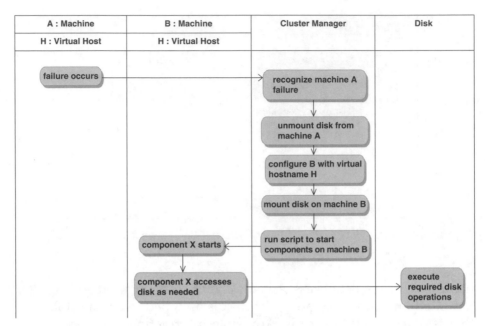

Figure 16-4: *Intra-Site Cluster Failover Management Process*

The process of managing the failover is shown in Figure 16-4. A cluster manager monitors the status of the machines. When it detects a failure, it unmounts the disk(s) from the failed machine, configures another machine with the same virtual identity, mounts the disk(s) on the new machine, and restarts the failed component (this is usually a script that gets run). The component reads the relevant state information from the disk and continues operation as before. There are a number of hardware and software vendors that provide these capabilities.

A similar approach is achievable using virtual operating system instances (generally referred to as virtual machines) and virtual disks. The identity of the instance is contained in the virtual machine, and the relevant state information is contained in the virtual disks. A virtual environment manager monitors the state of the virtual machine. When it detects a problem, it resurrects the virtual machine and related virtual disks on another piece of hardware.

There are, of course, other forms of failure besides a complete machine failure. These can be accommodated in this pattern by adding a monitor for those failures (e.g., Hawk) and having the monitor notify the cluster manager of the failure. The notification then triggers the failover process.

Generic Site Failover

The prevention of data loss within a data center is enabled through the use of fault-tolerant storage subsystems (e.g., RAID arrays). These allow data to be stored in a fault-tolerant manner and thus guarantee its availability to the recovered component.

Site failovers are complicated by the fact that the fault-tolerant storage subsystem used at one site will most likely not be available to components running at other sites. In this situation, preventing data loss requires replicating the information from the primary site to the backup site(s). The choice of replication strategy impacts the design patterns and performance characteristics for inter-site failover.

Storage Replication Strategies and the Recovery Point Objective

There are two possible storage replication strategies: synchronous and asynchronous. With synchronous storage replication, updates to data at one site are applied to the other site as part of the same update operation. When the component requesting the update gets confirmation that the update has occurred, the data is guaranteed to be saved at both sites. This capability is usually provided as a feature of the storage subsystem. EMC[1], for example, provides this capability in their Symmetrix Remote Data Facility (SRDF) family of software when the Synchronous option is chosen (referred to as SRDF/S).

There are obvious performance implications: Any write operation incurs a latency penalty of a round-trip communication to the remote site plus the time it takes to persist the data at the remote site. This is practical only when there is high-bandwidth, low-latency communications between the sites, which generally requires a combination of physical proximity (< 100 miles) and the use of dark fiber or similar low-latency network links. *However, synchronous update is the only storage replication strategy that can achieve an RPO of zero—no data loss during failover.*

With asynchronous storage replication, updates to the local storage subsystem are applied to the remote site after some delay. The extent of the delay is determined by the mechanism used for the replication. Many storage subsystems provide the capability to build a pipeline of

---

1. www.emc.com

updates that are then applied to the remote site. EMC, for example, provides this in the SRDF with Asynchronous option (SRDF/A). Remote updates are applied after the local component has been told the data has been successfully stored. Since there may be data in transit, this approach runs the risk of some data loss. For the updates managed in this manner by the storage subsystem, the RPO is generally in the range of seconds to a few minutes—but it is never zero.

Other asynchronous replication patterns involve taking snapshots of disks or performing tape backups. For these strategies to be appropriate, the RPO must be greater than the time interval between backups.

The sections that follow focus on design patterns involving synchronous file replication, since these are the most challenging. There are obvious variants of these patterns when asynchronous storage replication is used.

Inter-Site Failover with Different Host Identity Pattern

The most complicated site failover patterns arise when the component is resurrected on a machine with a different host identity (Figure 16-5). With this pattern it is necessary to distinguish between data files used by the component and configuration files that define the component. The reason for this is that some of the configuration files contain information about the host identity. These files must be different at the two sites. Similarly, the configuration files for other components that access this component may also require configuration files that are different at the two sites.

During normal operation, the storage subsystem synchronously replicates the changes to the data file to the remote site. It does not, however, do anything with the configuration files. These must be manually placed and managed on the remote site and edited to reflect differences between the host environments.

Figure 16-6 shows the configuration after an inter-site failover has occurred. The recovered component is now running on the B machine using the configuration files that were specifically created for operation on that machine. It is using the synchronously replicated copy of the data from the primary site, so no data is lost.

Note that in this configuration, there is no data replication from the secondary site back to the primary site. After the primary site is restored, data from the secondary site must be replicated back to the primary site. This will likely require a fail-back scenario using asynchronous replication since, as of this writing, the author was unaware of any

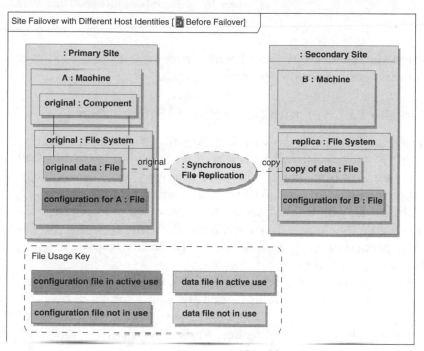

Figure 16-5: *Inter-Site Failover with Different Host Identities—Before Failover*

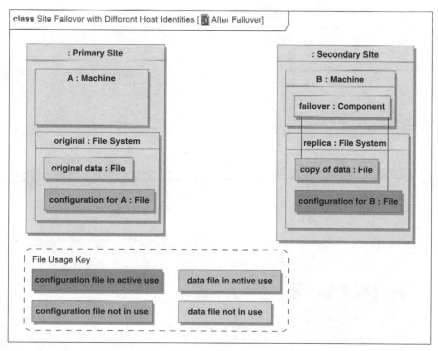

Figure 16-6: *Inter-Site Failover with Different Host Identities—After Failover*

storage subsystems with provisions for reversing the direction of synchronous replication after failover.

Inter-Site Failover with Same Host Identity Pattern

Inter-site failover with the same host identity is a bit easier (Figure 16-7). Since the component will be restored with the same host identity, the same configuration files can be used at both sites. Thus both the configuration and data files can be replicated at the remote site. This greatly simplifies the administration of the components. Furthermore, other components that access this one can use the same configuration as well. This approach does, however, require the ability to use the same hostnames and IP addresses at both sites.

After the failover (Figure 16-8) the component is running at the remote site with the same host identity using copies of both the configuration and data files. Note, once again, that after the primary site has been restored, file replication in the reverse direction to support fail-back remains an issue.

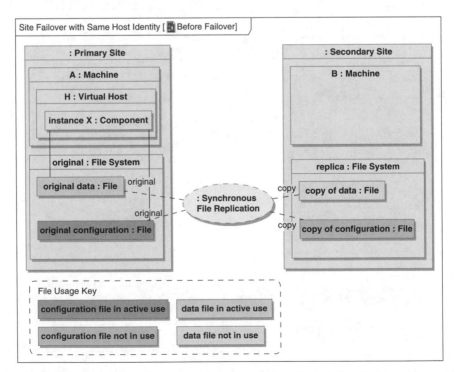

Figure 16-7: *Inter-Site Failover with Same Host Identity—Before Failover*

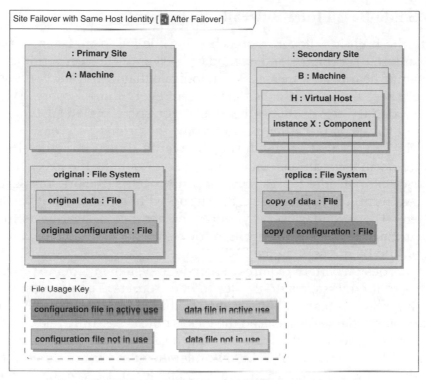

Figure 16-8: *Inter-Site Failover with Same Host Identity—After Failover*

This type of failover is readily implemented and automated with a combination of EMC SRDF/S and VMware vCenter Site Recovery Manager.[2] The Site Recovery Manager coordinates with EMC to stop the file replication as part of failover process.

Enterprise Message Service Failover

There are two types of design patterns that can be used for EMS failover: one is to use the generic intra-site and inter-site with same host identity failover patterns described earlier, and the other is to use the built-in capabilities of Enterprise Message Service.

---

2. www.vmware.com/support/pubs/srm_pubs.html

EMS File-Based Intra-Site Failover Pattern

With the built-in failover approach using file-based message storage (Figure 16-9), primary and secondary server instances periodically exchange heartbeats—messages that indicate that the primary server is alive. These messages are, by default, sent every three seconds. When the secondary server misses heartbeats for some period of time, by default ten seconds, it attempts to become the primary server.

The process that occurs during failover is shown in Figure 16-10. Under normal conditions, the primary server obtains file locks on the message storage files it uses. When a failure occurs (the primary server process terminates), these locks are supposed to be released by the file system. The secondary server notices the absence of heartbeats from the primary, obtains the file locks, retrieves the set of undelivered messages, and begins serving the EMS clients.

This design pattern requires a shared file system in order to provide access to the message storage files to both servers. The problem with this approach is that the most common shared file system, NFS, does not reliably release file locks.[3] If the lock is not successfully released the failover will, itself, fail. Please consult the *TIBCO® Enterprise Message Service™ User Guide* chapter on fault tolerance for a list of criteria that the shared file system must meet to be suitable for use as a shared message store.

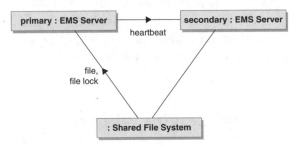

Figure 16-9: *Enterprise Message Service File-Based Intra-Site Failover*

---

3. Although NFS V4 is capable of reliably handling the file locks, the operating system must be properly configured to use these capabilities—most operating systems are not, by default, configured to do so. On Linux, at a minimum, disk mounts must use the nfs4 with tcp protocol with the "hard" option (retry failed NFS operations indefinitely), and both nfs and nfslock must be run as services that auto-start after reboot.

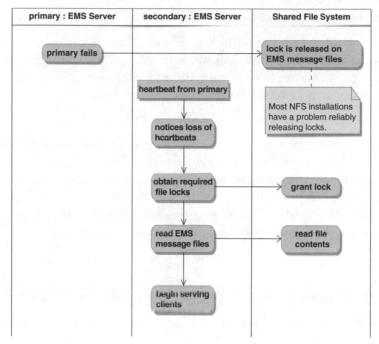

Figure 16-10: *Failover Process for File-Based Intra-Site Failover*

EMS Database-based Intra-Site Failover Pattern

An alternative approach is to use a database rather than a shared file system for the storage of undelivered messages (Figure 16-11). In this pattern there is no issue with file locking. However, storage and retrieval of messages in a database is generally slower than with a file system.

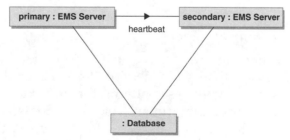

Figure 16-11: *Enterprise Message Service Database-Based Failover*

EMS Client Configuration for Failover

Regardless of the failover pattern selected, EMS clients must be appropriately configured or they will not automatically reconnect when the EMS server fails over. Specifically, the EMS client `serverUrl` parameter must contain at least two entries, for example:

```
serverUrl=tcp://server0:7222, tcp://server1:7344
```

For the file- and database-based intra-site failover patterns, the entries will identify the primary and secondary servers. For the generic approach, in which the server is resurrected with the same identity, both entries will be the same. Nevertheless, two entries must be present, as it is the presence of the second entry that triggers the EMS client to automatically reconnect after its connection to the EMS server is lost.

Considerations in Selecting an EMS Failover Strategy

Things that should be considered when selecting an EMS Failover Strategy include

- Secondary server start-up time
- Persisted message read time
- File locking reliability
- Administrative complexity

A major consideration in selecting an EMS failover strategy is the target recovery time objective (RTO): how quickly must service be restored. There are two components to this time:

1. The time it takes to get the back-up EMS server running
2. The time it takes for this server to read the persisted messages

Secondary Server Startup Time

From a server start-up perspective, patterns utilizing the built-in failover will be faster than the generic patterns. Since the secondary server is already running in these patterns, the time it takes for the secondary server to assume the primary role is the ten seconds or so it takes to realize that the primary has ceased to function. With the generic approach, the start-up time will be longer as the virtual host configuration must first be established (including the mounting of the disks) and then the EMS server instance can be started. Depending upon the environment, this may take several minutes.

Persisted Message Read Time

If there are persisted messages, the secondary server must read them before it can begin providing service. In doing this, reading from a file system will always be faster than reading from a database. The file-based read time can be further decreased by splitting the message storage among multiple files, which will be read concurrently.

File Locking Reliability

From an RTO perspective, the winning strategy appears to be file-based failover—but only if a shared file system with reliable file locking is available. Don't get trapped into trying to make it work with NFS V2 or V3 (many a group has tried and failed), and if you're looking at NFS V4 you need to ensure that your operating system is configured to use the locking properly (which it won't be by default). An unreliable file-locking mechanism means an unreliable failover pattern.

Administrative Complexity

From the perspective of administrative complexity, the generic failover approach is, by far, the winner. There is exactly one server configuration, and it can be used both for failover within a data center and between data centers. Client configurations remain the same as well. There is also the benefit of uniformity across different types of components: The management of the failover process is the same as for all components using cluster-style failover.

ActiveMatrix BusinessWorks Failover

There are three major patterns that can be used to achieve high availability with ActiveMatrix BusinessWorks engines. These patterns are available whether BusinessWorks is running as a stand-alone engine or embedded in an ActiveMatrix node:

1. ActiveMatrix BusinessWorks Deferred JMS Acknowledgement Pattern
2. ActiveMatrix BusinessWorks Built-In Intra-Site Failover Pattern
3. ActiveMatrix BusinessWorks Cluster Failover Pattern

ActiveMatrix BusinessWorks Deferred JMS Acknowledgement Pattern

When ActiveMatrix BusinessWorks jobs are started via the receipt of a JMS message, BusinessWorks provides the option of having the job acknowledge the receipt of the JMS message as an explicit activity in the job. This enables BusinessWorks to implement the Deferred JMS Acknowledgement Pattern.

The job starter receiving the JMS message must be configured to use this pattern. This is done via the job starter's `Acknowledge Mode` parameter by choosing the modes of `Client`, `Transactional`, `Local Transactional`, or `TIBCO EMS Explicit Client Acknowledge`. Figure 15-15, from Chapter 15, details the engine behavior for the `Client`, `Transactional`, and `Local Transactional` modes, and Figure 15-16, from the same chapter, details the engine behavior for the `TIBCO EMS Explicit Client Acknowledge` mode. These modes are summarized in Figure 16-12.

These deferred acknowledgement modes, coupled with the logic of JMS message redelivery, can be used to avoid loss of work. When these modes are being used and an ActiveMatrix BusinessWorks engine terminates (for whatever reason) in the middle of a job, the connection to the EMS server is lost and the message will be immediately eligible for redelivery. If you are using JMS queues to distribute load across multiple BusinessWorks engines (Figure 11-2), then the message will be

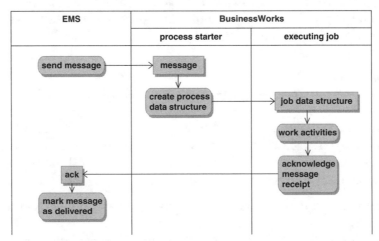

Figure 16-12: *Summarized Pattern for ActiveMatrix BusinessWorks Deferred JMS Acknowledgement*

immediately delivered to one of the other engines. If you are using generic cluster failover to recover the failed BusinessWorks engine, then the message will be redelivered when the engine restarts.

From a performance perspective, when messages are sent in a fire-and-forget message-exchange pattern and you have an RPO of zero, this is an efficient failover pattern. The alternative is to use Active-Matrix BusinessWorks checkpoints (described in the ActiveMatrix BusinessWorks Built-In Failover Pattern), which requires additional disk activity. The use of deferred acknowledgement avoids the disk access associated with checkpoints and is therefore more efficient.

Deferred acknowledgement is not, however, a panacea. Because a failed job is restarted from the beginning, the job activities that had been executed prior to the failure will be executed again. If these activities are idempotent, which means that they produce the same result no matter how many times they are executed, there is no problem. However, if you have non-idempotent activities—activities that cannot be safely repeated—then you must use a different design pattern. Database insertions are a common example of non-idempotent activities: The second time the insert will fail since the record already exists.

When you encounter non-idempotent activity and it can participate as part of a transaction, the simplest thing to do is to include it in an activity group and do the following things:

1. Specify the Group Action as a `Transaction` with an `XA Transaction` type.

2. Place the non-idempotent activity or activities in the group (typically a JDBC database insertion or a message publication).

3. On the Transaction Group configuration, set the `Include in Transaction` field to reference the activity requiring confirmation (e.g., a JMS Queue Receiver) and check `Include Checkpoint`.

If these things are done, the non-idempotent activities and the acknowledgement of message receipt will execute as a single transaction.

ActiveMatrix BusinessWorks Built-In Intra-Site Failover Pattern

ActiveMatrix BusinessWorks built-in failover (Figure 16-13) works very much the same way as the Enterprise Message Service failover using a database. When a BusinessWorks job hits a checkpoint activity or completes a transaction with a checkpoint option selected, it writes the current state of the job to a database.

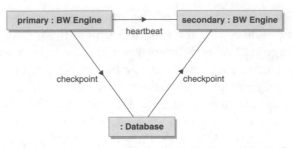

Figure 16-13: *ActiveMatrix BusinessWorks Built-In Intra-Site Failover Pattern*

The ActiveMatrix BusinessWorks engine, meanwhile, exchanges heartbeat messages with other engines in the BusinessWorks fault-tolerant group. This fault-tolerant group is defined at deployment time using the TIBCO Administrator. The engines may be configured either as a primary-secondary pair (the secondary is inactive unless the primary fails) or as peers (both are actively running the process). During deployment, the BusinessWorks processes for which fault-tolerant recovery is desired must also be marked to run fault tolerant.

In this configuration, should an engine running a job fail before its completion, the secondary or peer engine will recover the job from its last checkpoint. Note that any activities that have been executed since the checkpoint will be repeated after recovery, so the idempotency of these activities must be considered. To aid in dealing with non-idempotent activities, there is a predefined process variable that can be used to check whether the job has been recovered from a checkpoint. This can be used to implement alternate business logic in the event of a recovery.

The source of triggering events for process starters may be an issue with this failover pattern. Starters that are tied to a particular IP address (e.g., HTTP) will end up with a different IP address on the secondary ActiveMatrix BusinessWorks engine. An IP redirector must be used in this case to route requests to the correct machine.

ActiveMatrix BusinessWorks Cluster Failover Pattern

The third pattern for ActiveMatrix BusinessWorks failover is to use generic cluster failover. Figure 16-14 shows a configuration before failover. BusinessWorks is installed and running in a virtual host, and writing its checkpoints (if any) to a file (as opposed to a database).

When a failure occurs, the cluster manager resurrects the virtual host on a different machine after mounting the disk on that machine.

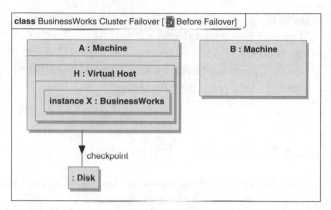

Figure 16-14: *ActiveMatrix BusinessWorks Cluster Failover—Before Failover*

The ActiveMatrix BusinessWorks engine retrieves its checkpoint files and resumes the execution of those jobs (Figure 16-15).

The use of cluster-style failover has some advantages over the built-in approach:

- The use of the file system as opposed to the database for storing checkpoints is faster.
- All the process starters will continue to work properly since the back-up instance of ActiveMatrix BusinessWorks is running in the same virtual environment.
- The same pattern can be used for both intra- and inter-site failover.

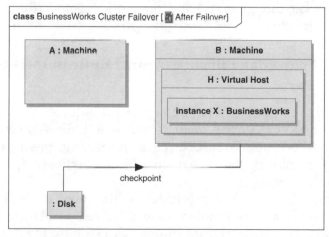

Figure 16-15: *ActiveMatrix BusinessWorks Cluster Failover—After Failover*

The disadvantage of this pattern is the recovery time: The cluster manager has to re-create the virtual environment and start ActiveMatrix BusinessWorks before service can be resumed. With the built-in approach, the back-up instance is already running—all it needs to do is read the checkpoints and resume processing.

ActiveMatrix Service Bus Failover

There are four failover patterns that can be used with ActiveMatrix nodes, all of which have already been described:

1. Deferred JMS Acknowledgement Pattern
2. ActiveMatrix BusinessWorks Built-In Intra-Site Failover Pattern
3. Intra-Site Cluster Failover Pattern
4. Inter-Site Failover with Same Host Identity Patterns

Using the Deferred JMS Acknowledgement Pattern

By default, ActiveMatrix nodes use the Deferred JMS Acknowledgement Pattern. The node confirms the receipt of a JMS message only when the JMS Binding worker thread is released. Thus any activities that are performed with this thread will be completed before the message is acknowledged.

Taking advantage of this capability, however, requires an understanding of the threading model of the ActiveMatrix node, as the JMS Binding worker thread may hand off work to other threads. Please review the threading model description in Chapter 15 for details.

Using the ActiveMatix BusinessWorks Built-In Intra-Site Failover Pattern

ActiveMatrix nodes do not have the general equivalent of an ActiveMatrix BusinessWorks checkpoint: There is no built-in mechanism for preserving the execution state of an entire node. Thus there is no generic capability for restoring the state of an arbitrary ActiveMatrix node that has work in progress.

However, this does not preclude a component in the node from explicitly saving and recovering state information. An ActiveMatrix BusinessWorks component, for example, can still use the ActiveMatrix

BusinessWorks Built-In Intra-Site Failover Pattern. See the *TIBCO ActiveMatrix BusinessWorks Service Engine User Guide* for configuration details.

Using the Intra-Site Cluster Failover and Inter-Site Failover with Same-Host Identity Patterns

Intra-site and inter-site failover for an ActiveMatrix node is readily accomplished by applying these patterns. Note that inter-site failover has a number of infrastructure constraints that must be satisfied before using this pattern.

An Example of a 99.999% Availability Environment for the Enterprise Message Service

Under the proper conditions, the patterns in this chapter can be combined to yield high-availability environments that span multiple data centers. These combinations all require

- Data centers located within 100 miles of one another.
- A dark fiber connection between the sites providing high-bandwidth and low-latency (<<10 milliseconds) network access.
- A reliable "stretch" VLAN across the two sites that allows the same IP addresses to be used at both sites. The reliability of the inter-site network must approach that of the individual data center networks.
- Synchronous real-time storage replication capability between sites.

If these prerequisites are all met, then the following patterns become possible.

EMS Multi-Site with No Message Persistence Pattern

This pattern is a combination of two patterns discussed earlier:

1. EMS File-Based Intra-Site Failover Pattern
2. Inter-Site Failover with Same-Host Identity Pattern

The combination of these patterns is shown in Figure 16-16, which presents the situation before failover. Two instances of the EMS server are deployed, one at each site. They are deployed in a variation of the EMS

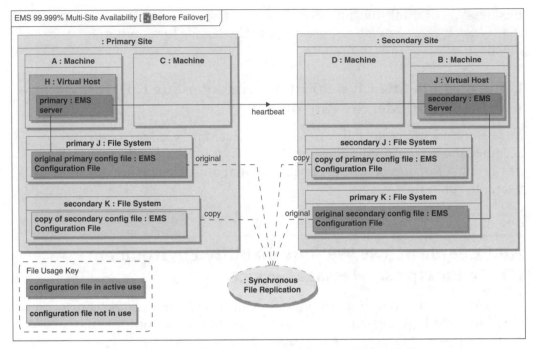

Figure 16-16: *EMS Multi-Site with No Message Persistence—Before Failover*

File-Based Intra-Site Failover Pattern, with the primary being deployed at one site and the secondary at the other site. A shared file system is not necessary, since there are no persisted messages. Synchronous file replication is used to maintain copies of each server's configuration files at the other site.

Note that there are two file systems being replicated, and in opposite directions. The J File System's primary is at the primary site, with a copy at the secondary site. The K File System's primary is at the secondary site, with a copy at the secondary site. This allows for initial failover in either direction.

The situation after the primary EMS server has failed but before it is recovered at the secondary site is shown in Figure 16-17. If the EMS servers are configured with the default heartbeat settings (three-second heartbeats, a ten-second absence triggering failover), this state is reached in ten seconds, well below the five minutes required for 99.999% availability. However, the reliability of the inter-site network comes into play: A failure will result in an apparent loss of heartbeats and the secondary

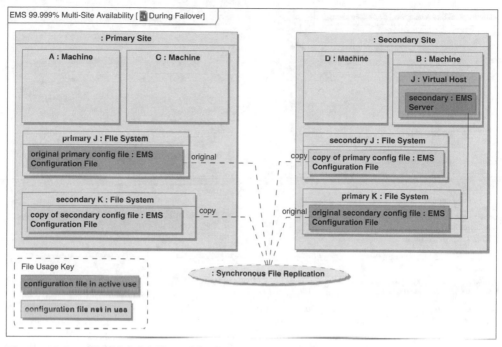

Figure 16-17: *EMS Multi-Site with No Message Persistence—During Failover*

server taking over when the primary is still operational. Message delivery behavior under these circumstances is undefined.

The failure of the primary server also triggers the Site Failover with Same Host Identity Pattern, which causes the primary EMS server to be resurrected at the secondary site. After this failover is completed, you have the situation shown in Figure 16-18. The fault-tolerant pair of EMS servers has been restored, now both at the same site. Note, however, that the synchronous file replication of the primary's configuration files (J File System) has been terminated. Restoration of the primary EMS server to the primary site will require additional design work.

EMS Multi-Site with Message Persistence Pattern

This pattern is a combination of three patterns discussed earlier:

- EMS File-Based Intra-Site Failover Pattern
- Inter-Site Failover with Same Host Identity Pattern
- EMS Client Load Distribution: Queue Pattern (from Chapter 11)

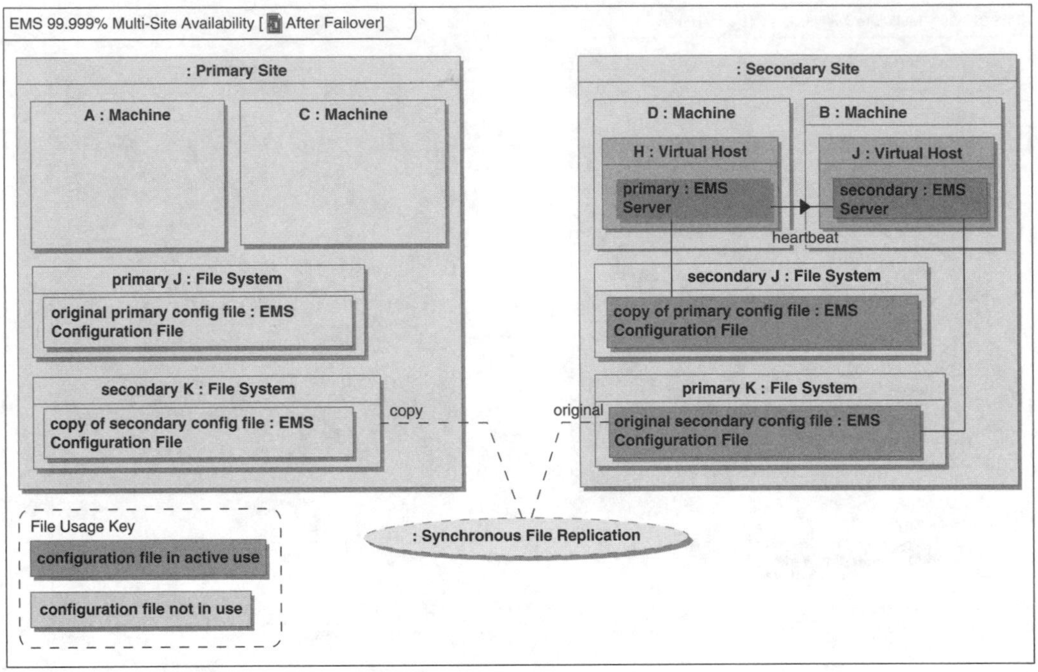

Figure 16-18: *EMS Multi-Site with No Message Persistence—After Failover*

The situation before failover is shown in Figure 16-19. Clients connect to either the primary or secondary EMS servers using a variation of the EMS Client Load Distribution Pattern in which the primary and secondary servers are deployed at different sites. The queues themselves reside on the queue EMS server. The message file on the primary J File System is being synchronously replicated at the secondary site.

When the queue EMS server fails, the Site Failover with Same Host Identity pattern is used to resurrect it at the remote site (Figure 16-20). During the failover period, clients can publish messages to the queue (these are held temporarily in the primary or secondary EMS servers). However, they cannot retrieve messages until the queue EMS server is recovered. Depending upon the period of time it takes to do this, queue delivery may or may not be restored within the five minutes required to achieve 99.999% availability.

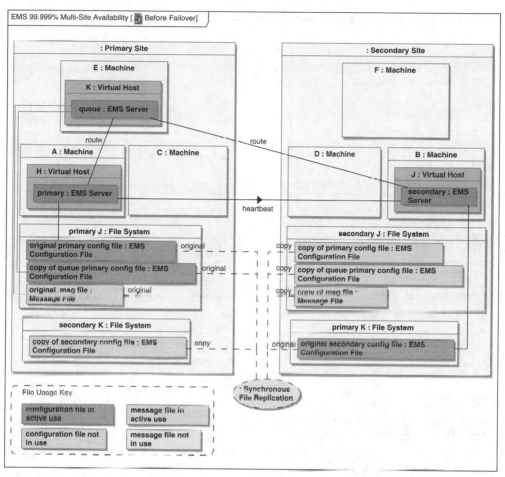

Figure 16-19: *EMS Multi-Site with Message Persistence— Before Failover*

The pattern, as shown, is not quite complete. The primary and secondary EMS servers also have message files that are used to temporarily store incoming messages in the event that the queue EMS server is down. To avoid any possibility of data loss, these files would have to be synchronously replicated at the opposite sites. Then, when the primary EMS server is recovered at the secondary site, it can read these messages and forward them to the queue EMS server.

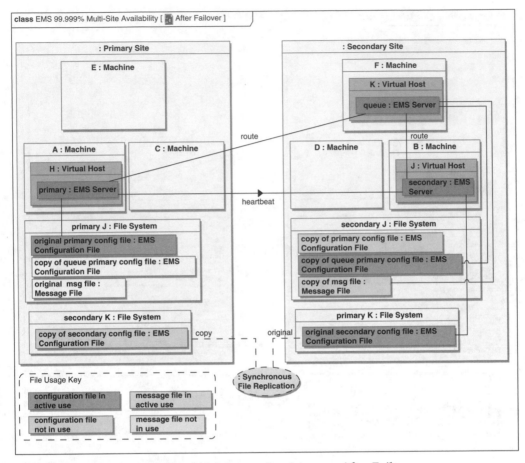

Figure 16-20: *EMS Multi-Site with Message Persistence—After Failover*

Summary

Fault tolerance, strictly speaking, refers to providing functionality without apparent loss of service despite the failure of one or more components. High availability refers to restoring service rapidly after the failure of one or more components. Few components in the IT world are truly fault tolerant—generally, networks and disk subsystems. Most other components are provisioned, when necessary, in a highly available manner.

In a high-availability setting, there are three key parameters that must be specified: overall availability, the time allowed to restore service (the recovery time objective or RTO), and the amount of data that is allowed to be lost when a failure occurs. The latter, referred to as the recovery point objective or RPO, is measured as the period of time for which data is allowed to be lost in the event of a failure. An RPO of zero means that no data loss is allowed.

A solution can actually be fault tolerant without requiring all of its components to be fault tolerant or even highly available. This is accomplished through the use of coordination patterns that automatically retry actions in the event of an individual component failure. A common pattern of this type involves the delivery of JMS messages to a component. If a component is designed to acknowledge message receipt only after its work is completed, then a failure of that component prior to acknowledgement will result in the JMS server redelivering the message. This is the Deferred JMS Acknowledgement Pattern.

One of the most common high-availability techniques is the Intra-Site Cluster Failover Pattern. With this pattern, a component operates in an environment with a virtual hostname and IP address and uses dedicated virtual disks. If the component fails, it is resurrected on another machine with the same virtual hostname, IP address, and disks. The component (and any other component that interacts with it) is unaware of any changes. This makes this pattern easy to implement for most components and provides a uniform mechanism that can be used for many different types of components.

Failover between sites is a bit more complicated and requires the replication of persistent information at the secondary site. There are two patterns that can be applied here. The Inter-Site Failover with Different Host Identity Pattern restores failed components at the secondary site but, because the hostname and IP address are different, different configuration files may be required and clients using the components may require alternate configurations as well.

The Inter-Site Failover with Same Host Identity Pattern is very similar to the Intra-Site Cluster Failover Pattern. The component is resurrected in a virtual environment at the secondary site with the same hostname and IP address that it had at the primary site. The difference is that instead of mounting the same virtual disks, the secondary site mounts replicas of those virtual disks. The strategy for disk replication determines how much data can be lost upon failover.

There are three patterns that can be used for Enterprise Message Service failover. One is the Intra-Site Cluster Failover Pattern. A second, the EMS File-Based Intra-Site Failover Pattern, uses a pair of EMS servers configured with a shared file system. The primary server's state is saved in the shared files. When the secondary detects a failure (loss of heartbeats from the primary), it reads the state information from the shared files and takes over. Most NFS file systems have problems with file locking and should not be used with this pattern.

The third option, the EMS Database-based Intra-Site Failover Pattern, is similar to the file-based pattern except that the messages are stored in a database instead of the file system. This takes care of the file locking problem, but is generally slower than the file-based approach.

With any of the EMS failover patterns, the EMS clients must be appropriately configured to take advantage of the failover.

There are three patterns that can be used with ActiveMatrix BusinessWorks. The first is the ActiveMatrix BusinessWorks Deferred JMS Acknowledgement Pattern, which is an extension of the Active-Matrix Deferred JMS Acknowledgement Pattern. It defers message acknowledgement until work is completed, and thus ensures that failure before that point will result in the redelivery of the message.

The second pattern is the ActiveMatrix BusinessWorks Built-In Intra-Site Failover Pattern, which uses two capabilities of the Active-Matrix BusinessWorks engines. One is the ability to save the state of an in-progress job as a checkpoint, and the other is the ability of the engines to monitor the status of other engines and recovery jobs from checkpoints. In this pattern, the BusinessWorks engine saves checkpoints in a database. When the back-up engine notices that the primary has failed, it retrieves the state of the checkpointed jobs from the database and resumes their execution.

The third pattern is the ActiveMatrix BusinessWorks Cluster Failover Pattern. This pattern uses file-based checkpointing in conjunction with the Intra-Site Cluster Failover Pattern. When the engine is resurrected, it retrieves the checkpointed jobs and resumes their execution.

There are four failover patterns that can be used with ActiveMatrix BusinessWorks nodes: ActiveMatrix Deferred JMS Acknowledgement, ActiveMatrix BusinessWorks Built-In Intra-Site Failover, Intra-Site Cluster Failover, and Inter-Site Failover with Same-Host Identity.

Given the right infrastructure, intra-site and inter-site failover patterns can be combined to yield multi-site high-availability patterns. For EMS and non-persistent messages, the EMS File-Based Intra-Site Failover Pattern and Inter-Site Failover with Same-Host Identity Pattern can be combined to yield a 99.999% availability solution across multiple sites. For persistent messages, adding the EMS Client Load Distribution: Queue Pattern gives client access with 99.999% availability, although delivery of in-flight messages might not quite meet the availability target.

Chapter 17

Service Federation

Objectives

A federation is a grouping of things in which each of the things retains a degree of autonomy. Historically the term arose in a political context to describe how regional political units (e.g., states or provinces) band together to form a nation while still retaining a level of regional autonomy.

The concept of federation applies equally well to the creation and management of services. It is not unusual for different organizations to independently develop services. At the same time, the need can arise for these organizations to share access to at least some of these services. These mutually shared services are said to be federated. Federation allows the different groups to work independently, yet share some of the results. What the groups agree to is a uniform way of locating and accessing the federated services.

This chapter explores the concept of federated services, discusses some of the issues that arise when federating services, and describes patterns for federation. After reading this chapter you will be able to

- Describe the concepts of service federation.
- Describe the issues that arise when federating services and approaches to addressing them.
- Identify and select appropriate federation patterns.

Factors Leading to Federation

At the core of service federation is the reality that different groups often develop services independently. Groups working in different functional areas, for example, may independently develop systems using a service-oriented approach. Groups working in different geographic locations, similarly, may develop their services independently. Federation arises when one of these groups has a need for services provided by another group. For the sake of uniformity, these areas will be referred to as service domains, regardless of whether the reason for separation is functional or geographic.

One fact that quickly becomes apparent in such situations is that most of the services in a service domain are intended to be used only within that domain. Only a small subset of the services is suitable for use by other domains. This is true even when two different groups develop services covering the same functional area: The different groups will likely modularize their functional areas in different ways. Consequently, most of their services will not be suitable for use by the other domain.

Issues in Federation

Access Control

Individual service domains often use different approaches for governing access to their services. The techniques and technologies employed for authentication, authorization, and encryption commonly vary from domain to domain.

These differences create problems when one domain needs to access the services of another. The domain requiring access must use the access techniques and technologies required by the other domain. The domain providing the service must administratively configure its access control to allow access to the other domain. Even worse, the access control rules for inter-domain interaction are often very different than those for intra-domain interactions.

The common solution to this problem is to create a single uniform access mechanism for the federated services. Only the services that are intended to be federated are exposed, and a uniform approach to access control is applied to all exposed services.

The ActiveMatrix Service Bus is well suited to this role. With minimal effort, it can re-expose selected domain services and provide uniform access control. If desired, exposed services can be presented with multiple transport bindings (e.g., SOAP/HTTP and SOAP/JMS). ActiveMatrix Service Bus also collects detailed statistics on service utilization.

Repositories

Before a service can be accessed, you must first know that it exists and learn how to use it. This is the role of a repository. Federation raises questions as to how repositories should be organized.

One approach is to place all the services from all the domains into a single repository. This runs counter to the idea of federation, but it has other issues as well. Finding the service you want could be a problem. Most of the services are intended only for use within a given domain. Placing all the services in the same repository makes it more difficult for people working in other domains to filter through and find the services that are intended for their use. This could be addressed by organizing the repository by domain and filtering the presented services based on the domain requiring access. However, this implies a level of central coordination that runs counter to the idea of independence lying at the heart of the federation concept.

The common solution to this problem is to create a repository that contains information about the federated services. The repository organizes the services so that they are easy to locate and contains all the information required to use them, including specifications, user guides, and WSDLs.

The TIBCO ActiveMatrix® Lifecycle Governance Framework product is well suited to this role. Its repository can manage the service-related artifacts as well as the contracts for individual service users. In addition, the governance workflow can manage the related life cycles for federating a service and granting access to a service consumer.

Basic Federation Pattern

If there are no geographic considerations, federation is fairly straight-forward (Figure 17-1). Services reside in their respective domains, each with its own access control policies and repository. To make a service available as a federated service, a new endpoint for accessing that

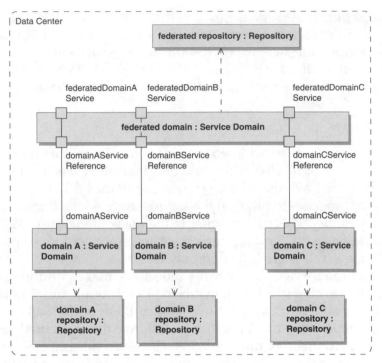

Figure 17-1: *Basic Federation Pattern*

service is added to the federated domain. Suitable access control policies are applied at the federated endpoint.

The federated domain maps its endpoint to the service domain's endpoint. As part of this mapping, the federated domain must comply with the access control requirements of the individual domain. Most likely the individual domain access control rules will have to be modified to grant access to the federated domain.

When a service is added to the federated domain, the relevant artifacts are added to the federated repository. Thus only federated services are presented in this repository, making it easier to locate the desired services. These artifacts are likely to be copies of artifacts present in the individual domain repositories.

When consumers of the federated service are added, a service utilization contract is established and the federated access control rules are updated. The utilization contract establishes the agreed-upon level of support for that service consumer. It is good practice to place the utilization contract in the repository.

Federation with Remote Domain Pattern

With today's global enterprises, it is not unusual to find some service domains located at different geographic locations. Such services can be federated using the Federation with Remote Domain Pattern shown in Figure 17-2. In this pattern, consumers of the federated services are not aware that some of the services are located remotely. In fact, all of the federated services could actually be located remotely.

In this pattern, the access points for all federated services are located at one site. Any consumer that requires these services must access that site, which may be remote from their location. This can complicate the federated access control rules if remote access requires different procedures than local access. Alternatively, the Distributed Federation Pattern can be used.

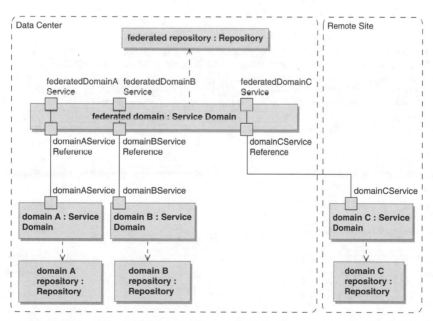

Figure 17-2: *Federation with Remote Domain Pattern*

Distributed Federation Pattern

A more general pattern for geographically distributed federation is shown in Figure 17-3. Here each site has its own federated service domain that provides local access to all federated services. When the actual service resides at another site, it is re-exposed through the local federated service domain. This approach consolidates all inter-site routine into the federated domains.

In distributed federation, each site maintains its own local repository of federated services, or at least its own local interface to that repository. Most of the repository content will be the same at each site, either replicated or using links to reference the source materials at a single site. Unique to each repository are the endpoints for accessing the federated services.

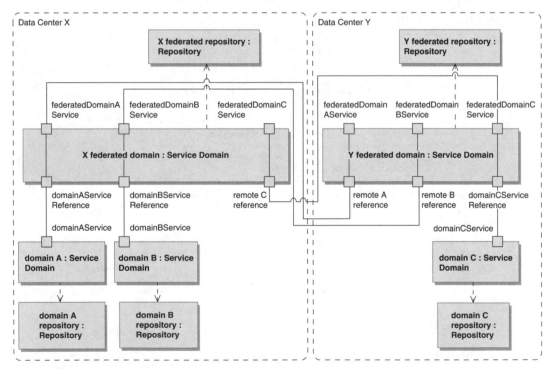

Figure 17-3: *Distributed Federation Pattern*

Standardizing Service Domain Technology

Although federation can accommodate the use of different technologies and techniques for different service domains, a proliferation of different techniques and technologies complicates development. Implementing a federated domain requires standardizing the set of technologies and techniques to be used for that domain. It is good practice to make these the preferred standards for individual service domains as well. Typically the policy is to allow existing domains using other approaches to continue to do so, but for any newly created domains to utilize the preferred technology.

Summary

Federation provides a standardized way for independently developed services to be shared across service domains by adding them to a federated domain. Adding them to the federated domain re-exposes the service, providing a new endpoint for its access and the ability to provide access control. The federated domain maps these endpoints to the individual services and complies with the access control specific to their individual service domains. The ActiveMatrix Service Bus is well suited to this role.

Federation requires a repository as well so that potential consumers can locate appropriate services and obtain the information required to use them properly. As with the individual service domains, the contents of the federated repository, for the most part, are extracts from the repositories of the individual service domains. The exception is the information about the service endpoints, which are specific to the federated domain. The ActiveMatrix® Lifecycle Governance Framework is well suited to this role.

Basic federation is straightforward at a single site. Since all services are local, mapping federated endpoints to their implementations involves just a local redirect and compliance with the service domain's access control policies.

When one or more of the service domains is remote, the mapping of the federated service must address the inter-site communications required along with any additional access control policies required for inter-site communications. Embedding this functionality within the federated domain eliminates the need for federated service consumers to deal with these requirements. However, federated service consumers located at other sites must still deal with these issues.

Distributed federation places a full federated service domain at each site, providing local access to all federated services. The required inter-site routing and access control compliance are completely contained within the federated domain. Since each site has different endpoints for its federated services, each site requires a slightly different view of the federated repository.

Chapter 18

Documenting a Solution Architecture

Throughout this book, various aspects of the Nouveau Health Care solution architecture have been presented, but these have been organized to support the topic discussions. This chapter presents an outline for presenting a solution architecture. An example of this outline containing the Nouveau Health Care Solution Architecture can be found at informit.com/title/9780321802057.

Business Objectives and Constraints

Provide the business context for the solution.

Quantified Business Expectations

Indicate, in measurable terms, the business objectives for this solution. If this is an incremental change to an existing solution, the quantification should reflect the expectations for the change being made.

Business Constraints

Indicate the business constraints being placed upon the project implementing the solution (or the change to the solution). Cost and schedule expectations are common constraints, but there may be others as well. Typically these are constraints on the business processes that comprise the solution.

Business Risks

Indicate the risks to the business that result from each of the impacted business processes failing to execute properly. Indicate the impact from a single failure and the impact from the process becoming unavailable for some period of time. This information is used by the architects to determine the level of fault tolerance to be built into each business process.

Solution Context

Most solutions are fragments of a larger architecture. Provide an overview of how the solution fits into the larger architecture.

Business Process Inventory

Provide an overview of the business processes that comprise this solution. Provide an overview of the artifacts that are exchanged between the business processes. Include all business processes involved in the exchange of artifacts. Even if a business process is not within the scope of this solution, if it is involved in an artifact exchange it must be shown.

Domain Model

Present an overview of the information used in the business processes. The focus should be on the concepts and their relationships, with particular emphasis on the multiplicities of the relationships. Only major attributes—identifiers and values that drive business process decision making—should be modeled. The domain model serves as an overview and guide to the detailed data structures used during the execution of the business processes.

Solution Architecture Pattern

Present the architecture pattern supporting the solution. The pattern should show the participants in the business processes (both human and machine) and their communications channels. Any constraints on the participants should be shown as well.

Business Process 1

Each major business process is described in its own chapter of the architecture document.

Business Process Design

Show the structure of the business process—its activities and the interactions between them. Show all artifacts required for the execution of each activity and all artifacts produced by each activity. This is typically done with a UML Activity Diagram or BPMN diagram.

Process-Pattern Mapping

Map the business process design onto the architecture pattern. The intent is to show how the components of the architecture pattern collaborate to execute the business process. All interactions between participants should be shown, and all artifacts exchanged between components should be identified and modeled. This is typically done with a UML Activity Diagram and one or more UML Class Diagrams to model the artifacts being exchanged. Interfaces should be identified and detailed.

Business Process 2

Document the second business process involved in the solution.

Business Process *n*

Document the last business process involved in the solution.

Addressing Nonfunctional Solution Requirements

Describe how the solution architecture addresses the nonfunctional requirements of the solution. The outline has sections for the most common categories, but additional sections should be added as required to address additional categories.

Performance and Scalability

Describe how the overall performance and scalability requirements for the solution were used to derive the performance and scalability requirements for the individual components. Where analysis indicates that more than one instance of a component may be required to handle the load, describe the mechanisms to be used for load distribution.

Availability within a Data Center

Describe how the availability requirements for the overall solution were used to determine the availability requirements for the individual components. Where meeting availability requirements results in the need for multiple components operating in a fault-tolerant or high-availability group, describe the manner in which the group will be managed and how work in progress will be handled.

Site Disaster Recovery

Describe how the site disaster recovery requirements (recovery point objective, recovery time objective) for the overall solution were used to determine the site disaster recovery requirements for the individual components. Be specific about how component state information is replicated between the sites and how work in progress will be handled.

Security

Describe how the security requirements for the overall solution were used to determine the security requirements for the individual components. Be specific about the roles of authentication and authorization servers and the points at which they interact with components. Be specific about how credentials will be managed, particularly when credentials can expire.

Component/Service A

There should be a chapter for each component or service involved in the architecture. The chapter summarizes the participation of the component in each of the business processes. The chapter is essentially the specification for the component's participation in the solution.

The level of detail in the chapter will depend somewhat on whether the component or service already exists. The following is what this might look like.

- *Existing Components and Services:* For existing components that require no modification or integration design to be used as part of the solution, the chapter will simply provide an overview of the component's utilization. To the extent that documentation on the component or service already exists, the sections of this chapter can be filled in with references to that documentation. This chapter should focus on the specifics of the utilization, identifying the interfaces to be used along with the volumes of utilization and required SLAs for those interactions.
- *New Components:* For new components, this chapter should be treated as the specification for the component unless the goal is to create a separate specification document.
- *New Services:* For new services, a separate service specification document should be created for each service. This chapter then references that document where appropriate and establishes the utilization contract between the solution and the service. In particular, this chapter should focus on the specifics of the utilization, identifying the interfaces to be used along with the volumes of utilization and required SLAs for those interactions.

Business Process Involvement

Indicate how the component participates in the solution's business processes. In most cases, this is detailed in the process-pattern mappings of the business process chapters. In such cases, a list of references to those diagrams is sufficient.

Interfaces

Document the component interfaces used by the solution. Use UML Class diagrams here, place textual details (WSDLs, etc.) in the appendices.

Observable Architecture

Document the observable architecture of the component (components upon which this component depends for proper operation).

Observable State

If the component has stateful information impacting its observable behavior, document the state and the manner in which it impacts the observable behavior.

Coordination

Indicate the patterns used to coordinate this component's activities with other solution activities. This is particularly important when these patterns involve multiple interactions.

Constraints

If there are constraints on when certain operations may be invoked, document them here. Some constraints are obvious: A cancelOrder() call is invalid when a placeOrder() call has not been made for that order. Others are less obvious: cancelOrder() cannot be called for an order that has already shipped.

Nonfunctional Behavior

Document the nonfunctional behaviors required of this component. These may be partially specified in the chapter "Addressing Non-Functional Solution Requirements." Use this section to add component-specific details, as needed.

Performance and Scalability

Describe how this component will achieve its performance and scalability requirements. Where analysis indicates that more than one instance of a component may be required to handle the load, describe the mechanisms to be used for load distribution.

Availability within a Data Center

Describe how the availability requirements for this component will be achieved. Where meeting availability requirements result in the need for multiple components operating in a fault-tolerant or high-availability group, describe the manner in which the group will be managed and how work in progress will be handled.

Site Disaster Recovery

Describe how the site disaster recovery requirements (recovery point objective, recovery time objective) for this component will be achieved. Be specific about how component state information is replicated between the sites and how work in progress will be handled.

Security

Describe how the security requirements for this component will be achieved. Be specific about the roles of authentication and authorization servers and the points at which they interact with components. Be specific about how credentials will be managed, particularly when credentials can expire.

Component/Service B

Document the component and its participation in the solution.

Component/Service *n*

Document the component and its participation in the solution.

Deployment

Deployment Environment Migration

Describe how the solution will be migrated from one environment to another. Pay specific attention to how code and configuration information will be migrated. Describe the role that source control and deployment scripts will play. Describe the configuration steps that are required once the solution has been migrated.

Development Configuration

Describe the development environment and the manner in which the solution will be assembled in this environment, including how many machines of which type and what components are installed on each. Describe the network topology.

Test Configuration

Describe the environment, including how many machines of which type and what components are installed on each. Describe the network topology.

Production Configuration

Describe the environment, including how many machines of which type and what components are installed on each. Describe the network topology.

Integration and Testing Requirements

Integration Strategy

Describe the sequence in which the components and services will be integrated and define the test harnesses and test data required at each step. Describe how the solution will be deployed in this environment.

Behavioral Testing

Describe how functional testing will be performed, including test cases and test data (may reference another document). Describe how the solution will be deployed in this environment. Pay particular attention to the test harness required and the mechanics of how test data are repeatably loaded so that test scenarios can be exactly repeated.

Failure Testing

Describe how failures testing will be performed. Identify the failure scenarios that will be tested and the environment into which the solution will be deployed for the test.

Performance Testing

Describe how the system's ability to meet performance goals will be established. Describe the additional requirements on components that may be necessary to support this testing (logging, time stamps, etc.). Describe how the solution will be deployed in this environment. If production-scale testing is not possible in this environment, describe how the testing results can be extrapolated to predict production performance.

Appendix A: Common Data Format Specifications

Place the textual versions of data format specifications (e.g., .xsd definitions of XML schema) for common (shared) data formats here.

Appendix B: Message Format Specifications

Place the textual versions of message format specifications (e.g., .xsd definitions of XML schema) here.

Appendix C: Service Interface Specifications

Place WSDLs and other textual interface specifications here.

Appendix D: Data Storage Specifications

Place textual definitions of database schema here.

Chapter 19

Documenting a Service Specification

A service specification serves two purposes. First, it specifies what the service implementation team needs to implement. Second, it serves as a guide for new service users to help them understand what the service is and what it is for.

Services that are intended to be reused must be usable in different solution contexts. This document should clearly indicate what those different solution contexts are, highlighting their similarities and differences. If the service is employed differently in the different contexts, this must be made clear as well.

Service Overview

Service One-Line Description

This description is the most concise possible statement of the service's purpose and is intended to help the naïve potential user quickly identify services of potential interest.

Service Abstract

The abstract is a short, one-paragraph description of the service's purpose, functionality, and intended usage. Its purpose is to help the naïve potential user further refine their identification of potentially interesting services.

Service Context

The context describes the architecture pattern into which the service is intended to fit. It shows both the consumer(s) of the service and the observable components having supporting behavior that is required for the service to execute properly. It summarizes the observable dependencies.

The context can be shown at different levels of detail. At the highest level of abstraction, the context shows all of the components and identifies the interfaces involved in their interaction. Some additional context information is required to complete the specification, specifically the details of the interface operations and data structures along with the communications channels over which the interactions occur.

This additional information may be shown in the context or included in other sections of the specification. In the accompanying example, the interface details are given in the triggered behavior descriptions and the communications channels are given in the deployment specifics section. Placing the interface details in the triggered behavior descriptions makes the context overview concise and easy to understand. Placing the communications channels in the deployment specifics allows different communications channels to be specified for different environments.

Intended Utilization Scenarios

The utilization scenarios provide a behavioral overview of how the service is intended to fit into the larger business processes. In simple situations in which the service's participation in the business process amounts to the invocation of a single service operation, these scenarios represent individual use cases for the individual operations. With more complex services, on the other hand, a single business process execution may involve multiple interactions with the service. Such is the case with the Payment Manager used in the accompanying example. In these cases, the utilization scenarios spell out the possible sequences of interactions. In all cases, the utilization scenarios should clearly indicate how the work of the service is coordinated with other work in the business process.

Interface Definitions

This section defines the interfaces provided by the service. It details the operations of each interface and the data structures used by those operations. Although the details for some interfaces can be provided by SOAP WSDL documents, for readability it is prudent to augment such detailed textual representations with graphical representations using UML class diagrams. Place the diagrams here and the text of the WSDL in an appendix.

Referenced Components

This section defines the interfaces of other external components that are used by the service. This information is generally taken from the specifications for those components, but it is useful to replicate those interface definitions in the present specification.

Observable State

Many services are stateful, with some operations of the service altering the state and other operations making that state visible to external components. This section identifies this information.

Services often statefully maintain replicas of information that originates in other components. This section identifies this information and the triggered behavior (if any) involved in maintaining its consistency.

Triggered Behaviors

The triggered behaviors define the service's behavior in response to triggering events, along with its dependencies on the behaviors of external components. This section enumerates those triggering events and provides details of the ensuing observable behaviors. These behaviors can include interactions with external components and interactions with the internal observable state maintained by the service.

Three broad categories of triggers should be included: operation invocations, notifications, and time-based events.

Coordination

The manner in which the service's activity can be coordinated with that of other components must be clearly understood by the service consumer. To the extent that the intended utilization scenarios document this coordination, simple reference to the scenarios suffices for documentation. Otherwise, this section should document the possible coordination as well as the behavior when coordination fails (e.g., observable behavior upon lack of response in a request-reply interaction).

Constraints

If there are constraints on the use of service operations, these must be documented. In some cases, such as allowed sequences of operations, the utilization scenarios may capture this in sufficient detail. In other cases, particularly involving business rule constraints, these need to be explicitly identified. Service consumers need to understand these restrictions.

Nonfunctional Behavior

This section documents the nonfunctional capabilities of the service. Throughput and corresponding response times for individual service operations should be documented. Required security constraints (authentication, authorization, encryption, non-repudiation) are specified on a per-operation or per-interface basis, as appropriate. Availability, outage constraints, and recovery times may be specified on a per-service, per-interface, or per-operation basis. Whether or not the service guarantees that requests are processed in the order received is another important nonfunctional behavior.

In some cases, the mechanisms used to achieve fault tolerance, high availability, or load distribution may require specific actions on the part of service consumers or the use of external components. To the extent that the service consumer must be aware of these mechanisms, they must be documented as part of the service specification. In these situations, it is important to clarify whether the performance-related specifications apply to a single instance of the service or to the aggregate capabilities of the multiple instances.

Deployment

Some observable characteristics of services vary depending upon the deployment environment. SOAP endpoints, for example, will likely be different in development, test, and production environments. Exposed fault-tolerance, high-availability, and load distribution mechanisms may also vary between environments, and these differences need to be documented.

Appendix A: Service Interface Specifications

Place the textual definitions of service interfaces (e.g., WSDLs) here.

Appendix B: Referenced Interface Specifications

Place the textual definitions of referenced service interfaces (e.g., WSDLs) here.

Afterword

The world of composite applications and services is large and complex. The material covered in this book and its companion *TIBCO® Architecture Fundamentals* lays the groundwork for successful solutions, but it is just a start. A more comprehensive discussion of the design issues you will encounter can be found in *Implementing SOA: Total Architecture in Practice.*[1]

Some problem areas will push your solutions into more specialized styles of architectures. Complex event processing is one, in which real-time events need to be evaluated as they occur and decisions need to be made as to what kind of action to take. Applications include tracking (e.g., following your luggage from airport check-in to your final destination), fraud detection, and real-time offers. This style of application will be the subject of the upcoming *Architecting Complex Event Processing Solutions with TIBCO®* from TIBCO Press and Addison-Wesley.

Another area of specialization is business process management. Here the problem is one of managing a complex process, often involving a mixture of human and system participants. The objective typically is to optimize both the execution of the process and the utilization of the workforce involved. These applications will be the subject of the

---

1. Paul C. Brown, *Implementing SOA: Total Architecture in Practice*, Boston: Addison-Wesley (2008).

upcoming *Architecting BPM Solutions with TIBCO®*, also from TIBCO Press and Addison-Wesley.

For additional information, you can go to www.tibco.com. To interact with other members of the TIBCO user community, please go to www.TIBCOmmunity.com.

Appendix A

UML Notation Reference

This appendix provides a brief overview of the UML notations used in this book. For a thorough examination of the notation, see *The Unified Modeling Language Reference Manual: Second Edition*.[1]

Class Diagram Basics

This section illustrates the basic UML Class Diagram notation. For the most part, explanations are presented as notes in the diagram.

Classes

Figure A-1 shows two examples of a UML Class, one representing a Person and the other representing a Banking Service. Classes may be used to represent abstractions or concrete things. By default, each class is represented by a box with three regions. The upper region contains

---

1. James Rumbaugh, Ivar Jacobson, and Grady Booch, *The Unified Modeling Language Reference Manual: Second Edition*, Boston: Addison-Wesley (2005).

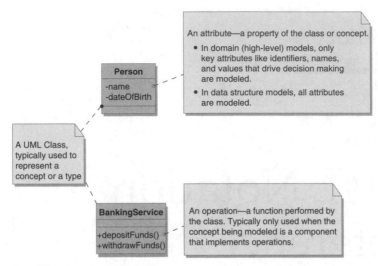

Figure A-1: *Classes*

the name of the class, the middle region its attributes, and the bottom region its operations (if applicable).

The display of these regions and the items within the regions is optional. The only mandatory part is the class name. There are also three additional optional regions that may be shown, one for structure, one for signals, and one for ports. Structure and ports will be discussed in the next section. Signals, in this context, are not used in this book.

Interfaces

A specialized concept, with its own notation, is the Interface (Figure A-2). A small circle appears in the name region to indicate that this is an interface (the coloring is just for convenience). Typically the operations region is the only one shown for an interface.

If you have a component that implements an interface, you can indicate this with a Realization relation, as shown in Figure A-2. A realization relation establishes the association between a specification (indicated by the triangle at one end of the line) and its implementation (at the other end of the line). In this case, the Banking Service Interface is an interface specification and the Banking Service component implements that interface.

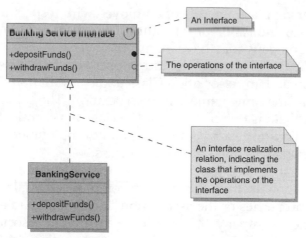

Figure A-2: *Interfaces*

Associations

A general association between classes is indicated by drawing a solid line between them (Figure A-3). The association has an optional name. At each end of the association a role name indicates the role that the class at that end plays with respect to the class at the other end. In the

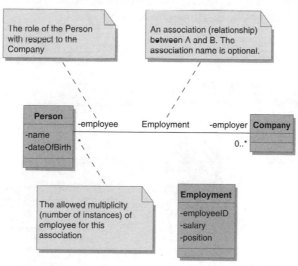

Figure A-3: *Associations*

example, Person plays the role of employee with respect to Company. There is also an indication of the multiplicity of the relationship. In the example, a Company may have many employees.

Sometimes there is a need to add information to the association. In this case, you add an Association Class to the association (Figure A-4). This class has the same name as the association. The semantics of this class is that there is one instance of the class for each instance of the association. Thus for each Person-Company Employment association, there is an instance of the Employment class.

The association class provides a home for information that is related to the association itself. In this case, the employeeID, salary, and position are all properties of the association. If a Person had a second job with a different company, that would be a different association with a different set of values.

Part-Whole Relationships: Aggregation and Composition

Sometimes you want to indicate something a little stronger than a simple association—you want to indicate the existence of a part-whole relationship between two classes. There are two variations on this in UML depending upon whether or not the class playing the part makes any sense on its own. If it does, the aggregation notation (Figure A-5) is used, adding a hollow diamond to the "whole" end of the association. In this example, the concept of an Account Reference makes sense in many contexts, but a Deposit Funds Request must indicate the account to which the funds will be deposited.

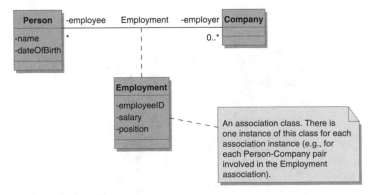

Figure A-4: *Association Class*

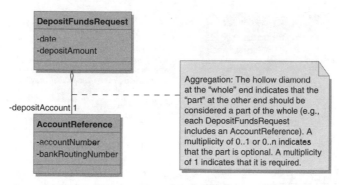

Figure A-5: *Aggregation*

When the part doesn't make any sense without the whole, a solid diamond is added at the "whole" end of the association (Figure A-6).

Generalization

Sometimes you will encounter a situation in which there is a core concept and then a number of variations (Figure A-7). A UML Generalization relation is used to indicate this type of relationship. Generalization indicates that each of the subclasses has *all* of the characteristics (attributes, relationships, structure, etc.) of the parent class. If you don't mean this, don't use generalization! Typically each of the subclasses has additional characteristics that are unique to the subclass.

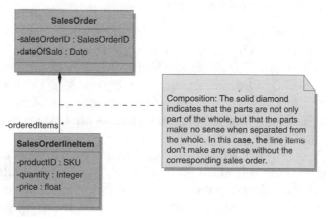

Figure A-6: *Composition*

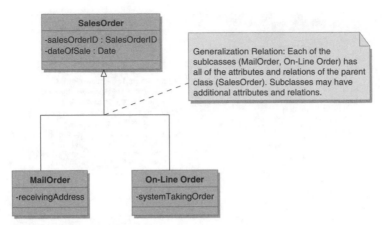

Figure A-7: *Generalization*

Structure

Structure is an important element of architecture, so you need to know how to indicate structure. In UML, structure can be indicated a number of ways. We have already seen two. One is the inclusion of attributes in a class: Each attribute is a structural element of the class. The other is an association with a role name at the opposite end, particularly when the association is an aggregation or a composition.

Composite Structure Diagrams

UML has another graphic notation for indicating structure called a Composite Structure Diagram. Each diagram represents the structure of a particular concept. For example, Figure A-8 is a composite structure diagram of the SalesOrder class shown in Figure A-6. The frame around the diagram identifies the concept whose structure is being shown.

Within the frame, the individual elements are known as parts. Each part has a name that is used to identify the part, with the overall concept being the whole. Part names must be unique. The part can indicate the type of object that is allowed to play the part and the allowed multiplicity of those objects. In the example, A SalesOrder has a part called orderedItems of type SalesOrderLineItem, and there may be zero or more instances of SalesOrderLineItem.

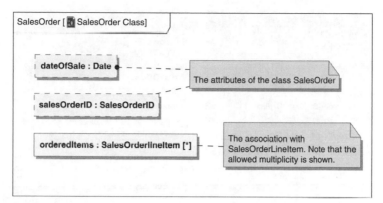

Figure A-8: *Composite Structure of the SalesOrder Class*

This notation can be used recursively to display the structure of the individual parts (Figure A-9). Thus you can expose as much or as little of the structure as is appropriate for the point you are trying to make.

Earlier we mentioned that there was a structure region of a Class in a class diagram. When you turn on the display of this region, what you get is a Composite Structure Diagram embedded in the class box (Figure A-10). Again, you have full control over how much or how little structure is displayed.

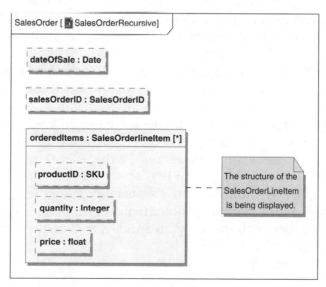

Figure A-9: *Nested Structure*

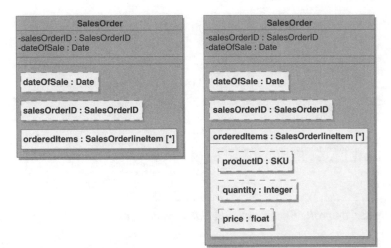

Figure A-10: *Displaying the Structure of a Class*

Avoiding Common Structure Editing Mistakes

A note on the mechanics of creating these diagrams is in order: Pay close attention or you will end up with a confusing model. The starting point is to remember that there is one, and only one, structure for each concept! Each of the diagrams is just a view of that structure. What does this mean for the mechanics of creating the diagrams? It means that if a structure has already been defined, your diagram should expose that existing structure.

The details of how to expose structure will vary from tool to tool. In MagicDraw (the tool used to create all of the UML diagrams in this book), when you select an element in a diagram and bring up the right mouse menu, there is a Related Elements menu choice. This provides the means of exposing existing structure. Learn how to use it!

What you do not want to do is create a duplicate structure. If there is already an association between two classes, display it—don't create another one! Then you'll have two associations. If there is already a part, display it—don't create another one. Then you will have two parts. Get familiar with this or your models will confuse, not clarify, your thinking.

Execution Environments

There are times when you want to describe how a collection of components are deployed and wired together. UML has a concept known as an Execution Environment that is ideal for this purpose. Figure A-11 shows an execution environment as it would be displayed in a class diagram. However, all this diagram shows is that the environment exists.

Execution Environment Structure

The usefulness of the execution environment concept emerges when you show its structure using a composite structure diagram (Figure A-12). Here an environment is shown with three parts: a service-Consumer (whose type is unspecified), an instance of a BankingService (with the instance unnamed), and an accountsDatabase. Also shown

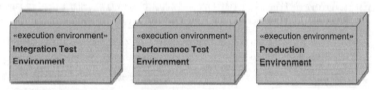

Figure A-11: *Execution Environments in a Class Diagram*

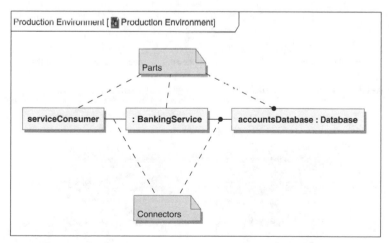

Figure A-12: *Composite Structure of an Execution Environment*

are connectors between the parts, here being used to represent commu-nications channels.

Ports

One thing that is missing from this picture is the Bank Service Interface and an understanding that this is the interface being used by the serviceConsumer. To indicate this, we add what is known as a port to the part (Figure A-13) and associate the Banking Service Interface with the port. The channel from the service consumer is now associ-ated with the port to indicate the use of that interface.

You've probably noticed another difference with this diagram: the surrounding frame indicating that this is a production environment has been removed. The display of this frame is optional, and in most of the diagrams used in this book the frame display has been removed.

Adding the port to this diagram did more than just add a box to the diagram: It altered the definition of the Banking Service. The newly added port can be displayed in a class diagram in two ways (Figure A-14). One is to turn on the display of the port region in the class, as has been done on the left. The other is to turn on the display of the port as a square on the margin of the class, as has been done on the right.

A port can be used to indicate either the presentation of a service interface or a reference to a service interface presented by another component.

Figure A-13: *Adding a Port in the Production Environment*

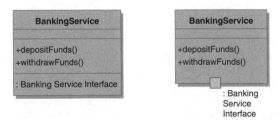

Figure A-14: *Showing a Port on the Banking Service Class*

Activity Diagrams

Actions and Control Flow

An activity diagram is used to describe behavior in the form of structured sequences of actions. Figure A-15 shows two actions related by a control flow. The semantics of this is that action A is performed and, when it is completed, action B is performed. The Control Flow arrow is used to indicate this sequencing.

Artifacts

Actions sometimes require inputs and produce outputs. These are generically referred to as artifacts and are represented as objects in UML. Figure A-16 shows an action consuming one artifact and producing another.

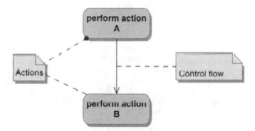

Figure A-15: *Actions in an Activity Diagram*

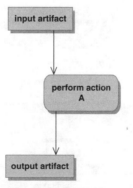

Figure A-16: *Artifacts Produced and Consumed by an Action*

Structured Activities

An action can be a structured activity (Figure A-17).

Call Operation Action

If you need to indicate that the action is the invocation of a specific interface operation, use the Call Operation Action (Figure A-18).

Decisions, Forks, and Joins

Activity diagrams have some specialized activities. Figure A-19(a) is a decision activity in which either action B or C is performed based on the logical outcome of the decision. In (b), a fork activity indicates that after action D is performed, both actions E and F occur in parallel. In (c), a join activity indicates that after both actions G and H are completed, action I is performed.

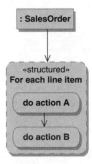

Figure A-17: *Structured Activity*

Figure A-18: *Call Operation Action*

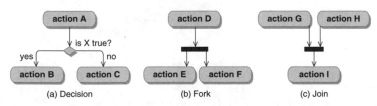

Figure A-19: *Decisions, Forks, and Joins*

Event Actions

Activity diagrams have special actions related to the occurrence of an event (Figure A-20). The Accept Event is used to indicate that the occurrence of some event, such as the arrival of a message, is the trigger for the subsequent action. The Time Event is used to indicate that some time-based event, such as the expiration of a timer, triggers the subsequent action.

Swimlanes

Swimlanes (Figure A-21) are used to indicate which participant in a process is performing which activity. In the example, Participant X performs action A, which generates an artifact. That artifact is then used by Participant Y's action B. The placement of the action in the swimlane indicates that the participant represented by that swimlane performs that activity. In contrast, the placement of an artifact (object) in a swimlane has no significance at all. In the example, the meaning would be the same if the artifact were placed in Participant X's swimlane.

The labels on the swimlanes may indicate either logical roles being played or the actual participant playing that role.

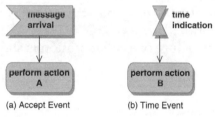

Figure A-20: *Event Actions*

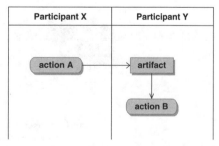

Figure A-21: *Swimlanes*

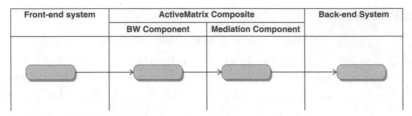

Figure A-22: *Swimlanes with Structure*

Swimlanes with Structure

The component represented by a swimlane may have a sub-structure. If so, you can indicate the actions being performed by the individual sub-components by adding structure to the corresponding swimlane (Figure A-22).

Collaborations

A collaboration is a structured set of interactions between a number of participants—in other words, a process. In a UML class diagram it is represented by an oval with a dotted-line boundary (Figure A-23). This enables you to indicate, for example, the artifacts that are generated and consumed by various processes.

The behavioral structure of a collaboration is shown using an activity diagram.

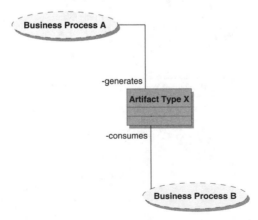

Figure A-23: *Collaboration*

State Machines

States and Transitions

State machines consist of states and transitions (Figure A-24). Each machine has an initial state, a final state, and one or more intermediate states. A machine may only be in one state at a time. Transitions between states are labeled with the conditions under which the state transition is taken.

Composite States

States can be composites of sub-states (Figure A-25). When State A transitions to the composite state, sub-state X is entered as indicated by the arrow from the composite to the sub-state. In this diagram, there are two possible exits from the composite state. If condition 1 occurs at any time, regardless of the sub-state, the machine will transition to state D. If condition 2 occurs while the composite is in sub-state Y, then a transition to State C will occur.

Orthogonal States

Sometimes a state is really a composition of two state machines. Such states are referred to as orthogonal states (Figure A-26). In the example, when the orthogonal state is entered, it is simultaneously in sub-state K and in sub-state X. Transitions between K and J are independent of transitions between X and Y.

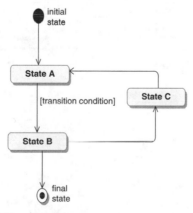

Figure A-24: *States and Transitions*

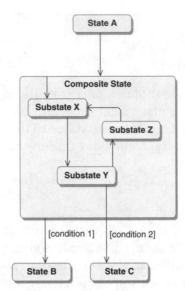

Figure A-25: *Composite States*

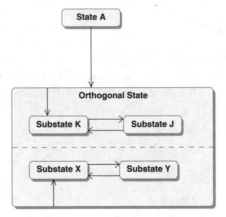

Figure A-26: *Orthogonal States*

Appendix B

WSDLs and Schemas
from Examples

Sales Order Example

This appendix contains a subset of the schema and WSDL definitions from the Sales Order example. The definitions included here are those corresponding to Figure 9-12, with the exception that the WSDL for the Sales Order Status Interface is not shown.

Sales Order Service Interface WSDL

The following shows the WSDL for the Sales Order Service Interface showing only the getOrderDetails() operation and its supporting definitions.

```
<?xml version="1.0" encoding="UTF-8"?>
<definitions
  xmlns="http://schemas.xmlsoap.org/wsdl/"
  xmlns:ns="http://enterprise.com/salesOrder/
    salesOrderInterface/
    schema/SalesOrderInterface1"
  xmlns:tns="http://exampe.com/sales/salesOrder/
    SalesOrderInterface/
    wsdl/salesOrderInterface1"
  xmlns:xsd="http://www.w3.org/2001/XMLSchema"
```

```
  targetNamespace="http://exampe.com/sales/salesOrder/
    SalesOrderInterface/wsdl/salesOrderInterface1">
  <import namespace="http://enterprise.com/salesOrder/
    salesOrderInterface/schema/SalesOrderInterface1"
    location="enterprise.com/salesOrder/salesOrderInterface
      /schema/salesOrderInterface1.xsd"/>

  <message name="getSalesOrderDetailRequest">
    <part name="part1" type="ns:GetOrderDetailsRequest"/>
  </message>

  <message name="getOrderDetailsResponse">
    <part name="part1" type="ns:GetOrderDetailsResponse"/>
  </message>

  <portType name="SalesOrderInterface">
    <operation name="getOrderDetails">
      <input message="tns:getSalesOrderDetailRequest"/>
      <output message="tns:getOrderDetailsResponse"/>
    </operation>
  </portType>
</definitions>
```

Address Schema

```
<?xml version="1.0" encoding="UTF-8"?>
<xsd:schema
  xmlns="http://enterprise.com/address/schema/address1"
  xmlns:xsd="http://www.w3.org/2001/XMLSchema"
  targetNamespace="http://enterprise.com/address/schema/
    address1"
  elementFormDefault="unqualified"
  attributeFormDefault="unqualified">

  <xsd:simpleType name="ISOCountryCode">
    <xsd:restriction base="xsd:int"/>
  </xsd:simpleType>

  <xsd:complexType name="Address">
    <xsd:sequence>
      <xsd:element name="address1" type="xsd:string"/>
      <xsd:element name="address2" type="xsd:string"/>
      <xsd:element name="city" type="xsd:string"/>
      <xsd:element name="state" type="xsd:string"/>
      <xsd:element name="postalCode" type="xsd:string"/>
      <xsd:element name="countryCode" type="ISOCountryCode"/>
```

```
    </xsd:sequence>
  </xsd:complexType>
</xsd:schema>
```

Carrier Schema

```
<?xml version="1.0" encoding="UTF-8"?>
<xsd:schema
  xmlns="http://enterprise.com/fulfillment/schema/carrier"
  xmlns:xsd="http://www.w3.org/2001/XMLSchema"
  xmlns:ns0="http://enterprise.com/address/schema/address1"
  xmlns:ns1="http://enterprise.com/phone/schema/phone1"
  targetNamespace="http://enterprise.com/fulfillment/schema/
    carrier"
  elementFormDefault="unqualified"
  attributeFormDefault="unqualified">
  <xsd:import
    namespace="http://enterprise.com/address/schema/address1"
    schemaLocation=
      "http://enterprise.com/address/schema/address1.0.xsd"/>
  <xsd:import
    namespace="http://enterprise.com/phone/schema/phone1"
    schemaLocation="http://enterprise.com/phone/schema/
      phone1.0.xsd"/>

  <xsd:simpleType name="TrackingNumber">
    <xsd:restriction base="xsd:string">
      <xsd:maxLength value="50"/>
    </xsd:restriction>
  </xsd:simpleType>

  <xsd:simpleType name="CarrierID">
    <xsd:restriction base="xsd:string">
      <xsd:maxLength value="50"/>
    </xsd:restriction>
  </xsd:simpleType>

  <xsd:complexType name="Carrier">
    <xsd:sequence>
      <xsd:element name="carrierID" type="CarrierID"/>
      <xsd:element name="name" type="xsd:string"/>
      <xsd:element name="address" type="ns0:Address"/>
      <xsd:element name="phone" type="ns1:Phone"/>
    </xsd:sequence>
  </xsd:complexType>
```

```
  <xsd:complexType name="CarrierRef">
    <xsd:sequence>
      <xsd:element name="carrierID" type="CarrierID"/>
      <xsd:element name="name" type="xsd:string"/>
    </xsd:sequence>
  </xsd:complexType>
</xsd:schema>
```

Customer Schema

```
<?xml version="1.0" encoding="UTF-8"?>
<xsd:schema
  xmlns="http://enterprise.com/customer/schema/customer1"
  xmlns:xsd="http://www.w3.org/2001/XMLSchema"
  xmlns:tns2="http://enterprise.com/address/schema/address1"
  xmlns:tns3="http://enterprise.com/phone/schema/phone1"
  targetNamespace="http://enterprise.com/customer/schema/
    customer1"
  elementFormDefault="unqualified"
  attributeFormDefault="unqualified">
  <xsd:import namespace=http://enterprise.com/address/schema/
    address1
    schemaLocation="http://enterprise.com/address/schema/
      address1.0.xsd"/>
  <xsd:import namespace=http://enterprise.com/phone/schema/
    phone1
    schemaLocation=" http://enterprise.com/phone/schema/
      phone1.0.xsd"/>

  <xsd:simpleType name="CustomerID">
    <xsd:restriction base="xsd:string">
      <xsd:maxLength value="50"/>
    </xsd:restriction>
  </xsd:simpleType>

  <xsd:complexType name="CustomerRef">
    <xsd:sequence>
      <xsd:element name="customerID" type="CustomerID"/>
      <xsd:element name="name" type="xsd:string"/>
    </xsd:sequence>
  </xsd:complexType>

  <xsd:complexType name="Customer">
    <xsd:sequence>
      <xsd:element name="customerID" type="CustomerID"/>
      <xsd:element name="name" type="xsd:string"/>
```

```
        <xsd:element name="address" type="tns2:Address"/>
        <xsd:element name="phone" type="tns3:Phone"/>
    </xsd:sequence>
  </xsd:complexType>
</xsd:schema>
```

Manufacturer Schema

```
<?xml version="1.0" encoding="UTF-8"?>
<xsd:schema
  xmlns="http://procurement.enterprise.com/manufacturer/schema/
    manufacturer1"
  xmlns:xsd="http://www.w3.org/2001/XMLSchema"
  xmlns:ns0="http://enterprise.com/address/schema/address1"
  xmlns:ns1="http://enterprise.com/phone/schema/phone1"
  targetNamespace="http://procurement.enterprise.com/
    manufacturer/schema/manufacturer1"
  elementFormDefault="unqualified"
  attributeFormDefault="unqualified">
  <xsd:import namespace=http://enterprise.com/address/schema/
    address1
    schemaLocation="http://enterprise.com/address/schema/
      address1.0.xsd"/>
  <xsd:import namespace=http://enterprise.com/phone/schema/
    phone1
    schemaLocation=" http://enterprise.com/phone/schema/
      phone1.0.xsd"/>

  <xsd:simpleType name="ManufacturerID">
    <xsd:restriction base="xsd:string">
      <xsd:maxLength value="50"/>
    </xsd:restriction>
  </xsd:simpleType>

  <xsd:complexType name="Manufacturer">
    <xsd:sequence>
      <xsd:element name="manufacturerID" type="ManufacturerID"/>
      <xsd:element name="name" type="xsd:string"/>
      <xsd:element name="address" type="ns0:Address"/>
      <xsd:element name="phone" type="ns1:Phone"/>
    </xsd:sequence>
  </xsd:complexType>

  <xsd:complexType name="ManufacturerRef">
    <xsd:sequence>
      <xsd:element name="manufacturerID" type="ManufacturerID"/>
```

```xml
      <xsd:element name="name" type="xsd:string"/>
    </xsd:sequence>
  </xsd:complexType>
</xsd:schema>
```

Phone Schema

```xml
<?xml version="1.0" encoding="UTF-8"?>
<xsd:schema
  xmlns="http://enterprise.com/phone/schema/phone1"
  xmlns:xsd="http://www.w3.org/2001/XMLSchema"
  targetNamespace="http://enterprise.com/phone/schema/phone1"
  elementFormDefault="unqualified"
  attributeFormDefault="unqualified">

  <xsd:complexType name="Phone">
    <xsd:sequence>
      <xsd:element name="phoneNumber" type="xsd:integer"/>
      <xsd:element name="regionCode" type="xsd:integer"/>
      <xsd:element name="countryCode" type="xsd:integer"/>
    </xsd:sequence>
  </xsd:complexType>
</xsd:schema>
```

Product Schema

```xml
<?xml version="1.0" encoding="UTF-8"?>
<xsd:schema
  xmlns="http://enterprise.com/product/schema/product1"
  xmlns:xsd="http://www.w3.org/2001/XMLSchema"
  xmlns:ns0="http://enterprise.com/procurement/manufacturer/
    schema/manufacturer1"
  targetNamespace="http://enterprise.com/product/schema/
    product1"
  elementFormDefault="unqualified"
  attributeFormDefault="unqualified">
  <xsd:import
    namespace="http://enterprise.com/procurement/manufacturer/
      schema/manufacturer1"
    schemaLocation="http://enterprise.com/procurement/
      manufacturer/schema/manufacturer1.0.xsd"/>

  <xsd:simpleType name="SKU">
    <xsd:restriction base="xsd:int"/>
  </xsd:simpleType>
```

```xsd
  <xsd:complexType name="Product">
    <xsd:sequence>
      <xsd:element name="productID" type="SKU"/>
      <xsd:element name="name" type="xsd:string"/>
      <xsd:element name="manufacturer"
        type="ns0:ManufacturerRef"/>
    </xsd:sequence>
  </xsd:complexType>

  <xsd:complexType name="ProductRef">
    <xsd:sequence>
      <xsd:element name="productID" type="SKU"/>
      <xsd:element name="name" type="xsd:string"/>
    </xsd:sequence>
  </xsd:complexType>
</xsd:schema>
```

Order Fulfillment Schema

```xsd
<?xml version="1.0" encoding="UTF-8"?>
<xsd:schema
  xmlns="http://enterprise.com/fulfillment/orderFulfillment/
    schema/orderFulfillment1"
  xmlns:xsd="http://www.w3.org/2001/XMLSchema"
  xmlns:ns0="http://enterprise.com/sales/salesOrder/schema/
SalesOrder1"
  xmlns:ns1="http://enterprise.com/product/schema/product1"
  xmlns:ns2="http://enterprise.com/fulfillment/carrier/schema/
    carrier1"
  targetNamespace="http://enterprise.com/fulfillment/
    orderFulfillment/schema/orderFulfillment1"
  elementFormDefault="unqualified"
  attributeFormDefault="unqualified">
  <xsd:import
    namespace="http://enterprise.com/sales/salesOrder/schema/
      SalesOrder1"
    schemaLocation="http://enterprise.com/sales/salesOrder/
      schema/salesOrder1.0.xsd"/>
  <xsd:import namespace=http://enterprise.com/product/schema/
    product1
    schemaLocation="http://enterprise.com/product/schema/
      product1.0.xsd"/>
  <xsd:import
    namespace="http://enterprise.com/fulfillment/carrier/
      schema/carrier1"
    schemaLocation="http://enterprise.com/fulfillment/carrier/
      schema/carrier1.0.xsd"/>
```

```xml
<xsd:simpleType name="ShipmentLineID">
  <xsd:restriction base="xsd:string">
    <xsd:maxLength value="50"/>
  </xsd:restriction>
</xsd:simpleType>

<xsd:simpleType name="ShipmentID">
  <xsd:restriction base="xsd:string">
    <xsd:maxLength value="50"/>
  </xsd:restriction>
</xsd:simpleType>

<xsd:simpleType name="ShipmentStatus">
  <xsd:restriction base="xsd:string">
    <xsd:maxLength value="50"/>
  </xsd:restriction>
</xsd:simpleType>

<xsd:complexType name="ShipmentLineItem">
  <xsd:sequence>
    <xsd:element name="quantity" type="xsd:int"/>
    <xsd:element name="shipmentLineID" type="ShipmentLineID"/>
    <xsd:element name="salesOrderLine"
      type="ns0:SalesOrderLineID"/>
    <xsd:element name="productShipped" type="ns1:ProductRef"/>
  </xsd:sequence>
</xsd:complexType>

<xsd:complexType name="Shipment">
  <xsd:sequence>
    <xsd:element name="shipmentlineitems"
      type="ShipmentLineItem" maxOccurs="unbounded"/>
    <xsd:element name="trackingNumber"
      type="ns2:TrackingNumber"/>
    <xsd:element name="shipmentID" type="ShipmentID"/>
    <xsd:element name="status" type="ShipmentStatus"/>
    <xsd:element name="salesOrder" type="ns0:SalesOrderID"/>
    <xsd:element name="carrier" type="ns2:CarrierRef"/>
  </xsd:sequence>
</xsd:complexType>
</xsd:schema>
```

Sales Order Interface Schema

```xml
<?xml version="1.0" encoding="UTF-8"?>
<xsd:schema
  xmlns="http://enterprise.com/salesOrder/salesOrderInterface/
    schema/SalesOrderInterface1"
```

```
  xmlns:xsd="http://www.w3.org/2001/XMLSchema"
  xmlns:ns0="http://enterprise.com/sales/salesOrder/schema/
    SalesOrder1"
  targetNamespace="http://enterprise.com/salesOrder/
    salesOrderInterface/schema/SalesOrderInterface1"
  elementFormDefault="unqualified"
  attributeFormDefault="unqualified">
  <xsd:import
    namespace="http://enterprise.com/sales/salesOrder/schema/
      SalesOrder1"
    schemaLocation="http://enterprise.com/schema/
      salesOrder1.0.xsd"/>

  <xsd:complexType name="GetOrderDetailsRequest">
    <xsd:sequence>
      <xsd:element name="orderID" type="ns0:SalesOrderID"/>
    </xsd:sequence>
  </xsd:complexType>

  <xsd:complexType name="GetOrderDetailsResponse">
    <xsd:sequence>
      <xsd:element name="salesOrder" type="ns0:SalesOrder"/>
    </xsd:sequence>
  </xsd:complexType>
</xsd:schema>
```

Sales Order Schema

```
<?xml version="1.0" encoding="UTF-8"?>
<xsd:schema
  xmlns="http://enterprise.com/sales/salesOrder/schema/
    SalesOrder1"
  xmlns:xsd="http://www.w3.org/2001/XMLSchema"
  xmlns:ns0="http://enterprise.com/address/schema/address1"
  xmlns:ns1="http://enterprise.com/product/schema/product1"
  targetNamespace="http://enterprise.com/sales/salesOrder/
    schema/SalesOrder1"
  elementFormDefault="unqualified"
  attributeFormDefault="unqualified">
  <xsd:import namespace=http://enterprise.com/address/schema/
    address1
    schemaLocation="http://enterprise.com/address/schema/
      address1.0.xsd"/>
  <xsd:import namespace=http://enterprise.com/product/schema/
    product1
    schemaLocation="http://enterprise.com/product/schema/
      product1.0.xsd"/>
```

```xml
    <xsd:simpleType name="SalesOrderLineID">
      <xsd:restriction base="xsd:string">
        <xsd:maxLength value="50"/>
      </xsd:restriction>
    </xsd:simpleType>

    <xsd:simpleType name="SalesOrderID">
      <xsd:restriction base="xsd:string">
        <xsd:maxLength value="50"/>
      </xsd:restriction>
    </xsd:simpleType>

    <xsd:simpleType name="SalesOrderLineStatus">
      <xsd:restriction base="xsd:string">
        <xsd:maxLength value="50"/>
      </xsd:restriction>
    </xsd:simpleType>

    <xsd:simpleType name="SalesOrderStatus">
      <xsd:restriction base="xsd:string">
        <xsd:maxLength value="50"/>
      </xsd:restriction>
    </xsd:simpleType>

    <xsd:complexType name="SalesOrder">
      <xsd:sequence>
        <xsd:element name="lineItems" type="SalesOrderLineItem"
          maxOccurs="unbounded"/>
        <xsd:element name="date" type="xsd:date"/>
        <xsd:element name="orderID" type="SalesOrderID"/>
        <xsd:element name="status" type="SalesOrderStatus"/>
        <xsd:element name="shippingAddress" type="ns0:Address"/>
        <xsd:element name="billingAddress" type="ns0:Address"/>
      </xsd:sequence>
    </xsd:complexType>

    <xsd:complexType name="SalesOrderLineItem">
      <xsd:sequence>
        <xsd:element name="quantity" type="xsd:int"/>
        <xsd:element name="price" type="xsd:double"/>
        <xsd:element name="orderLineID" type="SalesOrderLineID"/>
        <xsd:element name="status" type="SalesOrderLineStatus"/>
        <xsd:element name="product" type="ns1:ProductRef"/>
      </xsd:sequence>
    </xsd:complexType>
  </xsd:schema>
```

Index

TIBCO Education

You've read the book... now take action!

TIBCO Education is offering intense companion courses and a professional certification for each of the books in the architecture series from TIBCO Press. Each course will be released to coincide with the publication of its companion book. The planned series includes:

- ARC 701: TIBCO Architecture Fundamentals (available now)
- ARC 702: Architecting Composite Applications and Services with TIBCO (available now)
- ARC 703: Architecting BPM Solutions with TIBCO
- ARC 704: Architecting Complex Event Processing Solutions with TIBCO
- ARC 705: Architecting Master Data Management Solutions with TIBCO

Accelerate your career with TIBCO Certification.

TIBCO Certified Architect certifications are the highest level of accreditation in the TIBCO Certified Professional Program. These prestigious credentials recognize those individuals who demonstrate a clear understanding of the selected TIBCO products, a sound grasp of architecture concepts, methodology, and principles and how they may be combined to solve practical or challenging requirements.

To learn more about the courses and certification, visit the TIBCO Education website at http://www.tibco.com/services/educational

Your purchase of *Architecting Composite Applications and Services with TIBCO®* includes access to a free online edition for 45 days through the **Safari Books Online** subscription service. Nearly every Addison-Wesley Professional book is available online through **Safari Books Online**, along with thousands of books and videos from publishers such as Cisco Press, Exam Cram, IBM Press, O'Reilly Media, Prentice Hall, Que, Sams, and VMware Press.

Safari Books Online is a digital library providing searchable, on-demand access to thousands of technology, digital media, and professional development books and videos from leading publishers. With one monthly or yearly subscription price, you get unlimited access to learning tools and information on topics including mobile app and software development, tips and tricks on using your favorite gadgets, networking, project management, graphic design, and much more.

Activate your FREE Online Edition at
informit.com/safarifree

STEP 1:   Enter the coupon code: DEYZKCB.

STEP 2:   New Safari users, complete the brief registration form.
Safari subscribers, just log in.

If you have difficulty registering on Safari or accessing the online edition,
please e-mail customer-service@safaribooksonline.com